THE NEW IMMIGRANT WHITENESS

NATION OF NATIONS: IMMIGRANT HISTORY AS AMERICAN HISTORY

General Editor: Matthew Jacobson
Founding Editors: Matthew Jacobson and Werner Sollors

The New Immigrant Whiteness

Race, Neoliberalism, and
Post-Soviet Migration
to the United States

Claudia Sadowski-Smith

NEW YORK UNIVERSITY PRESS

New York

NEW YORK UNIVERSITY PRESS
New York
www.nyupress.org

References to Internet websites (URLs) were accurate at the time of writing. Neither the author nor New York University Press is responsible for URLs that may have expired or changed since the manuscript was prepared.

Library of Congress Cataloging-in-Publication Data
Names: Sadowski-Smith, Claudia, 1968– author.
Title: The new immigrant whiteness : race, neoliberalism, and post-Soviet migration to the United States / Claudia Sadowski-Smith.
Description: New York : NEW YORK UNIVERSITY PRESS, 2018. | Includes bibliographical references and index.
Identifiers: LCCN 2017034132 | ISBN 9781479847730 (cl : alk. paper) | ISBN 9781479806713 (pb : alk. paper)
Subjects: LCSH: Former Soviet republics—Emigration and immigration. | United States—Emigration and immigration. | Immigrants—United States. | Mass media and minorities—United States.
Classification: LCC E184.R9 S23 2018 | DDC 304.80973—dc23
LC record available at https://lccn.loc.gov/2017034132

New York University Press books are printed on acid-free paper, and their binding materials are chosen for strength and durability. We strive to use environmentally responsible suppliers and materials to the greatest extent possible in publishing our books.

Manufactured in the United States of America

10 9 8 7 6 5 4 3 2 1

Also available as an ebook

To Bryan and Nina

In loving memory of Manfred Sadowski

CONTENTS

Introduction

Presumed White: Race, Neoliberalism, and Modes of Migration in the Post-Soviet Diaspora

Over 1 million people identified as having been born in the former USSR or its successor nations in the 2010 US census.[1] They ranked as the ninth largest immigrant group after those from South Korea and before the much more widely studied group of immigrants from the Dominican Republic who are often considered in scholarship on Latina/o migration.[2] The 2010–2014 American Community Survey (ACS) estimated that 1.17 million post-Soviet immigrants now reside in the United States, outnumbering the 1.16 million from Korea. Post-Soviet migrants have arrived more recently than the largest contemporary groups from Asia and Latin America who benefited from the passage of the 1965 Immigration and Nationality Act. Even though small numbers of political dissidents and Jewish refugees were able to leave the Soviet Union in the 1970s, only the demise of the socialist East Bloc and the triumph of neoliberalism in the late 1980s initiated large-scale emigration from the former USSR.[3]

An ideology, collection of policies, and mode of governance, neoliberalism entered former East Bloc countries at a time when it had already been dominant in the United States and across Western Europe for about a decade. Neoliberalism promotes the idea that self-regulating markets best allow individuals to pursue the acquisition of wealth. While they took different forms in the United States and several Western European countries, depending on each nation's historical legacies and institutional structures (Hall and Soskice 2001), neoliberal policies have included the deregulation of markets, the liberalization of trade, the privatization of public sectors, the dismantling of social services and welfare programs, and the promotion of the financial sector over other economic activity (Harvey 2007).[4]

The Cold War constrained capitalism's tendency to gravitate toward growing inequalities until the fall of state socialism in the former Soviet Union and Eastern Europe allowed global corporate and political elites to more intensely promote neoliberal ideologies and practices in order to build consensus for the further upward redistribution of wealth and power (Piketty 2014; Duggan 2014). The subsequent dramatic widening of inequalities between individuals and communities in the United States, as measured in the 2000 Census (Steger and Roy 2010, 60), pushed this issue to the top of Democratic candidate Bernie Sanders's political agenda in the 2016 presidential election. Neoliberal transformations in the United States have been accompanied by the emergence of a "security state" apparatus (Hyatt 2011), which employs increasingly antidemocratic forms of governance to contain the growing dissent that accompanies increases in inequality. Differences among populations, such as those constituted by race or legal status, are further mobilized to justify increasingly segmented access to wealth and citizenship rights. While restrictions to legal entry and social rights, the rise in state-sponsored anti-immigrant sentiment, and tightened immigration enforcement are directed at all noncitizens, they have targeted the largest groups of immigrants from Mexico and Central America, and are also extended to those from Muslim nations. The overrepresentation of Latina/os and African Americans in prisons, the spate of police shootings of unarmed black men and children that have received increased public scrutiny since 2014, and the profiling of "Arab/Muslims" through "anti-terrorist" security measures further exemplify how racial profiling works to justify the deepening unequal treatment of various US populations.

Capitalism and its neoliberal variant were exported beyond the United States and Western Europe through free trade agreements, structural adjustment programs, and so-called shock therapy approaches to economic reform (Steger and Roy 2010, 10). Shock therapies serve to rapidly advance neoliberal policies that promote the liberalization of price and currency controls, the withdrawal of state benefits, and the large-scale privatization of public assets. First implemented in Chile in the 1970s, since the late 1980s these policies helped abolish socialist property regimes in Eastern Europe where they created some of the largest increases in social inequality *ever* (Harvey 2007, 17). Shock therapies found their deepest expression in the Soviet Union. They led to the country's dissolution in 1991 and the emergence of twelve successor states and three Baltic nations, which claim continuity with the pre–World War II states that existed prior to their annexation by the Soviet Union. The most rapid neoliberal transformations took place in Russia, the officially-recognized heir of the Soviet Union. As they occurred without financial mitigation or concern for the large-scale suffering of the populace, these processes led to years of severe economic stagnation, high unemployment, widespread impoverishment, and the rise of a small but powerful class of oligarchs who reaped most of the benefits of the transition (Klein 2007). Surging global commodity markets helped improve Russia's economy between the late 1990s and early 2000s, but after the global drop in oil prices and the imposition of international sanctions in response to its 2014 intervention in Ukraine, Russia has found itself in a period of prolonged economic stagnation.[5] While Ukraine, the second largest Soviet successor nation, was not subjected to the same level of shock therapy after it declared its independence in 1991, the country experienced a deeper crisis than other post-Soviet nations until its economy stabilized in the late 1990s. In 2008 Ukraine's economy slowed, and it lapsed into a second recession in 2013.

The massive social upheavals in post-Soviet countries have largely been attributed to the lingering effects of state socialism, such as corruption, authoritarianism, and the inability to commit to ethnic pluralism (Suchland 2015, 2011). But scholars of postsocialism have shown that developments in the former East Bloc, including the USSR and successor nations, also exemplify the delirious effects of neoliberalism (Keough 2006).[6] *The New Immigrant Whiteness* examines representations of migration from the former USSR and successor nations to the United States—in TV shows, memoirs, fiction, and interviews—as equally important responses to the extension of neoliberalism, which has reshaped the causes and forms of migration to the United States as well as the ways in which immigrants are received and in which they adapt and maintain connections to their regions of origin. Transformations in the USSR and successor nations propelled significant diasporic outmigration to the United States, Western Europe, and Israel throughout the 1990s and into the twenty-first century.[7] Ukraine has experienced an especially large population decline, partially as a result of emigration. The country's population has decreased every year since its peak of 53 million in 1993 to 45 million in 2016 (World Bank 2017). In 2007

Ukraine ranked third among top labor exporting countries in the world (Tolstokorova 2010a, 84–85).

Post-Soviet migrants employ virtually *all* forms of human movement available under current US migration law, which in turn afford them differentiated access to segmented citizenship rights. They have arrived as political and religious refugees, and as highly skilled, temporary labor, marriage, and adoptive migrants. Some also overstay nonimmigrant visitor or work visas. The majority of the early Soviet migrants were admitted as refugees from socialism (Logan and Rivera 2011, 30; Solari, 2010, 217). Large numbers also benefited from US legislation that established presumptive eligibility for asylum from religious persecution primarily for Jewish migrants, but also for Evangelical Christians and Ukrainian Catholics, who had sponsors in the United States (Korobkov and Zaionchkovskaia 2012, 328; Hardwick 2008, 38).[8] Between 1993 and 2000, close to 400,000 immigrants arrived annually from the former Soviet Union, a majority of whom came as Jewish refugees (Kasatkina 2010, 200). By the early 2000s, when it had become more difficult to receive refugee status, the proportion of Jewish migrants in the post-USSR migration decreased significantly (Korobkov and Zaionchkovskaia 2012, 328).[9] Throughout the 1990s, post-Soviet migrants became the second largest group of US marriage migrants and transnational adoptees (D'Aoust 2009, 7; H. Jacobson 2008). In addition, post-USSR migrants have participated in highly skilled migration in significant numbers.

Post-Soviet immigrants who overstay their nonimmigrant tourist, student, or work visas to become undocumented are placed in a position similar to that of other migrants who do not meet the increasingly restrictive requirements for legal entry or cannot endure the long processing times for visas or status adjustments, and thus arrive unauthorized at US borders.[10] Undocumented immigrants are not only denied the legal right to enter, reside, or work in the United States, but they are also excluded from access to most welfare rights. Available statistics on undocumented migration collapse arrivals from Europe and Canada. Their combined number surpasses migrants from the Caribbean and approximates those of migrants from South America (Passel and Cohn 2014).[11]

In addition to participating in all forms of migration to the United States, the post-Soviet diaspora is ethnically diverse, though the concept of ethnicity is defined differently in post-USSR nations and in the United States. In the former Soviet Union, major ethnic groups were often assigned their own republics (which have now become independent nations) and were considered "nationalities," while minorities residing within such administrative units were regarded as "ethnic." Substantial internal migration also led to the development of ethnicized identities where migrants lived in one Soviet republic but identified with another nationality (as ethnically Russian in Kazakhstan, for example), and where the descendants of a relatively high percentage of interethnic marriages may have identified with the national or ethnic origin of only one of their parents (Kolossov 2005).

Migration to the United States from Russia decreased after the country's economy doubled in size between 1998 and 2008 (Kotkin 2015), while the percentage of migrants from other Soviet successor nations increased.[12] In the 2000 Census, those who were born in Russia made up nearly 40 percent of the diaspora, followed by 31 percent from Ukraine, 7 percent from Armenia, and smaller numbers from Belarus, Lithuania, Latvia, Uzbekistan, Moldavia, and Azerbaijan. In the 2014 American Community Survey (ACS), the percentages of Russians, Ukrainians, and Armenians had changed to 35 percent, 27 percent, and 7 percent, respectively. The remainder of the diaspora had become more diverse, with Belarusians, Uzbeks, Moldavians, Lithuanians, Kazakhs, Azerbaijanis, Georgians, and Latvians making up between 2 and 5 percent of the population.

The ethnic and "national" identities that evolved in the former USSR continue to be assigned differential value in post-Soviet nations. So-called ethnic "Slavs" (Russians, Belarusians, or Ukrainians) rank higher than individuals residing in or with ties to Asian countries like Kazakhstan and Uzbekistan as well as those from the Caucasus region, which spans today's Russia, Armenia, Georgia, and Azerbaijan, and whose residents are called "Caucasian" and are often considered "black." Immigrants may self-identify with their nationality or ethnicity—rather than as Russian—even if they hold a Russian passport (Kasinitz 2013), and those with backgrounds in Asia or the Caucasus may not identify as white or be racialized as such in the United States. For example, in the 2006–2010 ACS, 4.3 percent of Kazakh migrants identified as "Other Asian or Pacific Islander," 7 percent of Kazakhs and 2.5 percent of Uzbeks as members of "two races," and 1.4 percent of Georgians saw themselves as "black."

An analysis of the legal and ethnic diversity of the post-Soviet diaspora complicates the emphasis in immigration studies on the significance of the *collective* characteristics of immigrant groups for their adaptation and transnationalism. These features include the human and cultural capital with which members arrive, such as their education, language and workplace skills, as well as their racialization into US specific ethnic and racial categories. Members of the post-Soviet diaspora share features that render them distinct from other contemporary arrivals. Both men and women generally arrive with high levels of education and work experience (Logan and Rivera 2011; Kasinitz 2013).[13] Despite their internal ethnic diversity, members of the diaspora are also collectively racialized as white in the United States. The diaspora is associated with views of the East Bloc as a monoracially white intolerant "other" that emerged during the Cold War (Atanasoski 2013) and with notions of a pan-European whiteness that is supposedly shared by all those of European descent in the United States and that consolidated after World War II.

The New Immigrant Whiteness examines the emergence of representations that not only associate the post-Soviet diaspora with these general ideas of a pan-European whiteness, but more specifically characterize its members as successors of turn of the twentieth century European immigrants who became fully incorporated into whiteness by the 1940s. These representations are especially visible in US reality TV shows, a genre that, like the post-Soviet diaspora itself, emerged in the context of global neoliberal transformations. In the early 1990s, demands for lower program production and airtime cost led the TV industry to adopt new techniques and genres that resulted in the development of reality TV shows (Friedman 2002; Dubrofsky 2006). In these shows, the new immigrants are uniquely associated with mythologized accounts of turn of the twentieth century European immigrant adaptation and upward mobility, which describe how immigrants lifted themselves up by their bootstraps to achieve the American Dream. This portrayal keeps alive the exceptionalist mythology of the United States as an immigrant nation. At a time of rapid national and global transformations that are characterized by increasingly segmented access to scarce resources, this narrative of exceptionalism ascribes to members of the post-Soviet diaspora the ability to access the same post–World War II regime of US citizenship rights that have linked a white racialized identity to upward mobility.

Their association with this narrative renders members of the new diaspora significantly different from other contemporary arrivals who are collectively racialized as nonwhite. In fact, just as the pan-European whiteness of turn of the century immigrants emerged in direct opposition to the "blackness" of African American populations and as immigrant descendants consolidated their white ethnic identities in reaction to the 1960s civil rights movement, representations of the post-USSR diaspora as white are explicitly contrasted with immigrant groups racialized as nonwhite. But rather than opposing the whiteness of the post-Soviet diaspora to notions of "blackness," it is most often contrasted with the "brownness" of Latina/os who have become the focus of anti-immigrant rhetoric and politics.

The extension of a historically constituted pan-European white identity and its association with a larger network of privileges to post-Soviet migrants assumes that whiteness has remained unchanged since World War II when it was consolidated through US federal policies in the context of a relatively well-functioning capitalist economy. While an ascribed white racial identity continues to shield individuals from systematic and institutionalized privilege and racialized violence that manifests itself, among other things, in the profiling and unequal treatment of diverse groups, such as the association of African Americans with crime, Latina/os with migrant illegality, and "Arabs/Muslims" with terrorism, other US citizenship rights, which were more readily available to immigrants racialized as white, have undergone significant transformations. Access to education, unemployment, retirement, and social security, which brought modest prosperity and security to an earlier European immigrant working class and its children, and ensured them fuller entry into the labor market, has markedly declined. Noncitizens have increasingly been excluded from what Linda Bosniak has called "internal citizenship rights," such as free choice of employment as well as access to public services, welfare benefits, and jobs in the public sector (Bosniak 2006, 34, 49). In addition, while European immigrants and their descendants benefited from discriminatory hiring in the industrial labor force when the working class was built, that labor market has largely disappeared in the context of a neoliberal economy. Unlike US-born whites, post-Soviet migrants also generally do not have access to intergenerational savings, which George Lipsitz (1998) identified as a decisive factor in the consolidation of white post–World War II privilege.

Through interviews with marriage migrants and the analysis of parental adoption memoirs that have proliferated as part of a boom in nonfiction since the 1990s, *The New Immigrant Whiteness* examines the extension of these mythologized and US-specific notions of whiteness to residents of the former East Bloc. The emphasis on family unification in US migration law has enabled the expansion of transnational marriage and adoptive migration—and the development of neoliberal migration markets—to the former USSR, in which post-Soviet immigrants are constituted as white even *before* they leave their countries of origin. In contrast, turn of the twentieth century Europeans were, in historian Thomas Guglielmo's words, only considered "white on arrival" (2003). While nineteenth-century immigrant men brought marriage partners from their countries of origin, today predominantly European-identified US citizens sponsor the migration of children or women from the former USSR so that they can create what they perceive as monoracial families. Older notions of a shared familial culture that is based on a common national or ethnic background have thus been replaced by the belief in a globalized form of US whiteness that signifies a shared racial identity. The attribution of this concept to residents of the former USSR or its successor nations transforms them into neoliberal commodities whose presumptive white racial identities increase their desirability and afford them preferred legal admission to the United States through sponsorship as wives and children.

The transnational expansion of US whiteness racializes the new immigrants as white even before their arrival in the United States, while their supposed turn of the twentieth century European immigrant predecessors often oscillated between efforts to assimilate into whiteness and to maintain their national, religious, ethnic, or cultural differences. Turn of the century European immigrants struggled to keep their cultural distinctiveness and group ties, and Jewish immigrants in particular resented assimilation pressures because they interfered with their efforts to assert a distinct racial identity (Goldstein 2006). Even though their ascribed white identities provide post-Soviet immigrants with immediate racialized privilege, the neoliberal value assigned to these identities exposes marriage and adoptive migrants to heightened expectations of their fast-track assimilation to a middle-class whiteness. This pressure obscures the neoliberal conditions occasioning post-Soviet migration and erases migrants' national, cultural, and linguistic differences, thus also impeding the maintenance or creation of bicultural or transnational identities. To differing degrees and with the exception of those who construct their identities exclusively in terms of their "nationality" or ethnicity, post-Soviet migrants are currently developing a "Russian" cultural identity through shared media, language, cultural institutions, and consumption patterns (Gold 2013; Kasinitz et al. 2004; Kasinitz et al. 2008, Kasinitz 2013). While this Russian identity can encompass Soviet Jewish immigrants, a minority of whom exclusively identify as Jewish (Kasinitz 2013), the emerging "Russiannenss" cannot simply expand upon an existing American Jewish identity that evolved from earlier immigration. The turn of the twentieth-century immigrants who largely came from the Russian empire, the geographical predecessor of the USSR, and often spoke Yiddish, assimilated to a Jewish American identity that had evolved from mid-nineteenth century central European Jewish immigration, has had a rather complex relationship to US notions of whiteness, and is simply not available to all post-Soviet migrants.

Through interviews and the study of an emerging body of fiction by first- and 1.5-generation (post-)Soviet writers, *The New Immigrant Whiteness* moves beyond histories of the consolidation of immigrant whiteness and the association of this racialized identity with the post-USSR diaspora toward examinations of contemporary immigrants who are racialized as white but differently positioned in their access to segmented citizenship rights based on their legal status. The book establishes a comparative perspective through which to study undocumented migration from the former Soviet Union, explores post-USSR immigrants' attitudes toward immigration from Mexico and Central America, and analyzes parallels between post-USSR and Asian immigrants who are similarly associated with the American immigrant dream of upward mobility. Such a focus renders members of the post-Soviet diaspora less exceptional from other contemporary arrivals and creates an agenda for further comparative work in a context where changes in the US economy and a declining welfare state are reshaping the US ethnoracial hierarchy. Even though race continues to function as a euphemism for geographical origin, ancestry, and culture, in the neoliberal context the concept also works to normalize deepening differential access to wealth (Melamed 2011, 44). Or as Ramón Saldívar has put it, while essentialist notions of race have given way to more complex understandings of multiethnic racial formations, structures of inequality continue to divide populations based on their perceived physical and behavioral characteristics within the larger context of white supremacy (Saldívar 2013, 2).

The New Immigrant Whiteness adds a focus on the importance of differential legal status on arrival (which moves beyond the familiar distinction between legal and undocumented status) to the emphasis on the significance of collective characteristics, such as racialization and educational achievements, for immigrant adaptation and transnationalism. Differential legal status or the lack thereof shapes migrant access to segmented citizenship rights. Post-Soviet migrants of Jewish descent who benefited from refugee policies in the 1980s and 1990s generally came with their families, were able to naturalize quickly, received assistance from Jewish organizations, and had access to welfare benefits, housing, as well as language and employment training. While they benefited from early eligibility for public assistance and a fast track to citizenship, these immigrants work in occupations with lower prestige and earnings when compared to immigrants from Western Europe and Canada who are also considered white (Logan and Rivera 2011, 29, 39). Migrants admitted on highly skilled visas tend to be inserted into temporary and flexible positions that illustrate how highly skilled jobs have become associated with conditions of precarity. At least initially, these migrants tend to earn less than US-born workers and have fewer employment opportunities because their visas are dependent on their employers and because the adjustment of their legal status generally takes a long time (Banerjee 2006).

For those who arrive with nonimmigrant work or visitor visas and overstay them, even higher levels of education, improved language skills, or longer stays in the United States usually do not translate into higher wages, and their upward mobility is severely restricted. Like other post-Soviet women migrants, marriage migrants who are incorporated into the middle-class lives of their US husbands often experience a loss of occupational status, although they are legally able to work in the United States and are generally well-educated. Post-Soviet immigrant women frequently end up working in the lower-skilled jobs that dominate the postindustrial US economy and that tend to be held by immigrants (Logan and Rivera 2011, 27).

Pan-European Whiteness

The field of whiteness studies, which consolidated in the late 1980s and 1990s in history, legal, and cultural studies, and later in sociology (Doane 2003), has emphasized the centrality of institutionalized white privilege and its link to white supremacy for any understanding of a white identity in the United States.[14] In its origins, this work rarely considered distinctions between native-born and immigrant populations. Historians have filled in the gap by exploring the emergence of a pan-European whiteness through a focus on the large numbers of so-called "new" immigrants who came to the United States between 1840 and 1920, primarily from Ireland, Italy, and the Russian empire. The size of this immigration far surpassed the Irish, Germans, and Scandinavians who had arrived primarily in the mid-nineteenth century.[15] While eastern Europeans came from diverse regions, including Romania and the Austro-Hungarian empire, most were Jewish and arrived from the Pale of Settlement in the Russian empire (Gold 1999, 115). Its borders largely correspond to the historical boundaries of the former Polish-Lithuanian Commonwealth that included much of present-day Lithuania, Belarus, Poland, Moldova, Ukraine, and Russia. Because the Russian empire controlled emigration by granting exit permits predominantly to ethnic minorities such as Jews, ethnic Poles, Lithuanians, Finns, and ethnic Germans, these groups were disproportionally represented among US migrants (Schneider 2013, 37).[16]

Whiteness historians have focused on the place of these "new" European immigrants in the US "color" hierarchy, which divided native-born/established immigrant Europeans from nonwhite populations, particularly African Americans and the smaller population of Chinese immigrants who had been arriving in the United States since the mid-nineteenth century. The black-white dichotomy, which originated in seventeenth-century African chattel slavery, informed legal definitions of US citizenship as limited to "free, white men." As this binary was extended to new arrivals, Asian migrants were excluded from naturalization until 1943 and Mexican migrants were treated as members of a nonwhite, persecuted minority in the Southwest at the turn of the twentieth century.[17]

Because they were ascribed a white *racial* identity despite their origins in different European countries, however, immigrants from Ireland, Italy, and the Russian empire had access to naturalization and to better jobs than African Americans or Asian immigrants who worked almost exclusively in their own communities or in domestic/personal service (T. Guglielmo 2003, 29). The new European immigrants were also largely exempt from the kind of systemic, institutionalized racial violence that was directed at African Americans, Chinese, and Mexican immigrants as well as Mexican Americans (Fox and Guglielmo 2012). Noel Ignatiev's work (1995) on the role of Irish immigrants as leaders in the crusade for Chinese Exclusion has shaped the view that European immigrants' efforts to access all facets of whiteness required their embrace of white supremacy, particularly hostility toward their nonwhite contemporaries (Satzewich 2000). The scholarship cites Irish immigrant support of slavery and of the 1917 Literacy Act, the participation of Irish immigrants in conflicts with indigenous people and Mexicans in the war with Mexico, as well as efforts by some Italian and Jewish immigrants to prevent the influx of larger numbers of African Americans into their neighborhoods in the early twentieth century (Guterl 2001; MacDonald 1998, 301; Garner 2006, 260; T. Guglielmo 2003, 146; Goldstein 2006).

The experiences of Jewish immigrants in particular question the notion that their efforts to enter the privileged echelon of the US racial hierarchy also necessitated their full support of white supremacy. Because they saw themselves as members of a racially and religiously distinct group that had been persecuted in several multinational empires, were exposed to revolutionary ideas about working-class unity, possessed skills that qualified them for occupations where they did not compete with African Americans, received coreligionist support that provided them with an avenue for economic mobility not available to other immigrant groups, and faced social exclusion, Jewish Americans tended to withhold strong support for white supremacy, especially state-sponsored racial violence or exclusion (Goldstein 2006, 59, 75–76).[18] Jewish newspapers and organizations systemically opposed Chinese Exclusion and the 1917 Literacy Act (Roediger 2005, 15; Barrett and Roediger 1997; Goldstein 2006, 31).

In addition, despite their acceptance as racially white which enabled them to naturalize, the new European arrivals were considered not "quite white" as they faced social stigma, including occasional exclusions from schools, public accommodations, labor unions, and institutions of elite society; and Italians in particular experienced some racialized violence and lynchings (J. Guglielmo 2003, 11). With the exception of eastern European Jewish immigrants who often worked as peddlers or in the Jewish-dominated garment industry, immigrants were also confined to unskilled occupations where they earned less than native-born whites (Schreuder 1989, 133; Garner 2006, 265). They tended to concentrate in ethnic ghettos (Goldstein 2006; Ignatiev 1995) and were selectively excluded from admission to the United States through 1920s Quota Laws that were based on pseudo-scientific racial theories of differences among European national origins. These laws created a system of annual quotas that allowed greater numbers of arrivals from northern Europe while restricting immigration from southern and eastern Europe and completing barring Asian immigration, thus anticipating the biopolitical racialization of contemporary immigrants from Latin America (Roediger 2008, 159).

Most of the new immigrants could only claim full inclusion into whiteness after World War II when they had achieved socioeconomic mobility from urban ethnic ghettos to suburbs, and had acquired educational and workplace skills (Alba and Waters 2011).[19] At this time, European immigrants, and particularly their descendants, began to disproportionally benefit from expanded social rights under New Deal legislation that built the postwar middle class and provided European immigrants with a path toward socioeconomic mobility not available to African Americans. These welfare rights included subsidized mortgage loans, unemployment, Social Security retirement funds, and GI Bill benefits as well as job protections. In fact, European immigrants became the greatest beneficiaries of FHA loans, having achieved higher rates of home ownership than native-born populations by 1940 (T. Guglielmo 2003, 147–148), and they were more likely than native-born whites to work in occupations covered by Social Security and nearing retirement when the program was instituted (T. Guglielmo 2015).

While the unequal distribution of welfare policies enabled immigrants who had come from different countries and regions of Europe with divergent migratory goals, skills, and human capital to achieve similar outcomes three generations later (Alba 2009), it also led to the kind of residential and educational segregation that still characterizes much of the United States (Roediger 2005; Alba 2009; Lipsitz 1998). George Lipsitz has also emphasized the important role that the intergenerational transfer of inherited wealth to succeeding generations has played in helping to solidify white economic privilege into the contemporary moment (Lipsitz 1998). The scholarly emphasis on the fact that opportunities for upward mobility were selectively provided to those racialized as white emerged in response to the ethnic revival of the 1960s. Descendants of immigrants consolidated what Mary Waters has called "symbolic" ethnicities by selectively borrowing elements from disparate European immigrant backgrounds at a time when these cultural and national distinctions had only a minimal impact on their daily lives (Waters 1990). Some white ethnics employed these identities to disavow their white privilege by arguing that the hardships experienced by their turn of the twentieth century immigrant ancestors were comparable to the treatment of contemporary nonwhite groups (M. Jacobson 1998, 2006; J. Guglielmo 2003).

The Chapters

This book brings together a variety of scholarly fields and perspectives to complicate the extension of a historically constituted pan-European white identity, and its association with an entire network of privileges, to post-Soviet migrants. A study of post-USSR migrants' participation in various forms of human movement bridges existing scholarship on refugee, highly skilled, marriage, adoptive, and irregular migration, which have largely been examined in isolation from one another and with an emphasis on the groups that dominate each type. As a result, separate bodies of work have emerged to explore refugee streams from various Third World countries, highly skilled migration from East and South Asia, low-skilled and often undocumented labor migration from south of the Mexico-US border, "mail-order brides" from the Philippines, and transnational adoptions from China and Korea.

Each chapter focuses on one such form of human movement in which members of the post-Soviet diaspora participate, and places it in dialogue with developments in the fields of American, media, whiteness, immigration, adoption, and Jewish studies, from which an analysis of this migration has largely been excluded. Historians and migration scholars have examined turn of the twentieth century migration from the Russian empire, predominantly by Jewish migrants from the Pale of Settlement, but have rarely explored post-1980s migration from geographies in Europe and Asia that made up the USSR. Some work in Slavic studies is emerging to examine historical outmigration from the former Russian empire to the United States—including the Russian colonization of Alaska as well as migrations after the 1917 revolution, World War II, and in the 1970s and 1980s—but, like US immigration scholarship more generally, the field has paid little attention to immigration since the late 1980s.[20]

Two separate forms of scholarship analyze the gendered movement of women who have migrated to the United States from the Global South and from the former East Bloc in the context of global economic restructuring (Suchland 2015, 6). The post-Soviet, Central European, and Eastern European women who have entered the intimate economy of sex work and marriage through migration tend to be examined from the perspective of human trafficking. They are treated as victims of criminal organizations, failed political systems, and corrupt political elites in former East Bloc countries. In contrast, migration from the Global South is considered in the context of the systemic structural exploitation of women under neoliberal conditions (Suchland 2015, 10).

A small body of scholarship in Jewish studies has focused on Soviet and post-Soviet migrants who came as religious refugees, by emphasizing their similarities to migration from the Pale of Settlement in the Russian empire (e.g., Gold 1999), or at times by including this group in studies of second-generation immigrants to New York City (Kasinitz et al. 2004; Kasinitz et al.2008; Waters et al. 2010). The latter work has found that while Soviet Jews who came in the early years of the diaspora were able to benefit from the help of coreligionists and Jewish assistance organizations, many are participating in the creation of a new ethnic "Russian" identity. However, some construct their identities by using Soviet and post-Soviet notions of national origin or ethnicity, which includes more specific considerations as Ukrainian or Russian Jews, with only a minority seeing themselves as exclusively Jewish (Kasinitz 2013). Some scholarship has also examined the role of religion in slowing the acculturation of Protestant post-Soviet immigrants who came as refugees (Hardwick 2008). Having arrived as entire congregations and settled in West Coast localities with preexisting religious networks, these groups do not seem to have acculturated well, and many migrants have suffered from a loss of occupational status or unemployment (Hardwick 2002, 269).

In the virtual absence of an established body of scholarly research on post-Soviet migration, this book employs analytical tools and theoretical frameworks from a variety of disciplines. My search for portrayals of post-USSR migrants led me to the medium of reality television, where some programs have turned their attention to the rise in global migration. I engage perspectives from media scholarship, including work on the development of the genre and the use of format adaptation, to understand how US reality TV represents post-Soviet immigrants as inheritors of the mythologized European immigrant dream in ways that diverge from their more established media portrayals as communists, terrorists, or villains.

In my search for alternative representations of the post-Soviet diaspora, I had to create my own "archive" of materials, using the methodologies of several scholarly fields. One of those is the interview method, which is integral to much scholarship in the social sciences. While scholars have explored Soviet Jewish immigrants on the East Coast, I focus on the smaller numbers of post-USSR migrants in the US Southwest and examine their migration experiences and return considerations as well as their attitudes toward anti-immigration policies that have targeted Latina/os and, so far, have taken their most visible form in Arizona's 2010 Senate Bill 1070. I also analyze the turn of the twenty-first century surge in memoirs by US parents who adopted children from Russia and Ukraine. Finally, I use my training as a literary scholar to examine fiction by first- and 1.5-generation immigrant writers, which places Soviet and post-Soviet migration into comparative frameworks with other forms of contemporary human movement to the United States. The medium of fiction allows authors to articulate alternative views of the present and of a speculative future that do not need to be based on empirical evidence. The use of fiction also enables writers to highlight connections between issues that have not yet been brought together in academic scholarship or popular discourses.

The first chapter, "The Post-Soviet Diaspora on Transnational Reality TV," examines Lifetime's short-lived series *Russian Dolls* and ABC's *Dancing with the Stars*, a widely watched US reality TV show. Both shows exemplify the emergence of new narratives that associate the post-Soviet diaspora with idealized accounts of turn of the twentieth century European immigrant adaptation and upward mobility. While they focus on 1.5-generation immigrant participants who came to the United States as young children or teenagers, most likely as religious refugees who initially dominated the diaspora, the two shows consistently downplay the Jewish identities of their cast members. As they give representational shape to the ongoing construction of a collective "Russian" identity, *Russian Dolls* and *DWTS* characterize this identity as another ethnicized version of pan-European whiteness. Post-Soviet migrant cast members are portrayed as following in the footsteps of idealized early European migrants, and they are set in firm opposition to Latina/os. The chapter also examines media commentary surrounding the two shows as well as interviews with participants, their own use of social media, and their participation in a Ukrainian TV show in order to highlight issues left unrepresented on *DWTS* and *Russian Dolls*, particularly post-Soviet migrants' engagement with growing anti-immigration sentiment and their efforts to establish transnational and diasporic identities. This approach opens up perspectives that render post-USSR migrants less exceptional from other contemporary US arrivals.

Chapter 2, "Highly Skilled and Marriage Migrants in Arizona," discusses the results of my interviews with post-USSR immigrants in Phoenix, Arizona, in order to place the post-Soviet diaspora in the context of US scholarship on adaptation and return migration. The majority of my interviewees participated in two highly gendered forms of movement—they either arrived on male-dominated highly skilled or female-dominated marriage migration. These migratory forms have been spurred by the interests of US men in creating monoracial families and by the neoliberalization of US academic institutions that has enabled the hiring of large numbers of academics in contingent and precarious positions. Their differential legal status upon arrival provides marriage and highly skilled migrants with diverging access to economic, social, and cultural forms of US citizenship, community building, and opportunities for return. Highly skilled migrants live middle-class lives, appear less interested in participating in a coethnic community, and maintain limited physical transnational connections. In contrast, marriage migrants experience downward mobility and dependency on their husbands, encounter greater difficulties connecting to post-Soviet migrants who arrived on other legal categories, and consider return more often. While they are immediately provided with temporary green cards and membership in their husbands' middle-class lives, the globalized form of US whiteness that the women were assigned even before they left their countries of origin also creates heightened expectations of their complete assimilation to a middle-class whiteness at the cost of their and often their children's bicultural and transnational identities.

Chapter 3, "The Desire for Adoptive Invisibility," explores the surge in US parental memoirs of adoption from Russia and Ukraine in the 1990s and early 2000s to complement scholarship on transnational adoption that has focused on questions of race when examining the largest and earliest forms of adoption from China and Korea. The chapter explores three of the most influential parental memoirs of adoption from the former Soviet Union—Margaret L. Schwartz's *The Pumpkin Patch* (2005), Theresa Reid's *Two Little Girls* (2007), and Brooks Hansen's *The Brotherhood of Joseph* (2008)—in order to highlight the centrality of race for adoptions from the former USSR. Like many other memoirs that have been produced since the boom of this genre, these three works propagate affective structures of neoliberalism that obscure growing domestic and global inequities (Gilmore 2010; Thoma 2014).

In these memoirs, parents explicitly eschew the traditional humanitarian narrative of adoption and portray themselves as neoliberal consumers who have the right to select healthy white children from an international adoption market in order to forge families whose members look as though they could be biologically related. The authors' belief that they share a preexisting white racial identity with post-Soviet children confers immense and immediate privilege onto adoptees. But this notion also reaffirms old-fashioned assumptions about immigrant adaptation. Because they are considered white like their parents, post-Soviet adoptees are expected to quickly and completely adapt to the middle- and upper-middle-class cultures of their new US families in ways that ignore their cultural and linguistic distinctiveness, the reasons for their relinquishment, and the many challenges associated with their status as adoptees. The belief that US adoptive parents share a racial identity with children in the former East Bloc not only turns them into preferred commodities but also renders them particularly vulnerable to rejections or adoption disruptions, which may help explain the significant numbers of abuse and death cases of post-Soviet adoptees at the hands of their US parents.

Chapter 4, "Fictions of Irregular Post-Soviet Migration," explores Sana Krasikov's short story collection *One More Year* (2008) and Anya Ulinich's novel *Petropolis* (2007) to develop a comparative approach to representations of contemporary irregular and unauthorized migration, a form of movement that has been largely associated with migrants from Mexico and Central America. The fiction by Krasikov and Ulinich represents ethnically and racially diverse protagonists from Russia, Georgia, and Uzbekistan who arrive in the United States on nonimmigrant visas and become undocumented migrants. Even though they are often associated with the tradition of American Jewish literature, these two works clearly move beyond the themes of assimilation and family migration that dominated twentieth-century cultural productions by eastern European immigrants of Jewish descent such as Mary Antin, Abraham Cahan, and Anzia Yezierska. Their work laid the foundation for a literature of assimilation to a middle-class white US racial identity that only became fully available to European immigrants by the mid-twentieth century. Rather than continuing the traditions of earlier Jewish American writing, the fiction by Krasikov and Ulinich emphasizes their post-Soviet characters' experiences of diminished access to the US labor market, residency, and citizenship rights, and thus places this fictional work in the larger context of contemporary US immigrant writing.

Chapter 5, "The Post-Soviet Diaspora in Comparative Perspective," analyzes additional data from my interviews with post-Soviet immigrants and Gary Shteyngart's novel *Super Sad True Love Story* (2010) to outline other areas of cross-ethnic comparative research. In the interviews, post-Soviet migrants largely stressed their ambivalence toward laws targeting undocumented migration like Arizona's 2010 Senate Bill 1070 from which they expected exemption because of their differential modes of entry as documented or highly skilled migrants (but rarely their ascribed whiteness). They also empathized with Mexican immigrants as the group most targeted by the law based on their shared status as immigrants or their experiences with state surveillance in the former USSR or in today's Russia. Their views are reminiscent of the ways in which turn of the twentieth century European immigrants insisted on differences from their nonwhite contemporaries who were targeted by institutionalized racial discrimination. But the attitudes of post-Soviet immigrants also recall how eastern European Jewish immigrants expressed overwhelming ambivalence toward or rejected expressions of white supremacy through empathy with African Americans, which was often based on comparisons with their own marginalization in the Russian empire (Goldstein 2006). The ambivalent or empathetic attitudes of many of my post-Soviet interviewees, most of whom are not Jewish, do not serve to shore up their racial identities but largely underscore their social distance from Latina/os.

Set in a near-future, dystopian United States that is undergoing similar shock therapies as the former Soviet Union, Shteyngart's novel speculatively explores the position of second-generation Russian Jewish immigrants in the US neoliberal racial hierarchy through comparisons with Asian Americans. Shteyngart arrived in the United States in the late 1970s, before the immense growth in post-Soviet migration, but his novel addresses how second-generation Korean and Russian Jewish immigrants are similarly linked to the myth of upward mobility while Latina/os and African Americans are marginalized as losers of neoliberalism.

The New Immigrant Whiteness calls for comparative studies of immigrant whiteness that set it alongside other racial formations through examinations of contemporary immigrants who are racialized as white but are differently positioned in their access to segmented citizenship rights based on legal status. Such an approach addresses the growing discrepancy between the ability of whiteness to deliver on many of its promises to newcomers racialized as white, such as social acceptance and upward mobility through cultural assimilation on the one hand, and its ideological function as a means of pressuring immigrants to assimilate to racialized power structures that benefit an increasingly smaller elite, on the other. Eric Goldstein has argued that early European immigrants' assimilation to whiteness was already less a matter of individual choice than the result of systemic pressures. While whiteness provided immigrants with significant economic and social privileges and largely exempted them from institutionalized racism and racial violence, the strongest pressures on immigrants to assimilate emanated from native-born elites who employed the black-white binary to obscure other fissures in US society and project an optimistic view of the US nation (Goldstein 2006, 3, 6). US elites have relied on this binary to gain the allegiance of the white underclass in order to retain their affluence and political power since the institution of chattel slavery (Morgan 1975). Anti-immigrant discourses and politics also served the interests of employers who promoted the belief that certain groups genetically fit specific jobs in order to undermine labor unity, depress wages, and spur competition (Barrett and Roediger 1997, 16–17). The extension of whiteness to new US arrivals and to populations who reside in countries of the former Second World that are portrayed as monoracially white provides them with even less of a choice over their own racialization and upholds the ideological dominance of a now globalized whiteness that obscures growing economic, social, and racial inequities among and within nations.

In its focus on the importance of differential legal status on arrival, *The New Immigrant Whiteness* points toward comparative approaches to whiteness that move beyond the currently prevailing emphasis on groups of migrants of the same geographical and national origins. This focus threatens to reaffirm narratives of stark historical and contemporary divisions between differently racialized immigrant groups, in part through an emphasis on the importance of shared group characteristics. While acknowledging the continued centrality of whiteness as a racial category to which many members of the post-Soviet diaspora have differential access, this book explores the participation of post-USSR migrants in various migratory forms in order to call for work that outlines similarities between individual segments of the diaspora and other contemporary migrants in their encounters with increased socioeconomic inequality, tightened immigration restrictions, segmented access to diminished citizenship rights, the growth in anti-immigrant sentiment, and the challenges of establishing new collective immigrant identities with transnational and diasporic dimensions.

1

The Post-Soviet Diaspora on Transnational Reality TV

While they have largely been neglected in academic scholarship, residents of the former Soviet Union are often represented in US popular culture. Throughout the 1990s, they continued to be portrayed in Cold War terms as US enemies and mail-order brides or fetishized as political refugees from socialism (Katchanovski 2007; Carruthers 2009). In the late 1990s and early 2000s many Hollywood movies featured criminal characters with Russian and Ukrainian names, referenced the existence of a "Russian mafia," and depicted "Russians" as terrorists and arms dealers (Katchanovski 2007). Popular serial dramas from the turn of the twenty-first century like *NYPD Blue* (1993–2005), *The Sopranos* (1999–2007), and *24* (2001–2010), similarly represented former USSR residents as terrorists or villains.[1] A newer series like *House of Cards* (2013–present) has portrayed Russia and its president as one of the main US adversaries in the contemporary era. At the time of this writing, Special counsel Robert Mueller is investigating Russia's involvement in the 2016 US presidential elections.

Even after the 9/11 terrorist attacks, highly stereotypical depictions of residents of the former Soviet Union as evil have tended to outnumber those of Muslim Arabs (Katchanovski 2007).[2] Since *24*'s first season in 2001, for example, its protagonist Jack Bauer of the fictional Counter Terrorist Unit tirelessly struggled to foil more "Russian" terrorist plots than attacks by Muslim Arabs. The "Russian" protagonists in *24* are always former military or KGB agents, come from some unspecified part of the former USSR, speak something barely resembling Russian, and are played by German, British, Irish, and US actors (Ohanyan-Tri 2015).[3] The fact that the USSR's largest successor nations, Russia and Ukraine, and their citizens are more frequently depicted as terrorists than are the residents of an equally homogeneously constructed ideological US opponent located in the "Middle East" shows that Cold War views of a world divided into two ideological camps remain entrenched. Different

US enemies are simply conflated to help justify the US wars on terror in the old binary Cold War terms.

As one of the newest and most widely watched media forms, reality TV shows from the 2000s have lent themselves especially well to portrayals of the post-Soviet diaspora that depart from these established media representations of Russians as major post–Cold War foes. The short-lived 2011 Lifetime show *Russian Dolls* (2011) and the immensely popular *Dancing with the Stars* (*DWTS*), which has been on ABC since 2005, exemplify the emergence of a new narrative that explicitly associates the post-Soviet diaspora with idealized accounts of turn of the twentieth century European immigration. *Russian Dolls* and *DWTS* highlight their cast members' cultural assimilation to a "Russian" ethnicity and their upward mobility into the white middle class as they appear to be following in the footsteps of their supposed European predecessors who assimilated to a pan-European whiteness and whose descendants developed ethnicized identities in the 1960s. Just as turn of the twentieth century European immigrants were often positioned and placed themselves in explicit contrast to African Americans, post-Soviet immigrants are assigned a pan-European whiteness or one of its ethnicized versions through contrast with the largest group of contemporary migrants from Latin America.

The reality TV genre emerged in the late 1990s at a time when the television industry was undergoing drastic transformations. The privatization and deregulation of large sectors of the industry and the subsequent arrival of new cable and satellite channels, created a need for programming that was predominantly driven by economic considerations, such as lower production and airtime cost (Biressi and Nunn 2005, 16). The use of program concepts or so-called formats is a cost-saving staple of reality TV. As they document and systematize the production knowledge gained from the development of a particular show, formats are duplicated or modified for introduction into other national markets in order to save money.[4] *DWTS* is an adaptation of the British Broadcasting Corporation's most successful reality show format *Strictly Come Dancing*. While it is not a format adaptation as such, *Russian Dolls* is modeled after MTV's notorious docusoap *Jersey Shore*. As additional cost-saving measures, reality TV shows typically cast nonactors and employ minimal scripting in order to eliminate the need to pay unionized writers and actors. Participants in reality TV shows are placed in highly constructed and often unusual situations that encourage behaviors and interactions designed to produce maximum emotional effect. The live or recorded surveillance footage of these responses is then edited into narrative structures that mimic the storytelling employed in other, more scripted shows and that play to audience expectations by reaffirming familiar views of the social world (Friedman 2002; Biressi and Nunn 2005, 3).

While reality TV thus actively constructs the "reality" it features through production and editing practices, the genre markets itself as providing audiences with unmediated, immediate, and intimate representations of ordinary people in unscripted situations, often by employing the tropes of revelation, truth telling, and exposure through interviews with participants (Biressi and Nunn 2005, 3–4). As it emphasizes drama and conflict to provide maximum entertainment, reality TV also engages with questions that other media forms rarely touch. The genre often addresses issues of individual and collective identity formation, and may even have taken over the task of constructing, not just representing, these identities (Turner 1996, 160).

Dancing with the Stars and *Russian Dolls* give representational shape to the ongoing construction of a collective "Russian" identity, which the two shows portray as a contemporary version of turn of the century European immigrant adaptation and upward mobility. A game show, *DWTS* focuses on the relationships between predominantly US-born B-list celebrities and their professional dance partners, many of whom are post-Soviet immigrants who have become stars in their own right through participation in the show. Reality TV promotes the notion that cast members can attain celebrity status through involvement in the genre as a way to gain access to upward mobility. While the two shows depict their post-Soviet participants as updated versions of generic turn of the twentieth century European immigrants, *Russian Dolls* models its portrayal of post-USSR participants more specifically after Italian Americans. This collective identity consolidated in the 1960s alongside other white ethnicized identities to reference the immigrant roots of European-descended Americans with ancestors from Ireland, Italy, and the Russian empire (M. Jacobson 2006, 5).

The mythologized accounts of turn of the twentieth century European migration that *DTWS* and *Russian Dolls* associate with the post-Soviet cast erases differences in the arrival and adaptation of various European immigrant groups. The identities of descendants of turn of the twentieth century Italian migrants thus become interchangeable with those of contemporary post-USSR immigrants. The two shows depict an equally homogeneous ethnic "Russianness" that obscures intradiasporic distinctions, such as cast members' diverse ethnicities and origins in different Soviet republics and their successor nations. While *DTWS* and *Russian Dolls* focus on 1.5-generation immigrant participants who most likely arrived as religious refugees, the two shows consistently downplay the Jewish identities of many of their cast members. Their association with a homogeneous whiteness or with one of its ethnic versions obscures the fact that, unlike other earlier migrants, turn of the twentieth century migration by those of primarily Jewish descent from Russia's Pale of Settlement did not result in the development of a "Russian" ethnic identity to which contemporary immigrants could assimilate. Turn of the twentieth century arrivals instead largely identified with a Jewish Americanness that had been created by earlier arrivals from Central Europe. To acknowledge that members of the post-Soviet diaspora may be connected to facets of an American Jewish identity, however, would severely complicate the emerging association of the diaspora with a mythologized and monolithic European immigrant whiteness to which Jewishness has a complicated relationship.

Just as the white ethnic identities that *DTWS* and *Russian Dolls* attribute to the new immigrants emerged in direct response to and in part as a backlash to the civil rights movements and growing immigration from Latin America and Asia in the 1960s, the two shows' cast members are ascribed a white racial identity through direct contrast with new arrivals from Latin America. Emerging academic scholarship has similarly associated post-Soviet migrants with processes of racialization that were experienced by earlier European immigrants. As historians of whiteness have established, these migrants first sought entry into and then worked to maintain membership in whiteness by differentiating themselves from nonwhite populations and simultaneously denying their white privilege. The two shows represent members of the post-Soviet diaspora as setting themselves deliberately apart from and often engaging in hostility toward Latina/os. Thus, *Russian Dolls* devoted an entire episode to addressing prohibitions against interracial dating with Latina/os, while social media and academic discourses surrounding *DWTS* have focused on how the spray tanning that is used by post-Soviet dancers underscores both their fascination with Latin American dance forms and their efforts to set themselves apart from Latina/os as the main target of anti-immigrant discourses.

Because the two shows' production of "Russianness" as an updated version of US immigrant whiteness relies on the idea that reality TV grants unmediated access to the "reality" it depicts, it is difficult to determine the degree to which the post-Soviet participants have been complicit in these portrayals. But some of the media commentary surrounding *Russian Dolls* and *DWTS*, particularly interviews with the shows' cast, their use of social media, and their participation in other non-US TV shows where their identity is differently constructed, foreground the neoliberal push factors for post-Soviet emigration, significant intradiasporic differences, and post-Soviet immigrants' efforts to engage with their homes and counter heightened US xenophobia. An acknowledgment of these factors underscores that post-USSR immigrants experience similar processes of adaptation and transnationalism as other contemporary new arrivals, which creates opportunities for comparative work across various diasporas.

Intergenerational Upward Mobility through Dancesport on *DWTS*

A BBC franchise, US *DWTS* is a dance competition and one of the most widely watched reality TV shows in which celebrities are cast. Created in 2005 after an Australian adaptation successfully debuted in the fall of 2004, the US version of *DWTS* format illustrates how the notion that celebrity status affords access to upward mobility has spread beyond elites and into the larger population (Turner 1996). By casting upcoming, established, or fading B-list celebrities who use the show as a springboard to jump- or restart their entertainment careers, *DTWS* highlights that reality TV now produces, markets, amplifies, and sells its own stars rather than simply features already established ones (Turner 1996, 156). *DWTS* follows its celebrities over the span of several months as they are trained by professionals in International ballroom dancing and related styles. Live footage of the couples' dance performances and of the judging are interspersed with recorded documentary footage of participants' back stories, rehearsals, behind the scenes moments, and confessional testimonials.

Because it is part of the BBC franchise, the US adaptation needs to reproduce the main generic elements of the original British format, particularly its use of the International style of ballroom, which originated in the United Kingdom in the mid-twentieth century and is considered the most prestigious style of dancing (McMains 2006, 95). This style differs significantly from the type of ballroom dancing that developed in the 1920s in the United States and has been most widely taught here. To be able to showcase International ballroom, the US version of *DWTS* cast a large number of foreign-born professionals who were trained in this style and participated in its dancesport version in locations outside the United States. Out of the original six professionals cast in the first season of *DWTS*, four were foreign born, and one, Alec Mazo, had emigrated from the former USSR as a child. When the cast was significantly expanded in 2006, several post-Soviet dancers were added as regulars. They included Maksim Chmerkovskiy, Karina Smirnoff, and Anna Trebunskaya. Maksim's younger brother, Valentin Chmerkovskiy joined the show as a regular in fall 2011. Inna Brayer, who came to the United States as a young child and several first-generation immigrants, including Elena Grinenko, Dmitry Chaplin, and Anna Demidova, have also appeared in several seasons of the show. Gleb Savchenko and Artem Chigvintsev, who both left Russia as adults, were added in the last few seasons.

In addition to hiring talent from Western Europe and Australia, *DWTS* was able to recruit from a large *domestic* pool of post-USSR immigrants whose arrival and settlement in the United States coincided with the adaptation of *DWTS*. Post-Soviet migrants brought with them a high regard for and training in ballroom. In the former Soviet Union, many parents sent their children—both boys and girls—to ballroom dance classes. Rigorous government-supported dance programs also prepared students for international competitions (Berger 2003). After the demise of the USSR, many highly trained ballroom dancers came to the United States and were able to make a living by teaching dance, opening dance studios, and seeking success as dancesport athletes (McMains 2006, 21; Berger 2003). Just as those fleeing Russia's 1917 Bolshevik revolution made important contributions to the development of US American theater, the much larger migration from the former USSR has initiated a surge in ballroom dancing and an astounding growth in the number of dance studios in the United States. Ballroom dancing continues to be most popular among immigrants from the former Soviet Union and their children, whose parents see participation in the dancesport as a way to achieve the American Dream (McMains 2006, 24; Solomon 2002; "Why Russian-American Jews" 2015). Participation in ballroom is also viewed as a sign of education and a means of creating community ("Why Russian-American Jews" 2015).

Even though the post-Soviet professionals in *DWTS* were originally envisioned as mere background to the celebrities whose apprenticeship as dancers was to be the focus of the show, over several seasons many of the dancers have become stars in their own right with a loyal following among the show's audience (Barnes 2011). While US critics have explored issues of gender, ethnicity, and disability on *DWTS* with regard to the stars featured on the show, the representation of its professionals has not yet received scholarly attention.[5] These cast members are not just hired to train celebrities. As members of a new diaspora, they act as what Anne Cooper-Chen (2005) has called "factors of glocalization" that facilitate the introduction of a global reality TV franchise like *DWTS* to another national media market like the United States. As regulars who have stayed on the show season after season, the professionals have increasingly been featured talking to the stars, the judges, or the show's hosts. Many of these interactions highlight the post-Soviet dancers' status as immigrants through an emphasis on their accents and their frequent lack of knowledge of older forms of US popular culture, with which the new immigrants tend to be unfamiliar.

In season 10 (2010) audiences learned more about the show's dancers through short videos that featured some of their biographies. These clips placed the post-Soviet cast squarely within established narratives of white immigrant success. The videos singled out these professionals from the show's other foreign-born dancers of Western European and Australian background to highlight their stories of intergenerational upward mobility through immigration and participation in US dancesport. The clips about Chmerkovskiy and Trebunskaya briefly address the migration experiences of the two dancers who came as young children with their families. Trebunskaya is shown talking about her hard childhood in industrial Chelyabinsk, Russia, without providing specific details about the difficulties she experienced, and declaring that dance functioned as a form of escape. Her mother states that the family emigrated to help alleviate her daughter's asthma. Chmerkovskiy's immigration story is told by his father, who recounts that the family left Ukraine to provide a better life for their children and to spare their boys mandatory military service.

The video clips reduce the push factors for the families' migration, including social upheavals following the introduction of neoliberalism, to a more universal immigrant story, according to which movement is driven by the parents' desire to provide better lives for their children. The clips also never address the legal circumstances under which the families of the two dancers were able to enter the United States. They make it seem as though any family that wanted a better life for their children, especially those from Europe, could just freely enter the United States. The videos thus reify the mythic notion of turn of the twentieth century European migration, particularly from the Pale of Settlement, in which entire families left behind their difficult lives in the "old" country so that the next generation could have better opportunities in the United States and in which immigration was not as tightly regulated as today. This myth of an immigrant America appeals to the show's audience, which is dominated by women over forty who tend to vote Republican (Harnick 2010).

It is unclear if the dancers and their families articulated their migration stories in these terms to the video producers. In her ethnographic work, Natalia Kasatkina has found that first-generation post-Soviet immigrants in Tucson, Arizona often provide rather vague reasons for their emigration (Kasatkina 2010, 125). In the narratives of Soviet and post-Soviet Jewish families, however, their emigration from the Soviet Union or successor nations tends to be more specifically framed as a way to provide better lives for the next generation (Senderovich 2016).

Compared to the *DWTS* portrayal of post-Soviet dancers as following in the footsteps of earlier European migrants on a path toward upward mobility, the large numbers of post-USSR dancers on the BBC original *Strictly Come Dancing* are depicted very differently. The BBC's 2015 documentary, "Strictly Russian," about two of its professional post-Soviet dancers who have most often won the show, instead highlights their exposure to government-sponsored training programs in the former Soviet Union.[6] The film also acknowledges that the dramatic changes in the former USSR and successor nations shaped their emigration, asserting that participation in dancesport enabled post-Soviet dancers an escape from poverty and from gangs, crime, and drugs (Creighton 2015).

The narrative of upward mobility that is so central to the videotaped biographies of US *DWTS*'s post-Soviet dancers not only reaffirms the exceptionalist notion of the United States as a nation of immigrants, but it also minimizes the national and ethnic diversity of the post-USSR diaspora. I was only able to verify that one of the post-Soviet professionals on the show, Inna Brayer, entered the United States with her family as religious refugees in 1989 ("Why Russian-American Jews" 2015). Asylum not only qualified Jewish migrants for public assistance, but it also allowed them to sponsor the migration of family members and provided them with shorter waiting periods for citizenship (Solari, 2010, 217). But other post-Soviet dancers on the show are also of Jewish desent. Karina Smornof has a Jewish father. Even though it is not stated in the *DTWS* video clip about him, Maksim Chmerkovskiy's father is Jewish (but his mother is not), and in season 18 viewers were introduced to his monolingual grandmother who lives in New York. In the Soviet Union, ethnic intermarriages like that of Chmerkovskiy's family were relatively common, so that a large number of post-Soviet family members arriving under US refugee policies were not Jewish, and even after 1989 small numbers of Jewish refugees were still allowed to enter the United States annually.

While his portrayal on *DWTS* completely ignores this facet of Chmerkovskiy's identity, judging by their social media presence he and his brother are highly aware of their Jewish background. They sometimes integrate symbols of Judaism into their self-representations, which is a relatively common practice even for secular post-Soviet immigrants of Jewish background. For example, in 2014 the Chmerkovskiy brothers used their Twitter accounts to post pictures of Maksim wearing a Star of David necklace and Val using arm tefillin in a Jewish weekday morning service.

In addition to downplaying Chmerkovskiy's Jewish descent and its likely significance for his family's migration, *DWTS*'s focus on portraying his "Russian" identity also never addresses his origins in the former

Ukrainian Soviet Socialist Republic (UkSSR) and its successor nation, Ukraine. Chmerkovskiy's family left Odessa in 1994, three years after Ukraine had declared its independence from the former USSR. But throughout most of its seasons, *DWTS* simply referred to him as "Russian," with host Tom Bergeron calling him a "blushing Russian" as late as May 2014. Probably because the ongoing conflict between Russia and Ukraine had by then been widely reported in the US press, media accounts surrounding the show in 2015 sometimes also described Chmerkovskiy as "Ukrainian" or "Ukrainian American."

In interviews and on social media Chmerkovskiy has also oscillated between calling himself "Russian" and "Ukrainian," but he did so using notions of ethnicity that were prevalent in the former USSR. While his use of the term "Russian" may simply refer to his identification with the Russian-speaking diaspora and the fact that Russian is his first language (Kolstø 1999; Wilson 1997, 181), Chmerkovskiy more likely employed it to refer to Soviet notions of ethnicity as denoting parental heritage. Both of Chmerkovskiy's parents identify as ethnic Russians who resided in Ukraine and Turkmenistan, a former republic in Asia, for long stretches of their lives (Skripnikova 2011). Although he must have been exposed to Ukrainian in the media and in school when he lived there until the age of fourteen, Chmerkovskiy seems to have little knowledge of the language (Litskevich 2011a), which has only limited mutual intelligibility with Russian. Such monolingualism is more common among the ethnically Russian, Russophone minority than among Ukrainian- or Russian-speaking Ukrainians (Wilson 2002, 35).[7]

DWTS's representation of post-USSR immigrants as homogeneously white Europeans who follow in the footsteps of earlier European migration is echoed in popular and academic discourses about the growing participation of post-USSR dancers in US dancesport, which contrast members of the diaspora with Latina/os. Instead of highlighting potential conflicts between post-Soviet dancers and the African American or Latina/o celebrities with whom they are often paired, discourses surrounding *DWTS* have focused on the centrality of spray tanning in International ballroom. Dance professionals use spray tan during competitions and performances as routinely as athletes in other sports, particularly in bodybuilding, to highlight their body image. A spray tan is assumed to make athletes appear healthier, slimmer, and more fit under harsh camera lights, and to accentuate their body shape and contours as well as their muscular definition.

The rise in the popularity of spray tanning is intricately linked to historical changes in attitudes toward skin color in Europe and the United States. Until the beginning of the twentieth century, pale skin was regarded as a marker of wealth and leisure, while a darker complexion was associated with those having to make their living by toiling outside. But when scientists in the 1920s determined that sunlight produced vitamin D and could prevent childhood diseases, the sun began to be regarded as a form of medication. Exposure to the environment was also prescribed as a treatment for tuberculosis, which was a leading cause of death. By the 1930s tan became a marker of vitality, beauty, and health, and beach resorts emerged as iconic vacation spots (Freund 2012, 3–4). As celebrities began to adopt and embody the trend toward tanned skin, the arrival of package holidays in the 1970s and 1980s made tanned skin accessible to a larger public. When health concerns about the negative effects of sun exposure arose, spray tanning products emerged to fill the gap.

Especially in the United States, where skin color has been central to determining questions of racial identity, tanning raises questions about racial identification. Even though tanned skin is sometimes theorized as indicating individuals' desire to change their race or become "the other," the practice also enables the performance of a modified form of ethnicity within accepted parameters of whiteness. Popular discourses surrounding *DWTS* that are invested in trying to determine the place of post-Soviet immigrants in the US racial hierarchy often associate cast members deemed to have a more ambiguous physical appearance with spray tanning. Though he has repeatedly denied subjecting himself to the procedure, Maksim Chmerkovskiy has frequently been accused of engaging in the practice (Carter 2012). The determination that he must have artificially darkened his skin places Chmerkovskiy within the parameters of established US racial categories and ignores the high degree of ethnic intermarriages and population shifts in the former USSR that have produced differential appearances and forms of ethnic identification. On *DWTS*, spray tanning has also been employed to maintain strict divisions between white immigrant and nonwhite cast members. When in season 6 (2008) Polish-born dancer Edyta Śliwińska supposedly "overtanned" and her skin looked darker than that of her partner African American football player Jason Taylor, for example, he also had to get spray tanned so as not to confuse accepted ways of differentiating between white (European) and nonwhite individuals in the United States in the interracial coupling (Chozick 2009).

Academic discourses about spray tanning in dancesport have made similar assertions. Like scholarship that has traced the emergence of twentieth-century European immigrants' white racial identity in opposition to "blackness," this work positions post-Soviet dancers who spray tan in explicit contrast to the "brownness" of Latina/os. Dance scholar Juliet McMains (2001) has likened spray tanned post-USSR dancers to nineteenth-century blackface minstrelsy performers. Minstrelsy shows were especially popular between the 1820s and 1840s, when issues of slavery were moving to the forefront of US national debates. White male performers used burned cork to blacken their skin in order to create racial stereotypes through public ridicule. Initially minstrelsy perpetuated negative stereotypes about several racialized groups. Though it was focused on African Americans, native-born white minstrels often made fun of Irish immigrants who were seen as racially other and similar to African Americans.

Whiteness scholars have posited that minstrelsy helped turn of the twentieth century European immigrants enter and assimilate into whiteness (Lott 1993; Rogin 1996). When Irish Americans began to dominate minstrelsy and became its most famous stars (Kibler 2015, 22), they challenged Irish stereotypes and asserted their Americanness, in part by ridiculing and thus distancing themselves from African Americans (Nowatzki 2006). These performers created an abject but fascinating blackness with which they partially identified in order to show that they shared a white racial identity with their audiences. When blackface reemerged in early twentieth-century film and on the stage, Jewish Americans took center stage (Kibler 2015, 23). Their use of blackface minstrelsy served to Americanize and whiten Jewish blackface performers against the backdrop of growing US anti-Semitism. By donning blackface, Jewish performers were able to distance themselves from negative perceptions of Jewishness and position themselves as both white and American (Rogin 1998). In a rare publication on the contemporary use of blackface by Asian American performers, Rachel Lee (2002) has argued that for them the practice may not just be functioning as a form of racial appropriation, which would reinforce existing power structures and allow Asian Americans to escape the cost of being black. Lee speculates that their use of blackface may instead be read as an allusion to Asian Americans' identification with African American struggles for emancipation and civil rights, and could thus be understood as a way of setting the grounds for potential alliances.

In contrast, McMains extends the US history of European immigrant minstrelsy performances into the contemporary moment to read the spray tanning by post-Soviet dance professionals as a cross-racial act of appropriation. Probably because post-Soviet immigrants and their children have come to dominate the sport, McMains singles out post-USSR dancers from the much larger number of (white) professionals who spray tan for performances and competitions. She argues that for the post-Soviet dancers, spray tan functions as a form of "brownface" that allows them to appear Latina/o, particularly when competing in the "Latin" dances that were inspired by Latin American and Caribbean dance forms, and in which post-USSR dancers often specialize. According to McMains, their spray tan signals the post-Soviet migrants' interest in Latin American dance forms and simultaneously their privileged white status, which indicates their difference from Latina/os who have been the focus of contemporary anti-immigration debates in the United States. As was the case with earlier European immigrants who had conflicted relationships with African Americans, McMains argues that spray tanning helps post-Soviet migrants assimilate to US whiteness at the expense of those who do not have that option because of their nonwhite appearance.

The historical comparison is fraught, however. Differently from turn of the twentieth century European immigrants who participated in minstrelsy as a cultural practice that had evolved *domestically* in explicit response to assimilation pressures, the post-Soviet dancers on the US version of *DWTS imported* spray tanning from the former USSR, its successor nations, or other countries where the practice has been as integral to the ballroom dance industry as it has to other sports. Unlike minstrelsy, spray tanning did not emerge as part of conscious efforts to solidify a white US racial identity through opposition to and the denigration of cultures and individuals deemed nonwhite. In a different national context, the spray tan that post-Soviet and other professionals employ on the BBC's original *Strictly Come Dancing* has also not been associated with racist attitudes or opposition to immigrants from other nations. Nevertheless, when used in the United States, spray tanning needs to be understood in the context of the US ethnoracial hierarchy, and post-Soviet and other dancers need to rethink their use of this practice.

Russian Dolls and Intergenerational Mobility through Ostentatious Consumption

While *DWTS* represents its post-USSR migrant cast as assimilated white "Russians" who have achieved the American immigrant dream of upward mobility through dancesport in order to appeal to the show's mostly conservative audience, the first short-lived reality show to focus exclusively on post-USSR migrants, Lifetime's *Russian Dolls*, was geared to an audience that also included the new immigrants and their children. The twelve twenty-minute episodes, which aired from August to October 2011, were cocreated by two post-Soviet Jewish immigrants. Alina Dizik arrived from Minsk, today's Belarus, in 1989 and Elina Miller came from Kharkov, today's Ukraine, in 1990. The two women met as teenagers in Chicago and fondly remembered New York City's Brighton Beach from childhood trips (Alston 2010).

Originally called "Brighton Beach," the docusoap set out to focus on the life stories of residents of this Russian-speaking enclave as representatives of a larger community in the process of assimilating to a white US racial identity. First settled by early twentieth century eastern European Jewish immigrants, many of whom worked in the garment industry, in the late 1960s Brighton Beach was inhabited by retirees from the Amalgamated Clothing Workers' Union. After the decline of this community, Jewish immigrants who were beginning to arrive in the 1970s, predominantly from today's Ukraine, were resettled there (Orleck 2001, 123–124). Popularized in the 1994 Tim Roth film *Little Odessa*, Brighton Beach has also been linked to organized crime syndicates. With the recent arrival of migrants from various former Soviet republics, the percentage of the Jewish population in Brighton Beach has decreased and the influence of migrants from post-Soviet Asian countries has become visible in ethnically mixed restaurants and other businesses. Dizik and Miller seem to have been aware of the ongoing transformation of the enclave and the post-Soviet diaspora before they created the show. They have stated that they wanted to cast a variety of "ethnic" archetypes on *Russian Dolls*, such as "a very straightforward ethnic Russian who's proud of the motherland," a Russian Jew, and someone from the Caucasus in order to "create a microcosm of the former Soviet Union" (Alston 2010).

But the show's cast does not reflect the diversification of Brighton Beach or engage with the internal ethnic and national composition of the former Soviet Union. Instead, Dizik and Miller selected mostly Jewish cast members who, like them, came mainly from today's Ukraine, Belarus, and also from Moldova as part of the large post-1980s migration. Many of the cast do not even live in Brighton Beach. As in *DWTS*, cast members are identified and at times are also shown to self-identify as "Russian," while their more complicated forms of association with various Soviet republics and successor nations are ignored, and their Jewish identities are downplayed. The show also perpetuates several stereotypes about "Russians." The change in the show's title from "Brighton Beach" to *Russian Dolls* introduced explicit visual imagery in its opening credits that placed the female cast inside Russian nesting dolls. Even though these dolls are traditionally associated with notions of motherhood, the term "Russian Dolls" also gestures toward escort services, prostitution rings, and mail-order brides. In addition, while the show's promotional slogan, "The Russians aren't coming, the Russians are here," signals that a sizable post-Soviet community has already developed in the United States, it also alludes to Cold War fears of the USSR as a country intent on invading the territory of the United States.

In its advertisement of the docusoap, Lifetime insisted that *Russian Dolls* provides "a glimpse into the lives of members of an immigrant community who are American without having yet become fully American" (Reddy 2011). *Russian Dolls* highlights how the cast's low-brow, conspicuous consumption patterns provide them with the illusion of upward mobility and also reveal that they are not yet fully assimilated, but remain part of the "ethnicized" lower class. Russian American novelist Michael Idov (2011) has described *Russian Dolls* as a form of minstrelsy, where members of one ethnic or racial group created and perpetuated stereotypes of other groups thought to be inferior. Idov has argued that the reality TV show similarly allows one segment of a particular group, namely "assimilated [middle-class] Russian-Americans," to enter show business by ridiculing and "exploit[ing] the image of the unassimilated Russian-American."

The majority of *Russian Dolls'* multigenerational female cast arrived in the United States as part of the post-USSR migration that started in the late 1980s. While details of the cast's migration background were rarely shared on the show, according to the Lifetime website and publications surrounding *Russian Dolls*, forty-seven-year-old Renata Krumer came from Belarus when she was in her twenties, thirty-four-year-old Marina Levitis came from Ukraine in 1991, twenty-three-year-old Diana Kosov arrived from Moldova in 1991, twenty-six-year-old Anastasia Kurinnaya came from Ukraine in 1988, and twenty-two-year-old Anna Khazanov arrived from Ukraine in 1998, at age nine.

But the show represents members of the two generations very differently. The lives of the younger, 1.5-immigrant generation cast are portrayed through parallels to the hedonistic ethnicized youth subculture embodied in the notorious MTV docusoap *Jersey Shore*. In contrast, representations of the first-generation immigrant women in their late thirties and fifties who are culturally less assimilated but have made it into the middle or upper-middle class, are modeled after the (supposedly ethnicity-free) culture of ostentatious consumption showcased on *The Real Housewives*, which was itself modeled after soap operas that focus on the lives of upper-class women. The women on *Russian Dolls*—a jeweler, a radio show host, and the wife of the owner of Brighton Beach's well-known nightclub, Rasputin—are identified by displays of their wealth in ways that also allude to the stereotype of the newly rich "New Russian" elite, which is associated with criminality and gaudy consumption habits. In keeping with this stereotype, Marina's husband, the owner of Rasputin, was convicted of felony charges during the airing of the show.[8]

Like *DTWS, Russian Dolls* emphasizes the stories of its 1.5-generation protagonists, whose experiences resemble those of the two shows' co-producers. These cast members have not yet arrived in the middle class and are aspiring to the kind of white ethnicized identity presented in the notorious *Jersey Shore* to which writers and producers explicitly compared *Russian Dolls*. A casting call for the show, posted in Brighton Beach, asked: "Are you the Russian Snooki or The Situation? Are you a super outgoing and fun-loving Russian-American that sometimes sneaks kalbaska, pel'meni and vodka from the fridge? Can people hear the Euro/Techno/Russian music blasting from your car before they see you pull up? . . . The cameras will roll as you do what you do best—eat, drink and PARTY." *Jersey Shore* was the first US reality show to sport a white ethnicized but ethnically homogeneous cast, which was supposedly Italian American. This premise very much contrasted with that of the earliest US reality show, MTV's *The Real World*, which assembled a racially and ethnically heterogeneous cast in order to generate conflict among cast members.

Jersey Shore highlights the persistence of remnants of twentieth-century southern European racialization by marking a white, working-class subcultural Italian American identity as ethnic. Many Italians remained poor and working class longer than most other European immigrants (J. Guglielmo 2003, 3). These migrants and their descendants came to be associated with an ethnicized group identity. Donald Tricarico (2007) has theorized that the Italian American youth subculture originated in pejorative views of new arrivals from Italy at the turn of the twentieth century, and was reinforced in the 1940s and 1950s—at the same time that a pan-European notion of whiteness emerged—through association with notions of the "Italian mafia," street gangs, and the movie *Saturday Night Fever*. In the film, working-class Italian American youngsters try to escape the restrictions of their class by participating in the glamorous world of disco clubs. Like these Italian American youths of the 1950s, *Jersey Shore*'s cast is not quite part of the middle class, but they are also not members of an oppositional youth culture that tends to be linked to urban youths who are racialized as nonwhite. Rather than escaping from the presumed constraints of their ethnic identity or its negative connotations, the Italian American youngsters reaffirm it by creating an ethnicized style that incorporates several sites of consumption such as tanning salons, gyms, pool halls, and beauty parlors.

Through analogy with *Jersey Shore*, *Russian Dolls* associates its younger cast with a similar consumer identity that is employed to turn their differences as 1.5-generation immigrants into a white ethnic identity deemed to be "Russian." Like the narrative of European immigrant whiteness, this analogy conflates descendants of turn of the twentieth century migrants with the children of contemporary arrivals who are themselves immigrants (rather than native-born ethnics). Cast members of *Jersey Shore* are several generations removed from the migration experiences of their ancestors and many are not of Italian background. Because *Russian Dolls* models itself after this show, it cannot highlight the biculturality of its immigrant cast members' identities. In a *Wall Street Journal* blog entitled "I can see Russia from my House," *Russian Dolls'* cocreator Dizik (2011) described herself as "having a foot in both worlds" and wrote that the show highlights "that this identity is in no way unique to me."[9] But the show does not represent the complexity and depth of this bicultural identity. Although the younger cast members are sometimes shown speaking some Russian with their parents, their cultural "Russianness" appears to be limited to visiting bathhouses and consuming Russian food.

Like the video portrayals of *DWTS*'s professional dancers, the immigration stories of these cast members are framed in the mythologized narrative of early European migration that emphasizes the intergenerational success stories of immigrants leaving behind their difficult lives in Europe so that the next generation can have better opportunities in the United States. At the same time that she is getting a spray tan, twenty-six-year-old Anastasia Kurinnaya, for example, tells audiences that her parents sacrificed their professional careers in Ukraine to emigrate to the United States when she was three so she could be educated here. Today, her parents continue to pay her university tuition, even in the face of mounting debt, as she keeps changing her major. Episode 3 features twenty-two-year-old Anna Khazanov, who came from Ukraine in 1998, as one of the latest arrivals among the women featured on the show. Her family lives in a small two-bedroom apartment and her grandmother sleeps on the couch. To help them financially, Anna started a modeling career at fifteen and opened her own modeling school.

Aside from this participant, the show creates story arcs of young cast members that highlight their search for intergenerational upward mobility through ostentatious consumption. Like the white ethnics of *Jersey Shore*, these participants are mainly interested in partying and self-beautification through tanning and workouts. Whereas the post-Soviet professional dancers on *DWTS* use spray tanning selectively as a form of body enhancement during competitions and performances, the female participants in *Russian Dolls* wear their deep tan on a daily basis so they appear to be part of a wealthier class for whom a tan symbolizes leisure and attractiveness. As their tan allows *Russian Dolls'* female participants to modify their body images to fit notions of class membership, they also stay within accepted parameters of an ethnicized whiteness. Because they lack the resources to finance the monied lifestyle to which they aspire, the female cast members talk frankly about seeking a wealthy husband.

In its focus on conspicuous consumption as a means to assimilate to an ethnicized and class-specific whiteness, the show never references the more unusual attitudes toward materialism among members of the post-USSR diaspora that, for many, were formed by years of material deprivation in the former Soviet Union. In her blog, Dizik wrote that "I still find it difficult to throw away uneaten food and am known to cave in to a designer bag splurge thanks to post-Communist era materialism. I always get pangs of guilt after not reusing perfectly good tea bags or paper towels. And can never forget that we left the U.S.S.R. with just $1,000 to our name, some bedding and, of course, a few leather jackets" (Dizik 2011). It is beyond the framework of the show to explore why members of this immigrant community who have experienced material deprivation in the former USSR or have heard stories about these experiences from their parents might choose ostentatious consumption to demonstrate that they are trying to assimilate to a version of white middle-class success in the United States.

Like the comments about spray tanning in dancesport and on *DTWS*, *Russian Dolls* also firmly contrasts its members with nonwhite US populations by emphasizing their hostility toward these groups. One episode focuses on post-Soviet cast members who oppose interracial marriage with Latina/os. Twenty-three-year-old Diana Kosov is shown to be breaking up with her "Spanish" boyfriend because he is not "Russian," and her mother later also tells her to marry a "Russian." Both women here use the term "Russian" when they actually mean "Jewish Russian." That they are Jewish is indicated by the fact that Diana wears a Star of David necklace when she breaks up with her boyfriend. There are clues that other cast members are also Jewish—and more observant than the Chmerkovskiy brothers from *DTWS* who sometimes tweet pictures of themselves wearing symbols of Judaism. As he is first introduced with his wife Marina, Michael Levitis is pictured with a kippah, and their front doorpost features a mezuzah parchment inscribed with verses from the Torah. The Levitises met as students at a Jewish high school and send their own children to a yeshiva elementary school (Hoffman 2011).

But *Russian Dolls* never explicitly identifies members of its cast as Jewish, probably because the show set out to create an ethnically white "Russianness" modeled after Italian and not Jewish Americans. Or perhaps participants in the show simply employ the term "Russian" as a shorthand because, as cocreator Dizik has stated, "For most Russian Jews . . . [y]ou really can't separate one from the other, and most of us are so secular that a lot of the Jewish traditions get mixed up with the Russian traditions" (Dizik 2011).

Because the cast of *Russian Dolls* is portrayed as white "Russian," the views of Diana's family toward interracial marriages, like their perspectives on spray tanning in dancesport, are interpreted as attempts by post-USSR immigrants to differentiate themselves from Latina/os—in this case, most likely from the largest Latina/o population in New York which is from Puerto Rico and is sometimes called "Spanish." But the Jewish identity of the post-Soviet dancers renders their attitudes toward intermarriage more complex. Jews have generally remained ambivalent about marriages to non-Jews. As Eric Goldstein (2006) has shown, from the time of their arrival in the United States, first east central and then eastern European Jews experienced pressures to assimilate to US whiteness while also wanting to retain notions of their distinctive racial identity that included opposition to intermarriages with non-Jews. While the rates of intermarriage have increased over the last few years, it remains more widespread among secular Jews in the United States (Pew Research Center 2013). The complexity of these attitudes toward interracial marriages, as embedded in Diana's comments to her boyfriend and her mother's remark to Diane, is lost in the show's effort to establish a white "Russian" consumerist identity.

Unlike the post-USSR migrants on *Russian Dolls* who position themselves and are set in explicit contrast to contemporary new arrivals who are racialized as nonwhite, docusoaps about 1.5-generation immigrants from East and West Asia that are similarly modeled after the *Jersey Shore* format do not set up a contrast between the residents of various US enclaves who participate in ethnically specific forms of ostentatious consumption and Latina/o immigrants. As in *Russian Dolls*, these shows highlight their casts' gaudy displays of consumerism as indicators that they are not yet fully assimilated, but on their way toward assimilation. Participants have access to various "shades" of whiteness, particularly forms of "honorary whiteness," through which they can enter the middle class. Called the "Persian" *Jersey Shore* and criticized for being even duller than *Russian Dolls* (Stasi 2012), for example, *Shahs of Sunset* reinforces the association of young, affluent Iranian Americans who work in Los Angeles's real estate market with vulgarity and materialism, while, like *Russian Dolls*, obscuring the immigration stories of their parents (Hale 2012). Another *Jersey Shore* offspring that never made it to network TV, called *K-Town*, cast eight Korean Americans who spend most of their time partying in LA's Koreatown.

Transnationalism, US Xenophobia, and the Post-USSR Diaspora

The representation of post-Soviet migrants as white in *Russian Dolls* and *DWTS* requires not only that they be placed in opposition to Latina/os, but also that they appear to be largely disassociated from their former homes. These immigrants are portrayed as different from other groups who are perceived as troubling the whiteness of the US nation because they supposedly resist assimilation by retaining ties to their countries of origin. But Michael Idov has drawn attention to the transnational identities of at least the first-generation immigrants cast on *Russian Dolls*, which largely remain offscreen. He has argued that even though the show's "creators . . . are more interested in presenting the 'Brighton Beach' identity as a stand-alone thing divorced from the old country, like *Jersey Shore*'s guido culture . . . [i]t's not, at least not yet." He continues, "were the cameras not trained on them, half of the cast [namely the older immigrant generation] wouldn't be speaking English" (Idov 2011).

The difficult migration experiences of these cast members and their reasons for leaving the Soviet Union have also only been depicted in spaces outside reality TV where the cast could wield more control over their self-representations. In interviews surrounding *Russian Dolls*, some of which were conducted in Russian by Russian-language TV stations, cast members told their often quite dramatic migration stories that are far more diverse than the narratives about bootstrapism and intergenerational mobility presented on the show. These stories included post-Soviet immigrants' persecution in the USSR because of their Jewish identities as well as periods of their material deprivation and reliance on public assistance in the United States before achieving economic success.

Michael Levitis recounted that his family's immigration to the United States in 1988 at age eleven was driven by his grandfather, who had been incarcerated in a gulag for financing Jewish schools ("Mikhail Levitis" 2011). In another interview, Levitis's mother Eva, a retired engineer, reported that "[m]y family started out on welfare when we first arrived here in 1988, but we worked very hard and climbed the corporate ladder, and now live an exciting life filled with colorful people" (Ruby 2011). Like accounts of turn of the twentieth century European migration that have shaped the myth of an immigrant America, *Russian Dolls* never mentions the importance of federal aid and welfare programs for the upward mobility of its first-generation cast members, many of whom also benefited from support for Jews from the former USSR and who now have achieved a level of wealth that can be openly displayed.

Like *Russian Dolls*, *DWTS* also obscures the complex transnationalism of some of its post-USSR migrant cast. Their transnational ties only become evident in media reports surrounding the show. When *DTWS* hired Gleb Savchenko to replace Chmerkovskiy as a professional dancer in season 17, the show employed a "pendular migrant," someone who emigrated from Moscow as an adult, has permanent residency in Australia where he worked on that country's version of *DTWS*, and then participated as a professional on the US version of *DWTS* after having been a member of the show's dance troupe. In 2015, Savchenko worked as a professional on the BBC's original *Strictly Come Dancing*, probably on a temporary work visa, and he also competed on the Russian version of *Dancing with the Stars*. Artem Chigvintsev, who is a permanent US resident, was originally cast as a professional on *Strictly* and then moved on to its US version, reportedly because of visa problems in the United Kingdom that were never mentioned on the US show.

Such transnational engagement is not just typical of post-Soviet migrants who came to the United States as adults and thus are perhaps more likely to become geographically mobile when new employment opportunities present themselves. Maksim Chmerkovskiy, a 1.5-generation immigrant, created perhaps even more significant transnational ties to Ukraine when he accepted the role as leading man in the first season of that country's *The Bachelor* (*Kholostiak*) in 2011. The reality TV show aired on the private channel STB in 2011, in between US *DWTS* seasons 11 and 12. Chmerkovskiy seems to have come to the attention of *Kholostiak*'s producers at STB, which also hosts the Ukrainian version of *DWTS*, when he took some time off from the US show's season 11 (2010) to visit his other, ailing grandmother in Ukraine. But Chmerkovskiy's stint on the Ukrainian show was only briefly mentioned in a "Dance Center" spoof routine in *DWTS* season 12.

Kholostiak highlighted a different yet also highly constructed aspect of Chmerkovskiy's identity than *DWTS*, which has squarely focused on his whiteness while also reminding viewers that he is foreign-born and ethnically "Russian." A dating show in which the leading man is expected to select a wife from among twenty-five contestants, *Kholostiak* portrayed Chmerkovskiy as a regular "Ukrainian" who lives in the United States but is "returning" to his "home" to look for a diasporic marriage partner. In a voiceover in this show's first episode, Chmerkovskiy explained that despite his US citizenship, he sees himself as Ukrainian, is proud of his Ukrainian heritage, and remembers fondly his first kiss and first fight in his native Odessa. The show's emphasis on Chmerkovskiy's US citizenship and Ukrainian roots served to signal the Western origins of *Kholostiak* in order to make the format more appealing to Ukrainian audiences. They have been exposed to a media market dominated by Russian imports and simultaneously also to a rhetoric expounding Ukraine's ongoing transformation from being a former part of the USSR to becoming a Westernized nation. A growing number of Western European and US format adaptations challenge the domination of Ukraine's TV market by Russian media products (Ryabinska 2011, 12–13) to convey the impression that Ukraine is increasing its cultural connections to its roots in the "West." In order to signal that a show is of "Western" origin, producers tend to make few changes to the original and often cast Western talent (Khinkulova 2012, 102).

While Chmerkovskiy's US citizenship helped him to play a similar role on *Kholostiak*, the focus on his Ukrainian roots and his continued self-definition as Ukrainian also gave the show an opportunity to emphasize the country's supposed attractiveness to members of the post-Soviet diaspora. To supply him with a credible motivation for his participation in the show since he had left Ukraine many years ago, the first episode highlighted his closeness to his mother and included footage of his relationship with his former fiancée and co-*DWTS* professional Karina Smirnoff, who is also from Ukraine. Stating that he wants his children to grow up with the kind of Ukrainian culture that only a Ukrainian wife can provide, Chmerkovskiy was shown to employ the same rhetoric as other immigrant men who marry women from their countries of origin because they are expected to uphold more traditional notions of gender and family, and to bring up their children in diaspora (Thai 2008). This representation alludes to the growing numbers of US migrants who are coming home as well as the increase in immigrant men who marry women from their homelands, thus following the nineteenth-century tradition whereby US immigrant men imported brides from their countries of origin (Cassarino 2004; Thai 2008). But the two phenomena have remained numerically negligible with regard to Ukraine. By thus presenting a highly constructed and idealized version of Chmerkovskiy as a "return migrant," *Kholostiak* tried to rebrand Ukraine as an increasingly Westernized destination for its male US diaspora and obscured the country's shortcomings that have manifested, among other things, in large out-migration, enormous economic problems, and armed hostilities between the country's major social groups, who often align their political attachments with their Russian or Ukrainian ethnicities and are supported by Ukraine and Russia.

Kholostiak's opening episode also gestured toward some of Chmerkovskiy's difficult immigration experiences as another reason for his interest in "return" and diasporic marriage. In a voiceover, he stated that the trials of immigration had brought his family closer together and that he desires a similar family for himself. In an interview about the show, Chmerkovskiy explained the obstacles that his family faced after their immigration to the United States, which were not represented in this much detail on *DWTS* or in the US media coverage of the show. He recounted that his father, a programmer by training, initially worked as a dishwasher in a pizzeria, while Chmerkovskiy supported the family by opening up his own dance studio at age sixteen (Men'shikova 2011). The family experienced downward mobility after their arrival in the United States. Better prospects emerged only through their sons' participation in dancesport for which they had been prepared in the former USSR and Ukraine, and which placed them on a path toward their present-day upper-middle-class status. Judging by Chmerkovskiy's general outspokenness while he was a regular on *DWTS* and during his many interviews, he probably also mentioned some of these details of his immigration experience to US outlets. But even though they could easily have become assimilated to the established narrative of European immigrant bootstrapism in the face of (initial) adversity, these details are usually not mentioned in the coverage of Chmerkovskiy. Episode 9 of *Kholostiak* also interspliced parts of a 2009 interview on US TV, in which Chmerkovskiy grows exasperated with the interviewer's difficulties in pronouncing his last name, and of a YouTube video by him, where he spells out his last name correctly. These incidents harken back to the turn of the twentieth century immigration to the United States when, as David Roediger writes, eastern European names were perceived to be "difficult" (Roediger 2005, 194).

If they had been more interested in the complexities of Chmerkovskiy's experiences as a US immigrant instead of his idealized relationship to his country of origin as a supposed marriage migrant, *Kholostiak's* producers could have used many more powerful examples from his coverage on US *DWTS* that attest to understudied anxieties about the place of the post-Soviet immigrant cast in the US nation and its ethnoracial hierarchy. Because *DWTS* contains these anxieties within narratives of white immigrant assimilation, they have only found expression outside the realm of the show. Here they took the form of anti-immigrant commentary that Bill Ong Hing (2002) has called narratives of "de-Americanization," which have surged since 9/11. These verbal affronts by members of the US public are designed to raise doubts about immigrants' rightful place in the US nation, independently of their actual residency or citizenship status. In interviews on the *Bonnie Hunt* and *Chelsea Lately* shows in 2010, for example, Chmerkovskiy's season 10 partner, US sportscaster Erin Andrews, called him "her Russian," imitated his accent, and remarked that she did not always understand his English even though Chmerkovskiy had lived in the United States for over twenty years by this time. When Chmerkovskiy talked to *People* magazine about his interest in the 2011 Women's World Cup in soccer, the interviewer questioned his allegiance to the US team since he was born in what is now Ukraine. Chmerkovskiy retorted, "Let's set the record straight. I've been a US citizen for 15 years. . . . That's my team, and it always has been!" (Alexander 2011).

In interviews on ABC's *The Jimmy Kimmel* show, which Kimmel conducts with couples who leave US *DWTS* each week, the host made similar de-Americanizing comments toward other post-USSR cast members. In an April 2011 interview he speculated that the audience may have voted off Dmitry Chaplin and his partner, Czech model Petra Němcová, "because it was the 'American theme' week; they [the audience] decided they had to get rid of the foreigners." When a surprised Chaplin retorted that he had "American citizenship," Jimmy responded, "[Y]eah, but still the accent; we are not sold." A few months later, Kimmel asked Valentin Chmerkovskiy, who came to the United States when he was eight, and his partner, Italian model Elizabetta Canetti, why they were eliminated. He said: "Do you think they are penalizing you for being a foreigner? . . . for both of you being foreigners coming into our country and trying to take our mirror ball?"

In an interview Maksim Chmerkovskiy gave to the Ukrainian press shortly after the final episode of *Kholostiak* aired in June 2011, he drew attention to his experience with xenophobia, which had not found expression on US *DWTS* or in the press coverage surrounding the show. Chmerkovskiy stated that many in the *DWTS* audience tended to regard him "only [as] an 'immigrant,' with sometimes an unpleasant word in front of it." He stressed the connection between anti-immigrant sentiment and US notions of race, saying, "I am Russian, a former Ukrainian, from the former Soviet Union, which is a stigma over there. . . . [I]t is called 'racial profiling,' which is when you are looked at not as a person, but as a representative of some nation, race, and all the rest." Chmerkovskiy also mentioned experiencing hate speech in the social media. He was told to "go back to his country" after especially negative "packages" about him were aired on US *DWTS* (Litskevich 2011b). On his *TV Guide* blog, Chmerkovskiy has speculated that these packages, which highlight what appear to be his physical and verbal abusiveness toward his partners as well as their frustrations with his demanding teaching style, were designed to predispose the audience to vote for other couples (Chmerkovskiy 2010a, 2010b).

Conclusion

Chmerkovskiy's lukewarm relationship with the "winner" of *Kholostiak* (who received a promise rather than an engagement ring) quickly faltered after the show. Amidst strong public criticism of his choice, Chmerkovskiy explained to the Ukrainian press his newfound understanding of the greater complexities of his diasporic identity, which was triggered by his visit to the neighborhood where he grew up (in episode 6). Even though at the start of the episode he reiterated to the remaining contestants that apart from his passport, "everything else in me is from Odessa," when he saw the neighborhood he was so overcome by emotion that he had to walk away from the cameras. While he never explained this outburst, in the postshow interview Chmerkovskiy declared that his participation in *Kholostiak* had led him to realize that he had idealized his Ukrainian identity, saying, "I never considered myself an American. But when I came here I understood that I have changed, and that I am no longer from here" (Litskevich 2011b).

As Chmerkovskiy's participation in *Kholostiak* failed to result in his "return" home in the form of a diasporic marriage and led him to realize that he was not "just" Ukrainian, it ironically also transformed him from a migrant with somewhat limited, mostly familial connections to Ukraine into that of an *actual* transnational subject, someone who lives in the United States but also accepts jobs in the booming Ukrainian reality TV market. After the conclusion of *Kholostiak*, Chmerkovskiy participated in several other STB adaptations of US and UK formats such as *Everybody Dance, Master Chef*, and *Culinary Dynasty*, and he hosted the second and third seasons of the game show *The Cube*. In Twitter messages he called Odessa his second home. Chmerkovskiy thus developed an elite form of migrant transnationalism that can also be found among post-USSR musicians, artists, scientists, and scholars who establish a "home base" from which to travel to pursue new opportunities in their fields of expertise (Dubinets 2013). Because of scheduling pressures and the ongoing conflicts in Ukraine, however, Chmerkovskiy's engagement with its booming reality TV market recently seems to have come to a halt.

The connections that post-USSR immigrants have retained or are (re)building with their former homes were also evident in the attention *Russian Dolls* received in Russia. Differently from some of the reactions to *Jersey Shore* in Italy, where the supposedly Italian American cast was received as "overtanned" and oversexed stereotypes of Italians after they moved abroad, a media observer in Russia wrote that *Russian Dolls* should be shown in Russia out of "patriotic considerations" because it would keep viewers from wanting to emigrate (Koniaev 2011). But *Russian Dolls* received the most attention from (post-)Soviet immigrants. Just as *Jersey Shore* evoked the ire of Italian American groups who demanded its cancellation because it reinforced ethnic stereotypes, community activists and officials protested *Russian Dolls*, and a Facebook group, "Russians against Russian Dolls," called for its boycott. The overwhelmingly negative reviews critiqued the show's use of the "botoxed immigrant stereotype" (Ruby 2011), its emphasis on materialism and hedonism in the search for wealth and status, the portrayal of women as second-class citizens, and the use of derogatory racial remarks. Novelist Lara Vapnyar also criticized the show's poor artistic quality in an opinion piece in the *Wall Street Journal*, writing that "even though *Russian Dolls* failed to offend me as a Russian Jewish American woman, in the end, I became deeply offended as a devoted television viewer" (Vapnyar 2011a). Because dismal audience ratings demonstrated that *Russian Dolls* had not succeeded in targeting mainstream populations, the show was quickly canceled.

While *Russian Dolls*'s representation of post-USSR immigrants as assimilating to a white ethnicized identity through conspicuous consumption was a commercial failure, ABC's *DWTS* has continued its portrayals of post-USSR immigrants as the "right" kind of contemporary immigrants who pursue the American immigrant dream through participation in dancesport. A 2014 video that purports to document Maksim Chmerkovskiy's "Road to Mirror Ball Victory," *DTWS*'s final prize which he won after almost a decade on the show, narrated "the heartfelt story of a little boy coming to America and realizing his dream as a professional dancer." This headline was chosen despite the fact that Chmerkovskiy has repeatedly said that he chose to pursue a career in ballroom dancing only *after* he came to the United States because he realized that it could serve as a means to financially assist his family. The video briefly recounts a small incident to illustrate the difficulties of Chmerkovskiy's migration, mentioning that his rollerblades were taken away from him on this second day in the country. But the video is silent about the much more severe economic hardships of his family's migration that Chmerkovskiy recounted to the Ukrainian press, not to mention the social fallout from neoliberal transitions that shaped large outmigration from the former USSR. Instead, the video focuses on Chmerkovskiy's intergenerational story of migration and the political reasons that supposedly motivated it, noting that he often thanks his parents "for bringing him to America to enjoy the freedoms here." Even Chmerkovskiy's transnational ties to Ukraine, as manifested in his interest in the country's ongoing conflict with Russia, were reconfigured as an affirmation of his political allegiance to the United States. Asked if he stayed informed about Ukraine, Chmerkovskiy stated, "We grew up here with the freedoms that nobody has over there" (Muir 2014).

Perhaps *DWTS* will soon be able to avoid the challenges of situating post-USSR migrants in existing US frameworks of race and immigration as producers seem to have initiated a trend toward casting young, US-born dancers as professionals. Because *DWTS* has spurred a growing interest in ballroom dancing, a new generation of "home-grown" performers, often of European descent, is now available to help boost declining audience ratings for a show with a largely conservative following. These performers, who are often pipelined through a dance competition reality show called *So You Think You Can Dance*, appeal to the assumed audience preference for traditional forms of national identification and circumvent the need to hire an even larger number of foreign-born and -trained performers.[10]

2

Highly Skilled and Marriage Migrants in Arizona

Segmented Assimilation and Return Migration

Popular attention to and a small body of scholarly work on the post-Soviet diaspora have primarily focused on migrants who came to the East Coast as religious refugees between the late 1980s and the early 2000s. But Russian-speaking migrants have also moved to the growing US West and Southwest, often under different legal circumstances.[1] In the last few decades, my home state of Arizona, for example, has attracted a record number of immigrants, predominantly from Mexico and various Asian nations. At the time of the 2010 census, 28.6 percent of Arizona's population was foreign-born. While the largest portion of that population came from Mexico, the fastest growing immigrant group is from Asia. Immigrants from India and China in particular either come directly to Arizona or move here from other US states, attracted by the lower cost of living, job opportunities or the presence of family members (Gonzáles 2012). Between 2004 and 2010, Arizona also ranked fourth per capita in refugee placement. Asylees primarily came from Bosnia, Kosovo, Sudan, Somalia, Myanmar, and Iraq (DeParle 2010). By 2016, the state had received the third-largest number of Syrian refugees after Michigan and California (Sunnucks 2016). The numbers of post-USSR migrants in Arizona also nearly tripled to 4,700 between the 1990 and 2000 Census. The 2006–2010 American Community Survey (ACS) estimates that this population doubled to 9,000,[2] and according to the 2014 ACS, approximately 14,000 post-Soviet migrants now reside in Arizona.

Between November 2010 and December 2011, I conducted semistructured interviews with twenty-seven post-USSR immigrant residents of Arizona in order to move the study of the post-Soviet diaspora beyond the focus on those who came as Jewish refugees, mainly to the East Coast, and who tend to be taken as representative of the entire group.[3] Arizona has a less extensive history of eastern European migration than other parts of the country. Early settlers like Jacob Isaacson who built the first trading post in present-day Nogales in 1880 and the approximately 150 families belonging to the Russian Spiritual Christian (Molokon) community who settled in northwest Phoenix in 1911 left few traces in the state (Brown 2007). By the second and third generations, many members of the Molokon community had abandoned their faith and retained little knowledge of their cultural heritage (Moorhead 2012).

The arrival of large numbers of post-Soviet migrants since the late 1980s has more markedly changed the landscape of the state's two major cities. Arizona has attracted a sizable number of Bukharan Jews from Central Asia. The Bukharan Jewish Congress of Arizona, which encompasses a synagogue, high school, Sunday school, and women's and youth organizations, comprises about 850 families. In addition, Phoenix has two Russian Orthodox churches. One has existed since 1949 and the second, which is part of Russia's Church Abroad, has offered services since the early 2000s. Post-Soviet migrants also attend Serbian Orthodox churches. There are several grocery stores, restaurants, and a Russian-language afterschool that offers music, theater, and language lessons. Arizona's second-largest city, Tucson, sports two Russian restaurants, several grocery stores, the Arizona Balalaika Orchestra, the Ukrainian American Society of Tucson, several Orthodox churches, including an Orthodox Ukrainian church, a bilingual School of the Performing Arts, and a Russian Martial Arts school. The International School of Tucson is considering adding a dual-immersion program in Russian to its offerings.

My interviews place the post-USSR diaspora in Arizona in the field of US immigration studies, which examines migrants' adaptation to US society and their connections to their former homelands. The Chicago School emerged about forty years after the beginning of European mass migration and predominantly focused on English-speaking second-generation descendants to develop theories of classical immigrant assimilation (Gans 2000, 78). This school has associated the economic success of early European migrants with their cultural assimilation to a pan-European whiteness, which involved the severing of ties with their countries or regions of origin. Many scholars of contemporary immigration assert that European immigrants assimilated because they were able to integrate into a white pan-European identity and had abundant access to opportunities for socioeconomic mobility that were not available to their contemporaries racialized as nonwhite. The large majority of post-1965 immigrants who came mainly from Asia and Latin America similarly faced higher or qualitatively distinct barriers to adaptation and assimilation because of racial discrimination and changes in US society (Alba and Nee 2003, 68). These changes included a shift to the postindustrial labor market, which is now sharply divided into college-educated professionals and low-paid, low-skilled service workers.

Segmentation theory identifies three ways in which contemporary immigrants and their descendants adapt to the different segments of such a racially and economically stratified society: through upward assimilation into the (white) mainstream, downward assimilation, or selective acculturation. The latter combines upward mobility with the preservation of an immigrant community's culture and values, as manifested by their residence or occupation in an ethnic enclave, their membership in ethnic organizations, or their consumption of transnational or ethnic media.[4] According to this theory, immigrants and their descendants either enter into highly paid professional or low-paid, low-skilled jobs, depending on their socioeconomic status; family structures, human and cultural capital, including their education, language, and workplace skills; and the context of their reception and incorporation, including their racialization in the United States (Portes and Rumbaut 2001).

The more recent interest in migrants' political, social, or economic engagement with their former homes has turned to a focus on return migration, which is a concept that encompasses immigrants' engagement in home visits or circular movement, their political activities or business investments, their participation in the remittance industry, and their physical return. But historians have noted that remittances, return migration, and involvement in homeland politics (Foner 1997; Sarna 1981), as well as an interest in the maintenance of ethnic cultures (Alba and Nee 2003, 145) also characterized participants in earlier mass migration. Rather than being a new phenomenon, transnationalism thus represents a new analytical perspective on migration. In fact, in the contemporary period of increased border controls people move less freely than at the turn of the twentieth century, and settlement often outweighs circular or return migration (Waldinger 2012). The scholarly focus on immigrant transnationalism and return has expanded the notion that migrants' differential educational achievement inserts them either into low- or highly skilled jobs (Cassarino 2004). There is some agreement that migrants with higher incomes and education levels are more likely to go back because of advantages in their home labor markets, whereas low-skilled workers with low levels of formal education are most interested in staying in the United States (Massey and Akresh 2006; Carrión-Flores 2006; Reagan and Olsen 2000).

The results of my interviews with post-Soviet immigrants complicate the emphasis on the effect of a group's educational achievement and collective racialization on their adaptation and transnational engagement, including their return considerations. With the exception of three interviewees, all the other participants were assigned a pan-European white racial identity once in the United States, and those who were educated in the Soviet Union or successor nations came with college degrees that, according to segmentation theory, should have slotted them into upwardly mobile professional jobs. Despite sharing these group characteristics, however, individual participants were inserted into two highly gendered forms of human movement: the majority of my male interviewees came to take positions in the contingent academic workforce, while most of the women arrived as "mail-order brides" to enter into relationships of dependency with US men. These findings correlate with demographic data about the post-Soviet diaspora in Arizona and the impression of individual participants. One interviewee noted: "Most of the people I know are the Russian girls that got married and met the same way, like I met my husband through the Internet. And the guys that I know here, the Russian guys, they are here with their Russian wives on a job thing. . . . So they came as a family, as a unit" (9f).[5]

Five of the eight male interviewees arrived from today's Russia (3) or Ukraine (2) on nonimmigrant student exchange (J-1) visas as postdoctoral researchers in the fundamental sciences such as physics, chemistry, and mathematics.[6] Because declining enrollment in these fields since the 1960s has led to the production of few graduates, academic positions are increasingly filled by foreign-born and -trained immigrants. Of the nineteen women in my study, the largest group (6) came on K-1 fiancé visas with the intention of marrying US citizens. An additional participant had married a US citizen in her country of origin and then moved to the United States on a temporary green card, and another had come here on a student visa and then married a US citizen.[7] These participants illustrate larger trends. While highly skilled and marriage migration to the United States have predominantly been studied with a focus on Filipina "mail-order brides" and South Asian IT workers, throughout the 1990s women from the former USSR became the second-largest group of transnational marriage migrants after Filipinas (D'Aoust 2009, 7), and about ten thousand scientists and engineers are estimated to have immigrated to the United States in the 1990s from Russia alone (Ganguli 2015, S258).

Whereas immigration scholarship has examined the impact of undocumented or uncertain legal status on an entire immigrant community's living and working conditions (Menjívar 2006), my interviews highlight the significance of *individual* immigrants' legal status at arrival for their transnational engagement and access to segmented layers of US whiteness. Even though it provides post-Soviet immigrants with significant privilege, my interviews show that the ascription of a white racial identity does not translate into access to the same economic forms of US citizenship, participation in a community of fellow ethnics/nationals, or opportunities for return. Male academics stressed that, despite the contingent nature of their academic jobs, upon their arrival in the United States they were immediately assigned a white middle-class identity. This is partly because their positions provided at least the promise of more permanent university appointments in the United States or other countries, and thus the possibility of a path toward middle- or upper-class status. Respondents had limited contact with fellow post-Soviet immigrants and, after obtaining more permanent university positions in the United States, many experienced long waiting times during which their legal status was adjusted and they could not leave the country. This prevented them from maintaining physical ties with their families in the Soviet successor nations or seeking employment there.

In contrast to postdoc migrants, the marriage migrants in my study were admitted to perform (unpaid) affective labor as wives and experienced a loss of occupational status as they took low-skilled and underpaid jobs.[8] Five of the women were from present-day Russia and one had grown up in Azerbaijan but was ethnically Russian. One additional interviewee had married in Ukraine and arrived with a temporary green card. All participants had college degrees, predominantly from the Soviet Union or successor nations. Their professional occupations exemplified the fact that in the USSR women were as well educated as men, participated at high rates in the labor force, and were well represented in professions that in the West were highly paid and dominated by men (Heyns 2005, 180). Large numbers of female migrants also come with professional and technical skills (Gold 1999, 127–128). In contrast to the Ph.D.s that enabled male scientists to accept postdoc positions in the United States, however, the women's degrees and their work experiences did not qualify them for highly skilled work visas or translate well into the US labor market. The extension of a white racial identity to women in post-Soviet nations—an identity that encompasses everyone of European descent in the United States—rendered them particularly attractive to US men who seek to create monoracial families. Like other marriage migrants, these post-Soviet migrants were provided with immediate access to US residency and work permits, a fast track toward permanent status, and at least in theory, participation in their husbands' middle-class status, since only individuals with such financial backgrounds can afford the cost of sponsoring marriage (Levchenko and Solheim 2013).

But marriage migrants were also at an increased risk of dependency and had access to limited forms of economic US citizenship. In the case of post-Soviet marriage migrants, their racialization as white exposed them to immense pressure to quickly assimilate to a middle-class whiteness at the cost of their and often their children's bicultural and transnational identities. While the marriage migrants in my sample were generally more interested than the postdocs in building coethnic or conational networks, they faced greater difficulty in connecting to post-Soviet migrants who had arrived in other legal categories. These factors negatively affected the women's adaptation and increased their rates of return considerations, since going home was one of the few ways available to them to become mobile.

Methodology

I located interviewees through acquaintances, colleagues, and friends, and through faculty and staff websites at a public Arizona university. A small number of interviewees were recruited through the snowball method, but participants usually referred me to only one other person even if they appeared to have a much larger coethnic network. With a few exceptions, I generally found the women participants through acquaintances, and met them in their homes or in restaurants, while I located almost all the male interviewees through university websites and met them in their offices. These websites often contain extensive biographies that helped me determine where individuals had grown up or acquired their degrees. A significant number of those I contacted via email after scouring these websites participated in the study, which explains the large portion of university employees in my sample. The interviews, which lasted approximately 40 to 120 minutes, were conducted in English, audiotaped, and transcribed. Participants were coded according to the date of their interview and their gender.

I only interviewed participants who had been born and raised in the former Soviet Union. Their national and ethnic diversity roughly mirrors the general makeup of post-USSR migrants in Arizona, where those from Russia have become less dominant. While they constituted nearly 60 percent of post-Soviet migrants in the 2000 Census, they represented less than half of this number (49%) in the 2006–2010 American Community Survey (ACS). The next largest groups in the 2006–2010 ACS were from Ukraine (19%), Uzbekistan (11%), Armenia (6%), Latvia (4%), Lithuania (4%), and Kazakhstan (1.4%). The majority (17) of my interviewees were from Russia, and a relatively high number (8) came from present-day Ukraine, with two identifying as Ukrainian-speaking ethnic Ukrainians. In addition, one interviewee was from Belarus and one hailed from Kazakhstan. Two other interviewees who grew up or moved to the United States from Kazakhstan and Azerbaijan were ethnically Russian. Another participant was Buryet, a member of the largest aboriginal group in Siberia, two were Armenian, and two Jewish. Participants ranged in age between their early twenties and late fifties, and represented first- and 1.5-generation immigrants. The vast majority of participants had arrived between the mid-1990s and the early 2000s, though a Jewish participant had come as early as 1990 and a student on an F-1 visa arrived as late as 2010. Marriage migrants came between 1992 and 2007, with three arriving in 2001. The majority of postdoc migrants came throughout the 1990s; only one arrived as late as 2003.

More than any other methodology I have employed in this book or in my prior scholarship, conducting these interviews forced me to acknowledge my personal stake in this work. I am used to being an outsider to the communities I study, even though the long history of academic debates about who can represent a particular community and the increasing acknowledgment of the need to recognize the complexity of intersectional identities have complicated any divisions between supposed insiders and outsiders. Scholarship in the social sciences, particularly in anthropology, has become centrally concerned with the role of the researcher in shaping and obtaining information through interactions with participants. Scholars have demanded that discussions of methodology also include details about the researchers, particularly about the cultural factors that structure their perceptions and interpretations, in order to better understand how the information they present was gathered and interpreted. The manner in which gender, ethnic, national, or religious social identities are attributed to researchers by participants and in which researchers negotiate their identities to gain access to the desired information influences their rapport with and acceptance by their informants (Tsuda 1998).

Many of my participants, especially those who were in their late twenties and older, wanted to know more about me, mainly because they were puzzled that I would even be interested in their migration experiences. I thus learned to provide that information at the beginning of each interview. I normally identify as a German who has lived in the United States for several decades and acquired US citizenship in order to avoid further intrusive questions about my background. But in these interviews I always stressed that I had immigrated to the United States just a few years after the dissolution of the former German Democratic Republic with the intention of obtaining a graduate degree and returning home to work in academia, but instead ended up staying in the United States.

My interviewees generally had little concrete knowledge of East Germany other than that it had been part of the Soviet-dominated East Bloc (and some participants even apologized for Soviet colonization). However, our shared status as immigrants from the former East Bloc and often, our common experiences of the rapid transition of socialist to market economies seemed to endear me to participants as someone who may understand their point of view. It also appeared to sufficiently answer their questions as to why I would be interested in their migration experiences in the first place. Some interviewees from Russia told me that they felt safer talking to me than to fellow compatriots. The unspoken assumption was that other post-Soviet immigrants were not always to be trusted. Other interviewees told me that speaking to me about their migration experiences had a therapeutic effect. Only once, toward the beginning of the interview process, was I accused of not being enough of a knowledgeable insider to conduct this research. One interviewee from Ukraine told me that had I known more about the former USSR (though not necessarily more Russian), I would have been able to tell from his last name that he was ethnically Russian (rather than Ukrainian).

While conducting these interviews, it became clear to me that my own migration experiences had shaped the wording of my semi-structured questions and follow-up inquiries as well as the way in which I often pressed interviewees on further details of their immigration experiences and their relationship to other immigrant groups.

Highly Skilled Migration to Contingent Academic Employment

Only two of my interviewees, both in their late twenties, arrived in the early 1990s as beneficiaries of US programs that granted presumptive refugee status to post-Soviet immigrants of Jewish descent with relatives or sponsors in the United States. To explain their families' motivations for emigration, these 1.5-generation immigrants initially employed the same narrative of intergenerational immigrant upward mobility that post-Soviet immigrant families in Arizona provided to an ethnographer (Kasatkina 2010, 125). This was also the narrative that Sasha Senderovich (2016) has identified as the dominant account among (post-)Soviet Jewish American families, and that was showcased in the biographies of post-Soviet professional dancers in the two reality TV shows discussed in the previous chapter.[9]

But while these shows present post-Soviet Jewish migration in ways that reaffirm the myth of an immigrant America to play to their predominantly conservative audience's assumptions, my participants provided more complex accounts of their migration and its effects on their identity formation. One interviewee pointed to economic considerations rather than anti-Semitism as the main reasons for his family's departure, but still described himself as both Jewish and Russian, saying that "[m]y parents kind of instilled this fact that we're Jewish to some extent. I myself identify with Russia just because I study [the country]" (23m). Arriving in Brooklyn as a young child, he grew up there amidst a large population of Russian Jews and his father worked for a Jewish assistance organization. In contrast, the second interviewee identified as Russian American rather than Jewish even though she highlighted religious persecution as one of the main reasons for her family's emigration. She was a teenager when her family arrived in Arizona and had to use Internet chatrooms to create the semblance of a Russian-speaking community. This was how she met her husband, an undocumented migrant from Russia, who at the time lived on the East Coast.

A much larger percentage of my interviewees had come as marriage and highly skilled migrants. One of these participants was able to immigrate under preferential categories for highly skilled scientists, which were available in the early years of post-Soviet emigration. He benefited from the 1992 Soviet Scientists Immigration Act (SSIA), which allotted 750 immigrant visas to eligible scientists or engineers who had expertise in nuclear, chemical, biological, or other high tech fields or worked on defense projects in these areas in the former USSR. The program was created to assuage fears that rogue nations or terrorist groups would recruit post-Soviet scientists to build weapons of mass destruction or entice them to sell their expertise. Even those who did not have an offer of employment were given permanent immigration status, and in 2002 the program was renewed for another four years and the visa cap increased to 950 (Ganguli 2015, S263). My interviewee was granted a green card even before he entered the United States, which significantly smoothed his arrival.[10]

In contrast to this migrant, the majority of my male interviewees arrived in the United States on J-1 visas to take up postdoctoral positions. Classified as *nonimmigrant* visas, J-1s are usually provided to those who are officially enumerated as students and expected to return home after completing their program of study or cultural exchange. While J-1 migration thus formally appears to be a form of study abroad, my interviewees all understood that their arrival in the United States to take up postdoc positions represented a form of highly skilled *labor* movement. While some participants reported that they had initially accepted their postdoc positions as a stepping stone toward more permanent migration, saying, "I was clearly planning to immigrate" (26m), others saw themselves as engaged in more temporary labor migration. They stated, "I moved to US but not as an immigrant but also a temporary worker . . . and then eventually we never moved back" (14m) or, "In my mind I wasn't immigrating really. I was essentially following the job" (13m).

When I conducted my interviews, I was not aware that the migration experiences of many of my male participants exemplified an underexamined aspect of the expansion of contingent and precarious forms of employment from low-skilled work into professional fields. US scholars have not paid much attention to the fact that postdoc positions have grown rapidly in US higher education. The surge in the number of postdocs is part of a larger process whereby a variety of temporary and flexible employment categories have replaced tenured and tenure-track full-time faculty appointments at US colleges and universities. In fact, the use of contingent labor in this industry has outpaced the private sector. While 40 percent of all US employment has become contingent, at universities the *majority* of faculty, two-thirds, now labor in contingent positions, and half of those work only part time (Fredrickson 2015). Their jobs are defined by tenuous employment security, limited instructional resources, and often such low pay that many have joined the working poor. The dramatic growth in these positions is gaining national attention because of public protests and unionizing activities.

Whereas the contingent teaching positions that have moved into the public spotlight are mainly held by women who tend to be US citizens,[11] the growth in the number of postdoc jobs at US universities has initiated a large-scale form of largely male, immigrant labor movement (Davis 2009, 3). Originally intended as a period of advanced specialized training for new Ph.D.s prior to embarking on faculty careers, in the last few decades postdoc positions have become a standard form of contingent academic employment. Between 1985 and 2006, the number of postdoc positions in US academic institutions grew by 100 percent (Black and Stephan 2010, 140–141). Ph.D.s are hired in these positions so they can perform activities that are normally required of full-time tenured and tenure-track faculty, including generating knowledge as well as directing undergraduate and graduate student research (Cantwell 2011, 107). The majority of temporary visa holders, 79 percent, are postdocs who received their Ph.D.s outside the United States, but some foreign-born postdocs also complete their degrees in the United States and then work on F-1 student visas that allow two years of practical training (Black and Stephan 2010, 142).

In contrast to contingent teaching jobs that are generally dead-end positions, postdocs can provide a path toward more permanent academic employment, usually at other institutions. Because I had identified many of my participants through faculty and staff website listings at an Arizona university, I had selected those who now held permanent academic jobs, usually after many years and several postdocs. But clearly the option of upward movement from postdoc to such permanent positions is not available to everyone. One respondent stressed that for those with foreign Ph.D.s it is far easier to enter the United States as postdocs than to obtain permanent academic jobs and residence. He said, "If you haven't done Ph.D. in this country, your chances for getting into the system are not that good really. . . . You come with an established network. . . . And you have to do it and you've got to do it [establishing networks] fast. Otherwise you just get thrown out" (13m). Two of my interviewees, perhaps not coincidentally the oldest, held research and administrative positions that were financed by external, federal grants rather than the university, and thus did not guarantee them permanent forms of employment after the expiration of the grants.

Not only are institutions of higher learning at the forefront of the use of contingent labor, but even those at least partially funded by taxpayers have constructed migration to postdoc positions to be even more exploitative than the highly skilled migration to temporary jobs in the private industry. A body of scholarship has emphasized the racialized nature of this H-1B migration to jobs in the private sector and its negative effects on migrants' economic and professional advancement in the United States. Created by the 1965 Immigration and Nationality Act, which allowed US firms to hire highly skilled immigrant workers on a temporary basis, the H-1B visa regime keeps workers dependent on employers for their immigration status and livelihood. If foreign workers want to transfer their visa in order to change jobs, they need special permission from the Department of Labor or require the assistance of another company (Banerjee 2006, 430, 440). In addition, employers can reduce employees' wages, increase commission rates, charge fees for providing health care, cut back on benefits, decline to increase salaries,

and threaten to fire their workers (Banerjee 2006, 437). The requirement that applicants for the H-1B hold at least a bachelor's degree fa-
vors the migration of those with schooling from emerging economies,
the majority of whom are from India (Banerjee 2006, 441; Banerjee and
Ridzi 2008).[12] In fact, the temporary nature of the H-1B visa encourages
the sojourner-like migration of men, which is reminiscent of turn of
the twentieth century labor migration for unskilled jobs, dominated by
men. Some H-1B holders come alone to first establish themselves and
then send for their families (Liu 2000, 177).[13] The H-1B visa regime has
thus created a gendered and racialized IT workforce, and Indian migrant
workers often also experience segregation and racial discrimination in
the workplace (Chakravartty 2006).

Even though universities are actually *exempt* from the caps on H-1B
visas that guide hiring by private businesses, institutions of higher learning prefer to request J-1 cultural student exchange visas for holders of
postdoc positions (Cantwell 2009, 42). Unlike the H-1B visa, the J-1 is
not tied to prevailing wage protections, and postdocs can be paid much
lower salaries than workers with H-1B visas in private industry. Around
2005, the average was about $40,000 a year (Davis 2009, 5). Unlike the
H-1B, which lets holders petition for adjustment to green card status, the
J-1 nonimmigrant visa does not provide a path toward permanent residency and even includes a provision that creates obstacles to changes in
legal status. Holders need to obtain an exemption from the requirement
that they return home for at least two years before applying for a status
change, such as an H-1B visa. Because the J-1 visa does not permit holders to work for another institution, it keeps postdocs even more tightly
locked into a specific job during the duration of the visa and minimizes
their chances of finding other employment that could provide a path toward permanent legal status (Cantwell 2011, 108). International postdocs
are also more likely to receive lower wages than native-born postdocs
and to work longer hours, even though they tend to be more productive
in terms of publications (Cantwell 2011, 103).

As is the case for H-1B migration, the J-1 visa regime has created a
gendered and racialized academic labor force, though it is slightly more
diverse than that produced by the H-1 visa requirements. Almost half
the postdoc positions at US universities are filled by male immigrants
from China, South Korea, and India (Black and Stephan 2010, 137). But

significant numbers of post-Soviet migrants have also arrived on J-1s. According to the Department of Homeland Security (DHS), which has provided detailed information on nonimmigrant visa arrivals by type since 2006, greater numbers of post-Soviet immigrants have come on J-1 visas than on F-1 (student) or H-1B visas, though not all J-1s are issued for postdoc positions. Between 2006 and 2014, the numbers of H-1B visa holders from the former Soviet Union remained relatively stable, hovering around 2,000 to 3,000 Russians and 1,000 Ukrainians.[14] In contrast, in 2008, at the height of J-1 migration, much larger numbers of post-USSR migrants—32,000 Russians, 12,000 Ukrainians, 6,000 Moldovans, and 4,400 Lithuanians—arrived in the United States. By 2014, these figures had declined to 13,000 Russians, 9,000 Ukrainians, 3,600 Moldovans, and 1,400 Lithuanians, but increased to 1,300 Kyrgyz and 5,000 Kazakh visa holders.[15] The numbers can only hint at the considerable size of the exodus by post-Soviet scientists, primarily to Western Europe and the United States, which started in the late 1980s. Korobkov and Zaionchkovskaia estimate that between 50,000 to 300,000 post-Soviet Russian academics worked abroad in 2006, between a quarter or one-third of whom lived in the United States (Korobkov and Zaionchkovskaia 2012, 330, 334). Other scholars suggest that, based on 2000 US Census figures, close to 10,000 Russian scientists and engineers immigrated to the United States in the 1990s (Ganguli 2015, S258). Forty-five thousand researchers and technical personnel are estimated to have moved from Ukraine to the United States (Tolstokorova 2010a, 76).

One of my respondents explained the reason behind the exodus of post-Soviet scientists thus: "[T]he level of physics in former Soviet Union was quite advanced on the world level . . . [but] it was quite clear that science disappeared from that landscape and will never appear there, at least in my lifetime" (13m). While the Soviet academic environment was highly respected with funding levels comparable to those in the United States (Ganguli 2013, 1), between 1991 and 1994 financial support for scientific research declined by roughly 75 percent (Ball and Gerber 2005, 52). In real terms, scientists in post-Soviet Russia lost nine-tenths of their incomes throughout the 1990s as the cost of living far surpassed their salaries. Scientists were forced to take second jobs, leave their research and academic positions for more lucrative job opportunities, or seek temporary or permanent work opportunities abroad (Mirskaya and Rabkin 2004, 6).

One of my interviewees reported that "in [the] mid-90s the salary of scientists was so low. . . . But prices were already very high. So it was hard to survive. It was possible because of visits to different countries to work for a couple of months" (14m). The interviewee engaged in frequent, cyclical border crossings into Western Europe in the early 1990s. He worked there a few months at a time to make enough money that would ensure his family's survival in Russia. In contrast to theories that describe similar temporary labor immigration to the United States from other parts of the Americas as the "pendular" or "shuttle" movement of low-skilled labor, these forms of highly skilled labor border crossings from Eastern to Western Europe have been theorized as a way to stay mobile in order to improve or maintain the quality of the family's life at home (Morokvasic 2004). In the late 1990s this kind of movement appears to have diminished, and my interviewee eventually migrated to Germany, then to Asia, and finally moved permanently to the United States.

In fact, all the participants who had obtained advanced degrees in the USSR or successor nations had held postdoc or similar appointments in Western European countries, usually before coming to the United States. This type of migration appears to be ongoing. Upon receiving his Ph.D. in Russia in the early 2000s, one interviewee immediately emigrated, first to Western Europe and then to the United States, because he could not find a job in Russia even though he wanted to stay there. Other interviewees reported that they decided to move to the United States from Europe because of the higher quality of the work environment. They said, for example, "Our initial goal was to find a place where I could enjoy what I'm doing, i.e., being a physicist" (17m) or, "I wanted to be able to go to the States. At that time it was the only place where you could go to do some real stuff" (13m). A participant from Ukraine said, "In terms of the physics research it's really very easy to work in physics here. . . . It's way much easier in terms of resources, in terms of your standing, in terms of your acknowledgment" (20m).

Men outnumbered women as postdoc migrants, despite the fact that female scientists were at near parity with men in the former USSR. In my sample, only two women scientists, as compared to six men, immigrated under postdoc or related highly skilled visa policies. These numbers reflect larger trends. In 2009, women scientists only accounted for about a quarter of emigrants (Korobkov and Zaionchkovskaia 2012, 336; Gokhberg and Nekipelova 2001, 185). While the existing research does not provide explanations for this gendered disparity, judging from my interviews migration to temporary positions is a risky undertaking for entire families, and women appear more willing to subordinate their careers to that of a partner, even if it is for a contingent job in another country. Just as South Asian H-1B visa holders sometimes come without their families, one of my interviewees initially arrived by himself with one of his children, while his wife and second child joined them later (26m). Other interviewees came with their wives and sometimes their children, but recognized that this kind of family migration constituted a considerable risk. As one interviewee said: "I was invited . . . to work for three months. And my wife asked me to go with me with two kids. . . . It was risky because we had to spend all the money just to get to America. So it was just strange behavior!" (14m). Other participants reported that, even after they had received more permanent legal status, their spouses ended up not working or found employment below their educational level (20m).

Even though my post-Soviet interviewees initially arrived on nonimmigrant visas to contingent positions at US universities, they reported that they were accepted and racialized into a white US identity that largely ignored markers of their foreign birth such as accent, dress, or behavior. One respondent said, "I never felt like they treat me differently because I'm from Russia or like enemy. . . . And also they don't care about your accent or because you are not able to express yourself in many cases" (14m). In addition to finding themselves in an environment that requires high levels of education and offers many middle-class positions, my interviewees had also entered a highly diverse and generally more accepting workplace. As one participant said: "I was lucky in a sense because I live in the university community, which is very international by itself" (26m).

The racialization of post-Soviet postdoc migrants as white, which often proceeded without acknowledgment of their foreign-born status, was especially evident to my interviewees, since they had all lived and worked in other European countries where they had had very different experiences. A respondent said, "When I came here, I essentially realized that this is a different planet really in terms of immigration. So in Europe you always feel that you are an outsider. Here you didn't feel you were an outsider" (13m). In Europe, linguistic and cultural differences—rather than primarily racial and ascriptive characteristics, as in the US context—are employed to assign "foreignness" to individuals and groups. In addition, many European countries have just recently acknowledged their status as immigrant-receiving nations and the value of migration to the country's economy and social and cultural life. Contemporary public and media discourses in Western European countries routinely assign negative attributes to migrants from a variety of Eastern European nations by evoking images of their "invasion" or by associating them with immorality and higher crime rates (Fox et al. 2012; Garner 2006; Kushner 2005). Respondents stated that in Western Europe they always felt like foreigners (14m), while "in the States we sort of fitted right in. This whole culture of a mixture of everything . . . fitted perfectly" (17m). Another interviewee reported that specifically in Germany, "foreigners are not as welcome. . . . The laws are in favor of immigrants, but people resist that. So it's more, I don't know, psychological than probably anything else" (20m).

Even though they were immediately accepted into a pan-European whiteness and many had obtained permanent residency or citizenship status by the time of the interview, respondents self-identified not simply as "American," but as Russian, Ukrainian, Russian American, or Ukrainian American. While they only had limited interest in surrounding themselves with fellow post-Soviet immigrants, they spoke their mother tongues at home, with most ensuring that their children also had at least some knowledge of that language. One respondent said that he "was not part of any kind of Russian community whatsoever" (26m), and another reported that the "Russian immigrant community is really spread [out] and I wouldn't call it a Russian immigrant community at all. We don't really communicate with each other" (17m). But respondents reported regularly reading the news in their mother tongues, usually on websites, or hearing about political and social developments in their homes from their families.

My interviewees were thus no different from most immigrants who are mainly interested in maintaining ties with immediate kin in their former homes rather than engaging in other forms of transnationalism.

While immigrants frequently conduct long-distance communication via phone- or Internet-based technologies like Skype which emerged in the early 2000s, they tend to take only occasional trips home (Waldinger 2012). Those among my respondents who had arrived in the United States in the early or mid-1990s reported that the emergence and popularization of Skype, a web-based service that provides free video chat and voice calls, had enabled them to stay in closer and more frequent contact with their families. For a variety of reasons, interviewees had also undertaken few return visits. Respondents reported that the temporary nature of their postdoc positions and the difficulty of adjusting their legal status after they found permanent positions at a US university made it difficult for them to visit their former homes. Backlogs of five to twenty-five years for processing changes in legal status impose severe travel limitations on migrants that affect their ability to maintain contact with their families as well as engage in professional travel (Jasso et al. 2010). One participant reported, "I was stuck here for seven years waiting for the green card. . . . So last year was the first time in seven years I went back to Moscow for a few weeks" (17m). Another interviewee had visited after a gap of fourteen years (13m). The relatively low pay for postdocs and the need to constantly compete in a tight job market for more permanent positions also affected migrants' ability to maintain physical connections with their homes, as overseas travel has remained very costly, especially when compared to the low price of communication technologies. One respondent reported, "There was a stretch of time when I actually went without going to Ukraine for probably like 5 to 6 years or so, especially when I was in postdoc. It was financially a little harder and it was also workwise basically competing for positions every time, because those positions are typically just one or two years, sometimes three years" (20m).

The postdoc immigrants I interviewed, and two of my participants who had come in the late 1990s and early 2000s on F-1 visas to obtain graduate degrees and subsequently accepted university positions in the United States, also exhibited little interest in returning to Soviet successor nations for academic jobs. A small number had considered the possibility, but none reported concrete plans for return. That post-Soviet academics, both those with foreign and US degrees, are reluctant to return complicates assumptions that highly skilled migrants whose movement tends to be shaped by job choices are the ones who most often go back home or move onward to third countries (Cassarino 2004) because of family ties or better economic opportunities in their countries of origin (Aranda and Vaquera 2011; Wadhwa et al. 2009; Hazen and Alberts 2006; Thorn and Holm-Nielsen 2008).

At the time of my interviews (2010–2011), Russia was doing economically much better than when many immigrants left in the 1990s because of the surging price of oil. Russia's economy had somewhat recovered from the 1997–98 crisis, which was marked by sharp decreases in earnings from oil and other resource exports as well as a decline in foreign investment that caused currency devaluation, inflation, and the breakdown of the country's banking system. Ukraine's economy had also improved and was being propped up by foreign investment. The Orange Revolution (2004–5) promoted the notion that the country was in the process of developing a stronger democracy than that of Russia. The academics I interviewed were very aware of these developments. For example, one scientist reported that he had considered returning as a postdoc after he received a job offer from former colleagues (17m), and another pointed to the global shift in economic power between the United States and his former home, declaring that "ten years ago it [emigration from the United States] was not in my mind, but now with the decline of my new country, it's not so unrealistic any more" (14m).

But these interviewees were in the minority, and their considerations did not translate into concrete plans for return. Since most of my interviewees had arrived in the United States in the 1990s or early 2000s they would be going back to different countries from the ones they had left, and those who had emigrated before or right after the dissolution of the USSR may not have considered the successor nations as their homes. A second issue is that improvements in several post-Soviet countries had not translated into a higher quality academic culture. Thus, one participant noted that he would only consider returning if the academic environment in Ukraine adopted US standards and moved toward more of a meritocracy (20m). Interviewees generally praised the merit-based and transparent research environment in the United States. One participant said, for example, "What I find the most important here is if I actually put up effort and I have talents, I can actually get something for it in the sense that I feel I have achieved something. Not because I know some-one, not because my parents know someone, but because this is what I have achieved, which is very different from home" (16f).

Russia appears to be the only post-Soviet country that has initiated any programs encouraging diasporic academics to return. The govern-ment has established grants promoting joint research groups between Russian academic institutions and post-USSR diasporic academics in order to facilitate the return of academic, cultural, and professional elites living abroad. In 2010, the Russian government, under Medvedev, cre-ated a new academic institution, the Skolkovo Research Center in Mos-cow, which was conceptualized as Russia's equivalent of Silicon Valley. The government even passed two bills to ease migration to positions at this school and to provide favorable working conditions for diasporic academics and venture capitalists willing to either return or engage in cooperation (Korobkov and Zaionchkovskaia 2012, 337–38). Several in-terviewees mentioned that they knew fellow diasporic colleagues who had returned to work at the Skolkovo (18f, 25f). Others pointed to post-USSR academics who had gone back to Russia because they were unable to find jobs in the United States after graduating from US institutions (16f). One interviewee also knew of colleagues who had started new re-search centers in Russia that were financed "with oil money" (15f). An-other participant mentioned that a second school, Moscow's School of New Economics, had been successful in attracting foreign or diasporic researchers (18f).

As compared to the relatively small numbers of physical returns and return visits, the highly trained migrants in my sample seemed to engage more frequently in diasporic research practices, in which individuals retain their employment in the United States and establish or main-tain connections with Russian institutions through grants or jobs (16f), sometimes also tapping into funds established for short-term visits or lectures for diasporic scientists (24m). These activities resemble the kind of migrant transnationalism that has developed among members of the diasporic post-USSR cultural elite (artists, athletes, performers), who pursue jobs in successor nations from their home base in the West. This practice is also exemplified by participants in the *Dancing with the Stars* reality TV show discussed in the previous chapter. The dancers accept temporary employment in the booming reality TV markets of Ukraine and Russia, while maintaining their main residence in the United States and continuing to participate in the entertainment industry here.

Marriage Migration: Global Whiteness and Entry into Dependency and Enforced Assimilation

The predominantly male post-USSR scientists who initially entered the contingent US academic workforce spoke positively about their incorporation into a white US racial identity, had achieved middle-class status after obtaining more permanent academic positions, and identified visa adjustment, job competition, and low pay as major obstacles for travel to their former homes but rarely considered returning. Because of the more exploitative nature of their migration, the interviewees who arrived on fiancé visas, however, had a more problematic relationship with their whiteness and faced greater difficulty in their efforts to create bicultural identities and maintain ties with their former homes. Like the prominence accorded to Indian nationals in studies of IT jobs, academic work on US marriage migration has focused on the largest group of "mail-order brides," who are from the Philippines (Simons 2001, 13; D'Aoust 2009, 1). Whereas the 1924 Immigration Act first established family reunification as one of the main pillars of US immigration, marriage migration only became a large-scale phenomenon after the 1946 passage of the Alien Fiancées and Fiancés Act, which expedited the admission of fiancés of the US armed forces stationed in Europe and Asia (particularly the Philippines).

The 1965 Immigration and Nationality Act, which gave preference to immediate relatives of US citizens and legal permanent residents, helped create a new pattern of marriages between US men and women from less economically developed countries (Levchenko and Solheim 2013). The growth in mail-order bride catalogs and the development of a highly commodified Internet marriage market in the 1990s (Constable 2003, 53) drew on existing gendered and raced hierarchies among nations. The extensive US military presence in the Philippines until the early 1990s, for example, was accompanied by a flourishing sex industry, which generated portrayals of Filipinas as hypersexualized prostitutes and submissive wives (Angeles and Sunanta 2007).

Many Filipinas became transnational wives in marriages based on the notion of status exchange. Predominantly white and older US men with above average incomes and relatively high education levels offer money and security to women from countries with weaker economies who are much younger, supposedly adhere to more traditional gender norms, and agree to become dependent on their spouses for their immigration status and livelihood (Patico 2009; Levchenko and Solheim 2013; Simons 2001, 10). On average, the difference in the spouses' ages is four times greater than in other US marriages (Levchenko and Solheim 2013). I observed a modified version of this status exchange in the situation of one of my interviewees. She came on a fiancé visa to marry an African American man she had met over the Internet. As a US citizen, he was able to offer her a higher socioeconomic status based on his citizenship in exchange for her more highly valued racialized identity.

Their union exemplified the reality that since the 1990s, marriage migration has expanded beyond the Philippines to other countries that include the former USSR (Simons 2001, 2). While women from the former USSR became the second-largest group of transnational marriage migrants after Filipinas throughout the 1990s (D'Aoust 2009, 7), more recently 47 percent have come from Asia, 27 percent from Latin America, and 8 percent from Eastern Europe, with Russia and Ukraine as the top two sending countries (Levchenko and Solheim 2013). In 2013, 26,046 migrants entered the United States on K-1 visas. The largest numbers (5,131) came from the Philippines, followed by migrants from China (1,397) and Mexico (1,268) (Pearce 2016). According to DHS data, which provide information on smaller migrant groups, in the same year 668 Russian and 680 Ukrainian women arrived on K-1 visas. In 2014, their numbers increased to levels comparable to 2013 marriage migration from Mexico—850 and 1,000, respectively.[16] While female US migrants from the former East Bloc tend to be understudied, probably because they appear racially similar to US women (Robila 2010), marriage migrants from the Global South and from the former East Bloc are examined from diverging theoretical lenses, which has stymied the emergence of comparative scholarship (D'Aoust 2009, 7; Suchland 2015, 6). Whereas female migration from the Global South is analyzed as an expression of the systemic structural exploitation of women under neoliberal conditions, Eastern European women tend to be viewed as victims of criminal

organizations, failed political systems, and corrupt political elites in former East Bloc countries (Suchland 2015, 10).

But marriage migration from the former Soviet Union also exemplifies global neoliberal developments. Post-Soviet migration surged
in response to the same drastic neoliberal transformations in the economic, social, and cultural realms after the dissolution of the USSR that
compelled scientists to leave in large numbers. Women lost their jobs
at a disproportionate rate, but were also affected by the shift away from
socialist family structures (made up of two working parents who often
received childrearing support from their extended families) toward the
unattainable ideal of the nuclear family, in which men are supposed to
be breadwinners and the women mothers and housewives (Solari 2010;
D'Aoust 2009). For men, these new expectations led to higher levels of
alcoholism, crime and suicide rates, and an alarming drop in life expec-
tancy (Rands Lyon 2007, 28), while many women emigrated.

In describing their motivations for marriage migration, interviewees spoke of losing their jobs or of not being able to find work in their
professions. Two participants had met their husbands in their native
countries—Russia or Ukraine—and stressed that, even though they
came on fiancé visas, they were pursuing love, not arranged marriages.
Some women were divorced or single mothers or they were above the
(very young) age deemed desirable for marriage in the former USSR and
its successor nations. One participant reported that, as she was about
to enter middle age, her marriage and emigration to the United States
had allowed her to become a mother and wife because in Russia women
are considered unmarriageable by the time they reach their late twenties. A divorced mother highlighted her infant son's need for a father.
Another participant spoke of US men's superiority to Russian men, who
are more likely to be unfaithful because they have many choices due to
the gender imbalance in the former USSR and several successor countries. The interviewee here referred to the demographic gap in Russia,
where mortality rates are higher for men than for women (Patico 2009,
315–316). Through migration, these women created the kind of traditional family structure that is now touted as the new norm in several
former Soviet republics, but they did so with foreign men who have the
financial means to enter the transnational marriage market. Or, as Jen-

nifer Patico theorizes, in these marriages romantic and marital desires become transnationalized (Patico 2009, 325).

Because women from the former East Bloc are collectively ascribed a white racial identity—even *before* their arrival in the United States—they are especially attractive to many US men who want to create monoracial families (Johnson 2007, 43). The whiteness attributed to these women is also sexualized, which places them at a high risk of exploitation. The expansion of the transnational marriage market to the former East Bloc has not coincidentally intersected with the growth in prostitution networks for Eastern European women who are deemed especially desirable because of their white racial identity. Just as they became a large part of marriage migration to the United States and Western Europe in the late 1980s, post-USSR women came to work in the sex trade all over the world. The large-scale trafficking of post-Soviet women to Asian countries, particularly of Ukrainian women to Turkey, the UAE, Syria, Korea, China, and Japan, and the presence of large numbers of Russian sex workers in Israel and Turkey, highlight the widespread interest in the consumption of a sexualized whiteness in non-Western countries. In fact, in the late 1990s Ukrainian women constituted the largest group of foreign sex workers in Turkey, and the second-largest group of foreign women in prostitution in Korea outside US military bases (Hughes 2000, 3).

The simultaneous rise in sex and marriage migration from the former USSR has historical antecedents in the transformation of prostitution into an international trade and its intersection with global migration in the second half of the nineteenth century. The so-called white slavery of eastern European women coincided with massive out-migration by women from the Pale of Settlement in the former Russian empire and from other parts of eastern Europe. Women constituted a disproportionately high number of US migrants from the Pale (namely, half), while they made up only 21 percent of southern Italians, the largest immigrant group at the time. Only the earlier Irish immigration had comprised a greater proportion of women, namely, 52.9 percent (Glenn 1990, 47). Promises of jobs, immigration certificates, and marriage proposals helped recruit women to Argentina and Brazil, the United States, South Africa, Turkey, and Egypt. In 1909 half the sex workers in Buenos Aires were eastern European Jewish women (Glenn 1990, 52).

The highly prized, sexualized whiteness attributed to post-USSR women that supposedly renders them racially similar to US men involved in the transnational marriage market represents their "admission ticket" to the United States. These women enter the country as prospective spouses under the most privileged family unification category that has no yearly caps, and they face shorter waiting times for temporary residency and work permits than extended family members. In addition, they become members of the middle-class US families of their husbands.

On the flip side of these immense privileges, US marriage migrants are exposed to a culture of dependency and enforced acculturation that negatively affects their adaptation to the US mainstream and increases their rate of return considerations. Dependency is usually discussed in the context of the highly publicized cases of marriage migrants as victims of domestic violence. The passage of the International Marriage Broker Regulation Act of 2005 (which is part of the Violence against Women and Department of Justice Reauthorization Act) exemplified the shift from viewing marriage migration as a form of sex trafficking to recognizing its linkage to domestic violence (D'Aoust 2009, 18).[17] But dependency extends far beyond physical abuse. Even more than the J-1 migrants who have to rely on their university employer for wages and immigration status, marriage migrants are highly dependent on a US man in both legal and financial terms. As one respondent described this phenomenon: "You lose your status, you lose everything, you come to the US as a nobody. You are totally dependent on the man for whom you come. Fiancé visa is probably the worst way to go. . . . You don't have a status, you can't do anything. . . . You are totally at the mercy of the other person" (10f). Another respondent described her financial dependency thus: "I'm dependent on my husband, and he's thirteen years older than me. And I don't have any savings. . . . I don't have it, he does, but I can't just rely on him" (1f). The lack of money also prevented her from getting a college degree and making return trips to Russia.

While this form of dependency is experienced by marriage migrants from all over the world, post-USSR (and other Eastern European) migrants face one additional, racialized form of cultural dependency that is underexplored. Because of their assigned white racial identity, marriage migrants experience unrealistic expectations to quickly assimilate to the ideal of white US American middle-class womanhood by completely detaching themselves from their linguistic and cultural identities. This imposed pressure to assimilate negatively shapes their migration experiences and increases their return considerations.

The post-USSR marriage migrants I interviewed reported being placed in the role of "fast track" immigrants who were expected to fully adapt to US cultural, linguistic, class, and ethnic norms, as exemplified in their new (supposedly monoracial) families and in the myth of an immigrant America. One interviewee summarized this pressure succinctly when she reported that her US husband criticized her inability to quickly adapt to the standards of white US middle-class femininity. She recounted that they "had a lot of fights about being socially awkward. Not being the way a middle-class American woman is, not being able to really adjust, socially awkward, not doing the right thing socially in social environments" (10f). Another participant reported her husband's frustration with what he saw as her inability to improve her accented and nonidiomatic English, saying, "From so many years of marriage, he just sometimes gives up on me. Like you still haven't . . . . What are you saying?" (1f).

The pressures to assimilate also manifested in the women's limited ability to raise their children bilingually or biculturally because their spouses did not speak their language and were not especially supportive of and at times even opposed to a bilingual home environment. While some husbands accepted their wives' efforts to raise their children with at least some knowledge of the Russian or Ukrainian language and culture, none of them knew or had made an effort to learn their wives' native languages. One participant described the difficulty of raising her child bilingually, given the presence of a family member who does not know the language, saying, "It's a family, how can I? No. My husband doesn't speak [Russian]" (11f).

Some spouses were downright opposed to language maintenance. One interviewee recounted that her spouse's rejection of her attempts to speak Russian to her child compelled her to consider returning home. She said that when "I talk to my son in Russian and he couldn't understand English, my husband told me that, 'I feel like I'm an alien in my own home.' . . . I felt him being upset about it. So I'm trying to creep in, trying to work this thing out because there was always an option to go back for me. He said, 'You know what? It's your decision. If you really insist on it, we can buy tickets and you can go home'" (1f). Most women reported that they no longer spoke to their children in their mother tongue, though some had found alternatives, such as building networks with other Russian-speaking families or having the children interact with their grandparents either via Skype, phone, or when the family visited them in the United States. Only two participants (9f, 12f) reported being able to take their children to visit their families in Soviet successor nations every summer, with one managing to temporarily return with her son for a few months so he could acquire some Russian (12f).

Marriage migrants faced the same obstacles as postdocs in their efforts to maintain physical contact with their homes, including a lack of funds and the travel restrictions that accompany the often lengthy process during which a temporary visa status, in this case a K-1, is converted into permanent residency. While most interviewees stayed in touch with their families via phone or Skype, marriage migrants faced greater financial obstacles than highly skilled migrants, and often, a lack of support from their US spouses, in their efforts to return for visits. Two of the marriage migrants I interviewed had never visited their homes the entire time they had lived in the United States—six and nineteen years, respectively (1f, 11f).

Expectations of their "fast track" adaptation, combined with dependency on their husbands and experience of social isolation, including separation from their families in their countries of origin, led many marriage migrants among my interviewees to suffer from depression or consider leaving their spouses and returning home. Typical responses included: "I almost went back home. That's how bad it was. I was homesick for about a year. It took me about a year to get used to the culture, to get used to the language, to get used to the food" (9f); "I was very lonely for three years. I was baking. For three years, even when my daughter was born, I was baking every single day. . . . Language-wise for six months was extremely difficult" (11f); "I felt totally out of place. . . . I was the housewife. . . . I was going nuts. . . . All of a sudden nothing is happening in your life. And I had [a] really hard time breaking into this life, finding my spot, finding what to do. And my husband, he didn't know how to help me" (10f). The last interviewee eventually divorced her US husband. Another participant reported briefly returning home but then rejoining her husband when she found out she was pregnant. She described her marriage and its effect on her well-being in the United States thus: "It's like a Palestinian and an Israeli living under the same roof. . . . And the more we live together, the more I realize we just never, never will come together. . . . [Our child] is the only thing in common. . . . We're not soul mates let's say, we're just so different. . . . I was isolated. I got into depression. Quit my job. I'm not interested in anything. It was like that on and off for five years" (12f). Her husband's politically conservative and fundamentalist religious views also led her to worry for her child's future. Another participant divorced her US husband and returned to Moscow—after having been in the United States for nine years and receiving an advanced US degree.

The pressure to assimilate had considerable effect on the women's identity formation as US immigrants. Unlike some of the male scientists, none of the women self-identified as Russian American or Ukrainian American. Instead, many reported experiencing a lack of identity or simply identified as Russian or Ukrainian. One participant said, "I don't fit [in] anywhere. And primarily it's not a language but an emotional barrier because it's very hard to connect sometimes" (11f). Another interviewee reported: "I'm stuck in between! . . . When I moved here, I felt like, 'OK. I cut off all the roots from Russia when I start going here.' But with time, I understand people start feeling nostalgia" (1f). Another participant self-identified as "Russian, doesn't matter what, first," but also noted her lack of ethnic engagement, saying, "I don't speak Russian too much and I don't have Russian TV" (12f).

Even though the conventions of the transnational marriage market induce women to portray themselves as family-oriented mothers and housewives who *willingly* entered into various forms of dependency, all the participants in my study had bachelor's or master's degrees, were trained in such occupations as engineering, architecture, education, philology, and the legal profession, and often had more extensive educational backgrounds than the US men they married. But their experiences in the US job market were very different from those post-Soviet migrants who came on J-1 visas to take up postdoc positions. Despite their advanced educational degrees and often the highly skilled positions they had held in the former USSR and successor nations, marriage migrants could not find jobs in their fields because, unlike the Ph.D.s in the fundamental sciences held by postdoc migrants, their degrees did not translate, or as one interviewee said, "It was difficult just to find a job probably because [of] . . . [the] lack of experience in the US market" (8f).

A few of my interviewees labored in low-prestige and low-paid occupations—as substitute teachers, as contract workers for temp agencies, or as employees in the social services or the service industry. Some had also created their own Internet or language teaching and translation businesses. These participants exemplify the finding that post-USSR women immigrants, though not specifically those who come as marriage migrants, are less likely to be working than male post-Soviet immigrants and if they are, they earn a quarter less than white female immigrants from Western Europe and Canada (Logan and Rivera 2011, 37–39). Even those who are college-educated and previously held highly skilled or technical occupations end up working in low-skilled jobs (Logan and Rivera 2011, 27).

In contrast to postdoc migrants, marriage migrants generally also made a more sustained effort to build coethnic networks, mostly to ameliorate their cultural and linguistic isolation and often, when they had children, to create the Russian-speaking environment that they could not build in their own homes. As one participant said, "I have a couple [of] close friends and most of them have kids so we can play, and while the kids play, we can talk" (1f). Because of their location both inside and outside immigrant communities (Johnson 2007, 126–127), however, marriage migrants also experienced difficulty in finding common ground with those who had come with their families, such as the wives of men who had arrived on highly skilled visa categories. Interviewees noted that other post-Soviet women who came with their husbands did not face as much pressure to assimilate and were better able to retain their native culture and language, transmit it to their children, and maintain connections with their home countries. As one interviewee said: "People who come as Russian community with Russian friends have a huge connection to Russia. I think they have more identity before they come, they live so simple, they have the same habits, the same jokes, the same background. I feel odd when I'm getting into completely Russian immigration groups here. I feel I don't fit [in] anywhere" (11f). She reported that she had more in common with other post-USSR marriage migrants, those who are "married to an American; it's very easy for us to communicate. Very easy. You have the same difficulties, you have the same transformations that you are going through" (11f).

One participant who had arrived on an F-1 student visa to take up graduate studies in the United States explained that she considered the migration motivations of marriage migrants amoral, which prevented her from forming friendships with women who had come with this visa status. She mentioned avoiding a fellow post-Soviet graduate student who had arrived as a marriage migrant. According to the interviewee, this person had come "for the wrong reasons. She didn't love her husband and actually just wanted to [immigrate]. I decided I really didn't need a contact like this, so I would rather be communicating with people from other countries than with my compatriots with this kind of attitude" (7f).

Conclusion

In the few studies that have been conducted on this issue, Jewish Russians have been found to have low rates of return and to engage in few return visits (Morawska 2004). They thus appear to be different from other contemporary US immigrants, an estimated 20 to 50 percent of whom return home permanently (Reagan and Olsen 2000, 339). On the surface, the small rates of return among post-Soviet migrants are reminiscent of the relative lack of return movement by turn of the twentieth century Jewish migrants from the Pale of Settlement in the Russian empire, especially compared to southern European migrants. Many Jewish migrants did not possess the required documentation to leave Russia and thus became denaturalized upon emigration, which made return much more difficult. While Jewish return migration was significantly lower than that of Italians, however, the numbers were higher than generally assumed. Between 1880 and 1900, as many as 15 to 20 percent of the migrants returned, some temporarily and most voluntarily, while deportations also increased after 1897 (Sarna 1981, 263, 368). Only in the early 1900s did return migration fall to the negligible rate of about 5 percent (Foner 2005, 359).

It would be too facile to explain the historical similarity between twentieth-century Jewish migrants and contemporary post-USSR migrants (including those who are not Jewish) in terms of their collective racialization as white and their desire to completely assimilate to US norms by cutting off transnational ties to their homes. This is the story portrayed in media representations of post-USSR migrants, which depict the new arrivals as updated versions of the mythologized turn of the twentieth century white European immigrant.

My interviews revealed a more complicated picture. The more negative immigration experiences of marriage migrants, especially the pressures they experienced to assimilate to the middle-class whiteness of their husbands, often induced them to either consider returning home or to actually return (if only temporarily) because this was the only alternative to their remaining in the United States. In contrast, the more limited instances of return considerations by the highly skilled migrants who are generally understood to be more mobile is the result of a *combination* of their generally favorable racial and economic integration into US society (despite their cultural and linguistic differences), especially when compared to their experiences of racialization in Europe; their family ties in the United States (especially the presence of children); problematic social and political developments in many Soviet successor nations; the high cost of physical transnational mobility; and the existence of fewer government-sponsored incentives that promote the return of post-Soviet diasporic intellectuals when compared to other immigrant-sending countries like China and India.

More generally, as a group my participants attributed their lack of return intentions to fears that Russia's economic growth had been almost entirely based on natural resource extraction and had entailed drastic increases in the cost of living, pollution, insecurity, and corruption. Participants also cited a lack of safety (6f, 16f, 21f), social security (17m), and democracy (26f); the presence of widespread corruption (9f, 14m, 26m), high prices (14m), pollution, and overcrowding (15f, 26m) in various post-Soviet nations. Ethnic hostilities toward those from Central Asia (12f) and ethnic conflicts in Ukraine also played a role in discouraging return. One scientist declared, "One of the reasons I decided to leave Ukraine is that I didn't like the political developments. So I would not go back even if I could find a job or anything. I just didn't like what happened after the Soviet Union collapsed and I still do not like what's happening over there. . . . [Particularly] the feelings towards Russians who became a minority, although it is still 30 percent of the population, are not very favorable" (13m).

My interviews highlight important distinctions in the choices available to post-Soviet migrants as they integrate into segmented layers of

US society, economy, and culture, and as they consider return. Because it shapes the insertion of individual migrants into various categories of the US immigration system, their arrival on highly gendered forms of legal status constitutes such an important factor in their adaptation and return considerations that it can outweigh shared group characteristics such as high levels of education and even, to an extent, the assignation of a white racial identity.

While the global extension of US notions of whiteness to post-Soviet women provides them with privileged forms of legal arrival and residence, it also places them at an increased risk of exploitation in the transnational marriage market and exposes them to pressures of enforced enculturation at the expense of retaining their ethnic and national differences or creating new bicultural and transnational identities. These two features have also characterized the transnational movement of post-USSR adoptees to the United States, which is examined in the next chapter. The rise of a neoliberal adoption market that for a while functioned largely unfettered by regulation and the attribution of a highly desired white racial identity to post-Soviet social orphans similarly fueled a highly problematic form of migration to the United States.

3

The Desire for Adoptive Invisibility

In April 2010, seven-year-old Artyom Savelyev came to the center of international attention when he arrived unaccompanied at the Moscow airport on a plane from the United States. Artyom carried a note from his US adoptive mother, Torry Ann Hansen, in which she stated that she wanted to "return" the boy to Russia because he was violent and mentally ill, and that the orphanage in Partizansk from which she had adopted him six months earlier had misled her about his condition. While the media initially condemned Hansen's actions as a form of adoption consumerism, they quickly turned their attention to the boy's mental and behavioral problems. In the only interview the adoptive family ever granted, the grandmother claimed that Artyom was physically abusive and that he threatened to kill family members and burn down their house (Hall 2010). In story after story, experts and adoptive parents expressed sympathy for Tory Ann Hansen's decision and speculatively associated Artyom's behavior with reactive attachment disorder (RAD) (Dell'Antonia 2010; Kershaw 2010; and Whitmire 2010). This controversial diagnosis, which attributes a child's failure to bond with her adoptive parents to attachment interruptions in early life, has gained in popularity among US parents with adopted children (Stryker 2010, 7). With all the attention on Artyom's problems, few reports addressed how his problematic treatment in the United States—where he was homeschooled and largely kept in the home—may have contributed to the termination of his adoption.[1]

In 2011, another scandal rekindled interest in post-Soviet adoptions when Alaska elementary schoolteacher and self-described member of the LDS church Jessica Beagley was convicted of misdemeanor child abuse. In November 2010, she had appeared on the Dr. Phil show to comment on a video that showed her disciplining one of her adoptive sons. Seven-year-old Kristoff Beagley (born Daniil Bukharov) had been adopted from an orphanage in Russia in 2008 at the age of five along with his fraternal twin brother Oleg. In addition to the twins, the Beagleys already had four biological children, one of whom had Downs syndrome (Grove 2011). In the video, which was filmed by Beagley's ten-year-old daughter, Beagley instructs Kristoff to hold hot sauce in his mouth and gives him a cold shower. The child's heart-wrenching screams brought many in the show's audience to tears and led host Phil McGraw to call Beagley's actions abusive. In her defense, Beagley alleged that her son had (undiagnosed) RAD and that other methods of discipline had not worked. Beagley's husband, a police officer who specializes in child abuse investigations, credited his Department of Defense training for the cold shower technique. He also explained his wife's behavior, saying, "Jessica is more frustrated than angry, because we've added more kids to the house" ("Mommy Confessions," 2010).

Artyom Savelyev's "return" and Jessica Beasley's appearance on the Dr. Phil show called attention to US adoptions from the two largest USSR successor nations, Russia and Ukraine, which opened their doors to transnational adoptions in 1991 at the onset of drastic transitions in Soviet successor nations. In terms of admission and access to US citizenship, transnational adoption represents an even more privileged form of migration than marriage migration, discussed in the previous chapter. Since the passage of the Child Citizenship Act of 2000, adoptees can enter the United States on IH-4 or IR-4 visas and automatically acquire US citizenship after their adoption is finalized.

Transnational adoption to the United States has been most often discussed with regard to children from Korea and China, but just as post-USSR women trailed Filipinas as US marriage migrants throughout the 1990s, children from Russia became the second-largest group of adoptees after Chinese children throughout that same decade. During the 1990s and into the early 2000s, Russia was a leading country of origin for US adoptees. A nation with a shrinking population, Ukraine ranked among the ten leading origin countries for US adoptees in 1999, and since 2000, has reclaimed that status (US Department of State, n.d.). While transnational adoptions to the United States declined from their peak of 22,989 in 2004 to just 5,370 in 2016, about 50,000 Russian children had been adopted by US parents between 1999 and the time the country ended adoptions in 2013 (US Department of State, n.d.). Since that period (and as in marriage migration, where Ukrainian women now outnumber Russians), Ukraine has taken over Russia's former role to become the third-largest sending country of US adoptees after China and Ethiopia. More Ukrainian children were adopted in 2014 than the previous year, while the numbers of adoptees from China and Ethiopia fell during the same one-year period (US Department of State 2015). In 2015, the numbers of South Korean adoptees increased so significantly that Korea displaced Ukraine from its position as third-largest origin country of US adoptees (US Department of State 2016).[2]

Similar to the reporting on Savelyev and Beagley, the US coverage of adoptions from the former Soviet Union has highlighted adoption failures or adoptee abuse, often by emphasizing the adoptees' mental and behavioral issues.[3] In contrast, discussion of adoptions from China has focused on attempts by the mostly white US adoptive parents to connect their children to Chinese culture (H. Jacobson 2014). This differential approach to the two adoptee populations also characterizes academic scholarship. Publications on Eastern European adoptees tend to employ medical or psychological perspectives to focus on adoptee disorders, even though Chinese adoptees also experience health issues and developmental delays as a result of institutionalization (H. Jacobson 2014). Research on transnational adoption that has focused on China and Korea, on the other hand, has emphasized race as a postadoption risk factor and has virtually excluded Eastern European children from its purview.[4] While humanities scholarship has examined issues of transracial international adoption, work in the social sciences has explored how adoptees from Asia accommodate to a US racial identity after having been sheltered by their mostly white, affluent parents from many of the challenges experienced by US immigrant and racialized groups.[5] In fact, South Korean adoptees who have grown into adults have produced creative and scholarly work that focuses on issues of race (Trenka 2003; Trenka et. al. 2006; Borshay Liem 2000).

Partially because adoptions from Eastern Europe began more recently, similar cultural productions by adoptees from the former Soviet Union are scarce. Instead, the memoir of transnational adoption has emerged as a new literary genre to chronicle *parents'* experiences of adoption. Traditionally employed by older public figures to recount how their lives reflected historical events, the memoir has expanded to include representations of a specific life experience (Gilmore 2001, 128), and representations of the genre have surged at the turn of the twenty-first century as part of a general boom in nonfiction. Parental memoirs of adoption from Russia and Ukraine mushroomed during the late 1990s and early 2000, at a time of surging US adoptions from this part of the world. Three of the most influential parental memoirs, Margaret L. Schwartz's *The Pumpkin Patch: A Single Woman's International Adoption Journey* (2005), Theresa Reid's *Two Little Girls: A Memoir of Adoption* (2007), and Brooks Hansen's *The Brotherhood of Joseph: A Father's Memoir of Infertility and Adoption in the 21st Century* (2008), exemplify the rise of this new genre.[6] While they cannot possibly represent the entire range of US adoptive parents with children from Soviet successor nations, these memoirs reveal how notions of a globalized whiteness have shaped adoptions from the former USSR. The memoirs cover a wide variety of experiences—by a single businesswoman, an expert in child maltreatment, and a creative writer. Schwartz writes as a newly minted adoption consultant, Reid's work has been endorsed by major adoption researchers, and Hansen's memoir has been touted as giving voice to the underrepresented heterosexual father's view of international adoption.

The rise in nonfiction coincided with the emergence of reality TV, as discussed in chapter 1. Both cultural forms purport to provide insight into events that occur in "reality." Unlike the surveys and interviews of adoptive parents employed in the small body of social science scholarship on Eastern European adoption, the use of the memoir allows parents to exert more direct control over the representation of their adoption experiences and to present them as guides for other prospective adoptive parents. Because memoirs appear to represent verifiable experiences in the physical world (Larson 2007, 15), the genre has lent itself especially well to efforts to understand transnational adoption. Laura Briggs has drawn attention to the fact that adoption has been "a surprisingly literary affair as adoptive parents, in particular (but also their children), struggle to make this unusual event make sense by narrativizing it" (Briggs 2006, 346).

A study of US parental memoirs adds to the impoverished media coverage of adoption failures a focus on the significance of whiteness for adoptions from Soviet successor nations. Even though they were intended as chronicles of success, these memoirs expose deeply problematic attitudes toward adoptions from the former USSR that render the cases of Artyom Savelyev and Kristoff Beagley less unique. The memoirs reveal how some US adoptive parents attribute adoption problems to the deficiencies and pathologies of their adopted children in order to legitimatize the parents' wish to create a particular kind of family. Like much other nonfiction from the turn of the twenty-first century, the three adoption memoirs propagate structures of affective neoliberalism (Gilmore 2010; Thoma 2014) that frame adoptions from Russia and Ukraine as acts of consumerism designed to help the authors fulfill their desire to form families which look as though its members are biologically related. Just as white US men use the transnational marriage market to create monoracial families, well-off white US parents employ the transnational adoption market to find white children who they think look like them so that the adoption can remain invisible to the outside world. The authors' declaration that adoption is designed to satisfy the *parental* desire for children who look like their parents represents a significant departure from the more traditional characterization of international adoption as a means to serve the needs of *children*. Often cloaked in the mantle of humanitarianism, the notion that international adoption helps "save" children from war, poverty, or the effects of communism has dominated US transnational adoption from its inception in the post–World War II period and initially also characterized adoptions from Eastern Europe in the early 1990s.

The three writers' conviction that they share *preexisting* racial identities with Eastern European children extends contemporary notions of US whiteness that encompass all those of European immigrant descent in the United States to prospective adoptees who reside in post-Soviet countries. Just like post-USSR women who come as marriage migrants, the designation of these children as white even *before* their arrival in the United States turns them into highly valued commodities in the neoliberal adoption market and enables their migration under privileged legal categories. But as in the case of "mail-order brides," the adoptees' assumed whiteness also creates unrealistic expectations of their quick and complete assimilation to their new families. This view not only ignores the trauma of children's displacement from their birth families, countries, languages, and culture, but also obfuscates global economic disparities between US adoptive parents and institutionalized children from the two Soviet successor nations, whose drastic and unmitigated neoliberal transitions enabled large-scale adoptions in the first place. Widespread unemployment, growing impoverishment, and changes in family patterns away from the model of two working parents who received child-rearing support from extended family led to a significant rise in child relinquishment following the neoliberal transitions in post-Soviet countries. The persistence of grave social disparities have carried this pattern into the current period. Since the early 1990s, the number of surrendered children in Russia has increased every year (Kostenko 2014, 347). Young, single mothers in particular relinquish their children, often those with disabilities or born prematurely (Kostenko 2014), to underfunded orphanages that are unable to cope with the influx of these social orphans. In response, large-scale transnational adoptions became normalized as the preferred child welfare option rather than as a measure of last resort, at least until Russia discontinued all adoptions in 2013, while adoptions from Ukraine are still ongoing.

The three memoirs by Schwartz, Reid, and Hansen show that the fiction of global whiteness, which turns post-Soviet adoptees into preferred commodities and privileged migrants, also renders them particularly vulnerable to rejection, adoption disruptions, abuse, or adoption failures. As paying consumers, parents feel empowered to reject referrals for adoptions simply because of the children's appearance and to subordinate considerations about their health to an emphasis on their racial and ethnic "fit" with their adoptive families. Adoption difficulties, such as the adoptees' perceived lack of progress in adapting to their new families, the existence of health issues, or racial identities that fail to live up to the parents' consumerist expectations of adoptive invisibility are blamed on the children. The fiction of global whiteness that shapes adoptions from Soviet successor nations and that is at work in the parental adoption memoirs thus provides one possible explanation for why post-USSR children have constituted the largest number of adoptees—nineteen—to die at the hands of their adoptive US parents, usually following prolonged periods of abuse.[7]

Beyond Humanitarianism in Eastern European Adoptions

The desire for adoptive invisibility has characterized US domestic adoptions since it was first formalized in the early twentieth century, at a time when the United States also experienced mass migration from eastern and southern Europe. As unmarried mothers were encouraged to surrender their children, sufficient numbers became available for adoption to mostly middle- and upper-middle-class parents experiencing infertility (Herman 2008, 147). Birth parents, private facilitators, or state-based adoption agencies tried to "match" adoptable children to prospective parents because shared outward appearance was believed to help facilitate bonding and to allow families avoid the stigma of adoption. Until the 1940s, when domestic adoptions were limited to children who were considered healthy and racially white, matching took into consideration a variety of factors, including the adoptees' physical appearance, intellectual abilities, as well as their religious, national, and ethnic backgrounds. While children were assigned religious identities based on either their own background or the orientation of the welfare organization that placed them, the national origin of adoptees was taken into account whenever it was deemed legible in the children's outward appearance (Herman 2008, 238).

While children started to move across national borders in World War I Europe (Briggs and Marre 2009, 2), in the United States transnational adoptions surged during World War II, at a time when the notion of a shared white racial identity had already began to encompass different European immigrant communities in the United States. Because sufficient numbers of children were available for domestic adoption, taking in children from European nations was seen as a humanitarian response to war. But already in the 1950s when the demand for children began to exceed the number of infants available in the United States and around the same time that US military men could marry overseas spouses, new regulations were implemented to allow military and government employees stationed in Western Europe and Asia to also adopt children from these areas (Lovelock 2000). Following the Korean War, concerns about the discriminatory treatment of racially mixed children fathered by US soldiers inspired humanitarian responses from Christian organizations and families. These responses were also linked to the rejection of international communism (Bergquist 2009).

The connection between humanitarianism and anticommunism continued to shape the second wave of intercountry adoptions from Cuba and Vietnam in the 1960s and 1970s. The 1960s clandestine "Peter Pan"

Operation was designed to "rescue" the children of parents opposed to the Castro government and was later expanded to include children whose parents believed rumors that their children would be shipped to work camps. At the end of the Vietnam conflict in 1975, US parents who wanted to adopt South Vietnamese children—many of whom were of mixed race, fathered by US military personnel—also framed their adoptions as humanitarian responses to a sense of guilt for the US involvement in Vietnam (Varzally 2009).

Beginning in the late 1960s, when transnational marriages between US men and women from less economically developed countries were taking place on a large scale, South Korean adoptions were no longer dominated by mixed-race children but began to include large numbers of social orphans who had been relinquished by unmarried mothers. Yet these adoptions continued to be legitimized in humanitarian terms as a means of rescuing destitute children from the "miseries of the Third World" (Hübinette 2004). Similarly, when US adoptions from Latin America increased in the 1980s, largely in response to the difficulties prospective US parents were experiencing in conceiving or in adopting domestically, they were presented as humanitarian efforts to rescue children from conditions of poverty. As Laura Briggs has argued, adoptions from Latin America became cloaked in sentimental narratives that invoked the specter of endangered children, desperate US adoptive parents, and a corrupt adoption system. These narratives figured US adoptive parents as rescuing children from poverty, while birth parents were portrayed as "(at best) happily sending their children off to a land where they will have more material benefits" (Briggs 2006, 348).

The dramatic post-1990s surge in US adoptions from former socialist countries, which coincided with a rise in marriage migration, revived the connection between anticommunism and humanitarianism. This association obscures the main reasons for the surge in child relinquishment in former East Bloc nations undergoing neoliberal transformations, namely, parental impoverishment and the disappearance of welfare services and childrearing support from extended family. At the same time, parental poverty has become the main explanatory model for the increase in social orphans in Latin America. As Lisa Cartwright has argued, in the early 1990s the US media focused on the increased number of institutionalized children in formerly socialist countries like

Romania, the Soviet successor republics, and China to create a mediated politics of pity that prompted humanitarian aid efforts to rescue orphans (Cartwright 2005, 188). In the United States, documentaries like ABC's "20/20" special, "Shame of a Nation" (1990), presented images of child suffering in underfunded and overcrowded state-run orphanages, while also highlighting the possibility of unregulated and low-cost adoptions.

Focusing on Romania, from which the largest number of documented adopted children entered the United States in 1991, "Shame of a Nation" emphasized malnourished and disabled bodies that framed institutionalization as a form of disability (Cartwright 2005).[8] Because the conditions for large-scale child relinquishment were created by the policies of the Ceaușescu regime, which penalized small families, banned birth control, and criminalized abortion (Wilson 2003), appeals to viewers' compassion to rescue children from these institutions were also cloaked in anticommunist sentiment. Would-be US parents traveled to Romania to adopt children on their own or with the help of independent facilitators, thus participating in the fantasy of direct transnational crisis intervention through parenthood, which was understood as an act of humanitarian aid (Cartwright 2005, 194–197). Drawn to Romania by images of institutionalized orphans, adoptive parents soon found, however, that the vast majority of institutionalized children had severe mental or physical disabilities or were not available for adoption because they had been housed there only temporarily by their families. As child relinquishment surged in response to high inflation, rising unemployment, and cutbacks in state welfare benefits, which caused even wider impoverishment during Romania's transition to a market economy (Dickens 2002, 77), visitors from the United States and other Western countries started adopting children who were not institutionalized. Adoptions from the country were shaped by such high levels of abuse and corruption that, to this day, Romania is unable to document the majority of adoptions that took place between 1991 and 1997 (Conolly 2000).

The link between mass-mediated humanitarian responses to global crises and the potential for abuse in an unregulated adoption market reemerged in the aftermath of Haiti's 2010 earthquake. As a reaction to US media coverage which centered on institutionalized children awaiting adoption, the governor of Pennsylvania chartered a plane to take some fifty Haitian infants from the rubble of their orphanages, but ended up also removing twelve children who were not available for adoption. Shortly thereafter, ten Baptist missionaries from Idaho were arrested for attempting to move thirty-three Haitian children into the neighboring Dominican Republic without the required documents. Though the Idaho Baptists claimed the children were orphans whose homes had been destroyed in the earthquake, the parents had actually entrusted their children to the temporary care of the group in the hope of securing them an education (Rowe 2010; G. Thompson 2010). That adoptions from contemporary Haiti and early 1990s Romania relied on similar narratives of child rescue, which focused on saving institutionalized children from the effects of natural disaster or from communism-induced disability, suggests that the story of humanitarianism is deeply dependent upon its association with other perceived conditions of crisis.

The adoption memoirs by Schwartz, Reid, and Hansen show, however, that the rhetoric of anticommunist humanitarianism is no longer necessary to justify adoptions from Eastern Europe, since child relinquishment in several nations there cannot be exclusively linked to the failures of socialism or with the policies of communist dictators like Ceaușescu. Instead, these adoptions can now be framed as explicit admissions of adoptive parents' consumerist desire for the kind of child that best fits their notions of a family in which everyone looks alike. One could speculate that this shift was possible because, in contrast to adoptions from Latin America, adoptions from formerly socialist countries were never primarily presented as a response to growing poverty and the decimation of social welfare in states in transition, but as rescue missions to save children from the lingering effects of communism, figured as literal and symbolic disablement. As Lisa Cartwright writes, already by the end of the 1990s the US media focus on institutionalized children's disability, which sought to evoke a humanitarian response, began to transform into an emphasis on hidden impairments in Eastern European adoptees that included a new attention to attachment disorders (Cartwright 2005, 201–202, 206). In distinct contrast, the justifications for adoptions from China shifted from an emphasis on the children's disabilities to a focus on the country's one-child policy. In addition to the centrality of US constructions of race, this differential focus has shaped the divergent approaches to the two populations that were leading US adoptions at the height of this phenomenon.

Schwartz, Reid, and Hansen move the rhetoric of humanitarianism to the background of their narratives and instead portray their adoptions from post-USSR countries primarily as a means of achieving a form of adoptive invisibility that they understand as a shared familial whiteness. This emphasis on racial sameness obscures the fact that, as in other adoptee-sending countries, the rise in child relinquishment in Ukraine and Russia was a response to widespread impoverishment, the disappearance of social services, and the dissolution of family structures. In the case of these two countries these developments followed the neoliberal transition from socialist to capitalist property regimes.

Only remnants of the humanitarian justification survive in the authors' occasional claims that, apart from fulfilling their own desire for children who look like them, transnational adoption may also improve the adoptees' economic, educational, medical, or family status. Thus, in *Pumpkin Patch*, Margaret Schwartz, a business consultant and single woman in her mid-forties, writes that she settled on adoption from Ukraine in the early 2000s because "I am fair skinned with hazel eyes and dark blond hair, and want my children to look like me" (17). Only upon arriving in Ukraine and hearing of the often dire medical diagnoses of children available for adoption did Schwartz realize that, besides fulfilling her own desire for a family, she may also be "rescuing" institutionalized children from an underfunctioning medical system.

Similarly, in *Two Little Girls* child maltreatment expert Theresa Reid explains her desire for "adoption privacy"—which she defines as the ability to "retain the prerogative of disclosing our adoption status to the world" (13)—as the main reason why she and her husband Marc, a pediatrician, chose to adopt from Eastern Europe. Reid explains that the couple selected Russia in the mid-1990s because her husband's ancestors came from what she says is the same geographical area, that is, the Russian empire. She admits that her "primary goal" was "to build a healthy family," even though she also fashions a dramatic child rescue story, according to which adopting a girl from Russia could possibly save her from "end[ing] up a victim of the international sex trade" (18). About her second adoption from Ukraine in 2002 Reid writes, however, that it was motivated "not primarily to do good in the world, not primarily to rescue an unknown-but-already-loved child, but primarily to complete our family as we saw fit" (66). Brooks Hansen in *The Brotherhood of*

Joseph casts his motivation for adopting from Eastern Europe in even more explicitly selfish terms. After four years of unsuccessful fertility treatments, he and his wife saw themselves as the "aggrieved party . . . the sick ones . . . the ones in need." Only when they got further along in the adoption process did Hansen begin to realize that "there were the children, too" (91). The couple rejected adoptions from Korea in favor of first, Romania and then Russia, because, as Hansen writes, "all our reasons for considering Korea were borne of fear, not excitement—and what excited me was the idea of adopting a child from a part of the world to which I felt a visceral connection" (96–97).[9]

Fictions of Global Whiteness, Adoptive Invisibility Consumerism

Throughout their narratives, the three writers cast themselves in the role of adoption consumers who have the right to select healthy, white children from the international adoption market, even if it means working with unethical adoption providers who circumvent the few rules that regulated transnational adoption from Soviet successor nations to the United States at the time. The authors chose Russia and Ukraine not only because they thought that white children were available there, but also because in the 1990s and early 2000s these two countries encouraged largely unregulated adoptions of children to overseas parents after other former socialist countries such as Romania had ended or restricted international adoption. Russia permitted adoptions through unlicensed agencies as well as through independent and uncertified providers such as lawyers and other adoptive parents. Ukraine allowed parents to select adoptable children from a photolisted database at the Ministry of Education and then visit the children in their orphanages to make a final decision.

The US government undertook no significant attempts to curb its citizens' adoption consumerism. Unlike the US child care system which focuses on involuntarily relinquished children, there is no public infrastructure to facilitate transnational adoptions. Instead, international adoption extends the domestic practice of placing voluntarily relinquished children with adoptive families through largely unregulated third parties or private commercial or nonprofit agencies (O'Halloran 2006, 210). Until the United States ratified the Hague Adoption Convention in 2008 and designated a central entity to accredit and approve adoption service providers in member countries, the US government generally only became involved in international adoptions when it granted visas to adoptees under the so-called "orphan process." Under this process, transnational adoption is considered a private legal matter between adoptive parents and a foreign court, in which US authorities cannot intervene. The Child Citizenship Act of 2000 grants adoptees automatic citizenship when they enter the United States as lawful permanent residents. Under the Hague Convention, private adoptions from nonmember states continue under the older orphan process.

Schwartz, Reid, and Hansen chose to work with US agencies or individuals that violated the few existing rules governing Russian and Ukrainian adoptions at the time. Schwartz describes that she turned to Ukraine—instead of other Eastern European nations where white children were supposedly also available—because of the country's adoption procedures that at the time of her writing, between 2001 and 2003, allowed high parental involvement in the selection of children. The 1996 Resolution on Adoption includes a provision that bars adoptive parents from receiving information about available children prior to completing an application process and travelling to Ukraine. At the State Department of Adoption and Protection of Child's Rights, a part of the Ministry of Social Policy, adoptive parents are shown a database of adoptable children from which they can choose. Asserting her neoliberal consumer choice, Schwartz writes, "I want to be the one to decide what children I bring home. Many countries, including Russia, pre-select children for adoptive parents. It is illegal in Ukraine to do this; instead people go directly to the orphanage and select the child they want" (17). Schwartz also chose to work with an independent facilitator, Cathy Harris, whose expertise was based mainly on her own adoption of five Ukrainian children. Harris's Ukrainian contacts bribed officials and engaged in other questionable practices to speed up the adoption process; as Schwartz writes, one of the facilitators even "told me that I was not to discuss financial terms with anyone except him, nor was I to mention his name at the NAC or other government agencies" (80).

Once she arrived at Ukraine's Ministry, Schwartz rejected several children based on their medical diagnoses or inferences about their health that she drew from their photolisted appearances. When Schwartz met the reportedly healthy girl whom she had selected at the Ministry, the author immediately diagnosed her with Fetal Alcohol Syndrome (FAS), a condition that other adoptive parents had warned her was widespread among Eastern European adoptees. In the absence of any documented history of maternal alcohol consumption or a physician's confirmation, Schwartz's diagnosis was based solely on her own assessment of the child's facial features. In a key moment of her memoir, Schwartz highlights the centrality of the child's appearance for her consumerist decision making, writing: "I felt as if I were looking at a fabric sample and had to decide if I wanted to buy the whole bolt without seeing what was under all the folds" (95).

The other two authors also rejected adoptable children whose appearance (as ascertained by photos, videos, and meetings) appeared to signal potential problems with their health status or racial identities. The children's outward features became central to the parents' adoption consumerism as they chose children they deemed "right" for their families and rejected those who were not. As Lisa Cartwright has shown, whereas pictures were originally introduced into the process of international adoption to document abandoned or lost children, today parents use visual representations to assign ethnic and racial identities as well as health and ability status to the prospective adoptees (Cartwright 2003, 89). While parents' attempts to ascertain the health status of adoptees can be partially explained by the unreliability of the medical information provided, this being a major cause of adoption failures, their efforts to deduce adoptable children's racial "fit" with the preexisting family clearly serves their desire to attain adoptive invisibility.

Reid almost rejected a referred child because her appearance clashed with what she had imagined for her biological child. That she was searching for a daughter who looked as though she could have been her biological kin highlights Reid's view of an adoptee as a substitute for the child she could not have. This view evokes more well-known parental fantasies of replacing a lost or deceased child, which are grounded in an often unconscious economy of seriality and substitution. Because in the unconscious the boundaries between discrete entities are permeable, different children can be condensed into one and the same child, regardless of the biological or psychic differences between them (Schwab 2009, 285). The adoption market promises to fulfill such parental fantasies of substitution by transforming children into replaceable commodities.

The referred girl's appearance not only clashed with Reid's imagined biological child, but it also severely complicated Reid's fantasy of a shared white racial identity with Eastern European adoptees. This child was too blonde (and what's not said: "too white") to fit Reid's husband's ethnic background, which, readers now find out, was actually Jewish. He was apparently a descendant of turn of the twentieth century migration from Russia's Pale of Settlement, which has often been compared to post-Soviet migration in terms of migrants' similar geographical background and white racial identity. The case of the potential adoptive child underscores the limitations of such fantasies of a shared whiteness between descendants of early eastern European migrants, who were mostly Jewish, and residents of post-USSR nations who are racially and ethnically diverse. In fact, the picture of the little blonde girl brought to Reid's mind "grainy images of the anonymous hordes who persecuted Europe's Jews" (28). But Reid quickly dismissed this thought, which severely complicated her view that the couple shared a racial identity with the girl they were adopting from Russia, and decided to move forward with the adoption. But when the couple visited Russia to adopt the referred child, the perceived "misfit" between the girl's and the couple's outward appearance negatively shaped their entire experience. As they ignored a host of unethical practices by their placing agency, the couple were preoccupied with comparing the "too white" appearance of the child they were about to adopt with what they perceived as the more favorable looks of children with curly dark hair and dark eyes who more closely resembled the Reids.[10]

During her second adoption, which was designed to produce a sibling for her blonde, blue-eyed daughter, Reid again prioritized her desire for a shared familial appearance—this time between their daughter and the potential second adoptee—and did so even at the expense of concerns about the prospective adoptee's health. When they no longer qualified for adoption from Russia because of their age, the couple chose another agency with a brand new program in Ukraine, but only after they received a money-back guarantee if they failed to locate a suitable adoptee. This agency worked with Ukrainian attorneys who violated one of the few existing regulations by "reserving" a child in the Ministry's database even before she became officially available for adoption. When the child was claimed by a Ukrainian citizen who had priority in the adoption process, Reid settled on another girl, called Sniezhana (little snowflake). Even though they were happy to have found a child (any child?), the couple developed such serious concerns about the girl's physical and mental health—and her outward dissimilarity from their daughter—that they considered terminating her adoption and leaving her in the orphanage. In ways that resemble many adoptive parents' reaction to Artyom Savelyev's case, Reid even identified with another US family who abandoned their five-year-old adopted boy at the Kiev airport because, as reported by the Ukrainian adoption facilitators, they "could not find relation with him" (260). Reid describes her sympathy for this couple as follows: "We were a little in awe of what it took to do what they had done. Did it show extreme callousness or had they perceived (or thought they perceived) in their week with this child a profound inability to connect?" (261).

Whereas Reid eventually overcame her reservations about adopting Sniezhana, Hansen's memoir culminates in the rejection of a healthy infant whom he perceived to be racially different from himself and his wife. In their quest for adoption, the Hansens settled on an agency that miraculously referred them a six-month-old healthy infant, even though children without reported medical conditions were rare among those available for adoption from Russia at the time, most adoptable children were at least eight months old, and the Hansens had previously rejected several referrals on the basis of the children's reported medical diagnoses. Upon his first meeting with this boy, Hansen remarked on the child's physical resemblance to his wife, especially his dark hair color and olive skin tone. But Hansen also noted a more distressing feature: the boy's eyes "showed a slightly more Asian than Indo-European influence; that pleat at the edge pulled to a nearly Oriental length" (160–161). After spending a few hours with the child, the couple rejected the referral.

Affirming the difference between adoption humanitarianism and his family's consumerism, Hansen states that the couple would have made a different decision if "this boy's parents had been good friends of ours and they'd died in a car crash" (172). To provide a "clear-cut, easy-to-understand reason" for why they felt as though the referred baby boy "was not meant to be [their] son," the Hansens cited "confusion about the boy's race." As Hansen writes, "[T]he referral had listed him as Caucasian, but there was reason to think this might not have been entirely true." Hansen's statement that the couple's decision against forming a transracial family was "part of the reason [they had] come to Russia" (190) reveals their inability to grasp how differently the concept of race works outside the United States, specifically their ignorance of the internal diversity of the former USSR, which was comprised of peoples of European, Central Asian, and West Asian heritage (Cartwright 2003, 86).

The rejection of this child led the Hansens to prioritize their desire for an adoptee who looked "Caucasian" even if he had possible health issues. In violation of another of the few existing rules for transnational adoption at the time, their agency referred to them a baby boy who was still in the hospital rather than already institutionalized in an orphanage. This child suffered from first-degree prematurity and other health problems. The Hansens nevertheless decided to adopt him, even though prematurity was one of the medical diagnoses that had led them to reject another referral when they were still in the United States. Hansen admits, "[I]f we had seen his numbers on a referral back in the safe confines of our apartment in New York, we would have made a paper airplane out of it" (202). While Hansen's memoir does not provide updates on the boy's postplacement condition, in 2008 Hansen reported on his blog his efforts to adopt another child. This time the couple set out to adopt a young girl from Kazakhstan, an Asian country with a majority Kazakh population that traces its origin to Turkic and Mongol tribes.

As in Reid's case, Hansen writes that the couple's desire to adopt a little girl was grounded in the wish to "find [their first child] a sister, and ourselves a daughter," while he does not appear to consider the prospective adoptee's needs.[11] In a 2012 blog entry, a commencement speech Hansen gave to high school graduates six years after his son's adoption from Siberia, he rewrites the central storyline of his book. Perhaps influenced by their more recent adoption of a daughter from Kazakhstan, he now attributes the couple's earlier rejection of the baby boy in Siberia who had an insufficiently "Caucasian" appearance to "intuition" rather than "confusion about his race." Brooks states that "my wife and I were literally handed a gift that for some mysterious and inexplicable reason—born of intuition—we could not bring ourselves to accept."[12]

Rendering Post-Soviet Adoption Invisible

Even though their transnational adoptions were marked by their search for adoptive invisibility, some of the writers initially paid lip service to the idea that their adopted children may need to maintain cultural connections to their countries of birth. At the beginning of her narrative, Schwartz thus imagines locating "people who speak Ukrainian near where we will live" and sharing Ukrainian Christmas stories and ornaments with her adopted children (20). This proclamation is similar to the statements many potential adoptive parents make when they blog about their experiences and, prior to their visits to Russia or Ukraine, often mention that they want to make sure they will retain some elements of their adoptees' cultures (Hall 2012).

The notion that a "birth culture" is important for the well-being of transnational adoptees has emerged from the public activism and cultural productions of Korean adult adoptees. Widely articulated in scholarship on adoptions from Asia, this notion now also shapes the practices of the adoption industry, which stresses that adoptive parents need to expose their adopted children to their "birth culture." Following these admonitions, many parents of Asian adoptees enroll their children in language classes or expose them to some of the culture, foods, and holidays of their birth countries. Because these practices are grounded in assumptions that culture encompasses stable traditional practices, they often uncritically construct what Margaret Homans has called "a simulacrum . . . birth culture'" (Homans 2006).[13] The insistence on the need for a "birth culture" (simulacrum) for Asian adoptees primarily acknowledges their differential racialization from their mostly white adoptive families. The notion of a "birth culture" implies that because transnational adoptees are racialized as nonwhite, they need to know at least some elements of a national (Chinese or Korean) culture. Through the acquisition of this "birth culture," adoptees can be imagined as inheritors of their adoptive parents' national culture (and class status) while still maintaining their pluralistic ethnic and cultural inheritance (Briggs 2006, 346).

In contrast, because Eastern European adoptees are racialized into the same notion of pan-European whiteness as their adoptive parents, a comparable systematic notion of "birth culture" is not available to them.

The absence of this concept makes it even more difficult for adoptive parents who might actually want to retain their children's connections to their countries of birth in the former East Bloc. But in her interviews with adoptive parents, Heather Jacobson found that while parents with children from Russia spoke of themselves as committed to preserving their children's birth culture, they did not actually engage in the practice for fear of drawing attention to the adopted status of their children (2008, 129). In their quest for adoptive invisibility, these parents thus often denied even the "birth culture simulacrum" option to the children they adopted from Ukraine and Russia.

Schwartz, Reid, and Hansen similarly not only withheld access to such a "birth culture" but they set out to eradicate their children's national differences so as to keep their adoptions private and invisible. Despite her initial pronouncements to the contrary, Schwartz's postadoption account of the four months she spent with her children never once chronicles attempts at maintaining any part of her children's connection to Ukraine, and neither do the other two memoirs. All the authors changed their children's first names in an attempt to naturalize their adoptees' new identities and to render the children more "American" and connected to the symbolic "ethnicized" European identities that the parents had constructed for themselves. Schwartz assigned her children the names of her own European ancestral kin in order to give them "part of [her] heritage so they will grow up knowing that they belong to a family with whom they will be forever entwined" (120). Likewise, Reid believed that her second daughter's name, Sniezhana, was "too difficult . . . for an American child to pronounce" (181), and the Hansens renamed their son Sergej to shield him from "teachers asking . . . about [his name] every year on the first day of school" (216). The authors seemed to fear that their children's unpronounceable first names could become grounds for a form of othering and thus also withheld from them the possibility to access an emerging ethnicized "Russian" identity and culture, which is represented in the US reality TV shows discussed in chapter 1 and claimed by some post-USSR migrants themselves.

The extension of a US white racial identity to post-Soviet adoptees also obscures economic disparities between nations through the myth of an assumed racial homogeneity among adoptees and their parents. That is why Hansen was completely taken aback when a Russian judge

asked him if the couple had considered that their adopted son "probably came from a different social class than we did." He writes, "I almost
didn't even understand the question . . . we didn't consider [the adoptee]
to be of any class" (232). As the adoptees' national and class differences
from their adoptive parents—and their importance for the creation and
maintenance of global inequities that allow the transnational exchange
of children—are hidden in notions of a shared racial identity, the children are placed in the role of ideal immigrants who, like post-USSR
marriage migrants, are expected to fully assimilate to the majority US
cultural, linguistic, class, and ethnic norms represented by their adoptive family.

Even though the writers do not address the impact of the adoption
industry on their decision-making process, many adoption providers
have not only de-emphasized the need for a "birth culture" for children
adopted from eastern European countries (H. Jacobson 2008, 55), but
have encouraged a belief in the infinite adaptability of post-USSR adoptees. One online guide to Ukraine that is sponsored by a dating agency
specializing in "Ukrainian Brides," for example, asserts that "adaptation to the new family, culture, and language takes place very rapidly—
usually within just a few months. Unless children are taken to special
classes (say, from the local Ukrainian/Russian community), they soon
forget how to speak their native language."[14] In fact, even though he was
already seven years old when he was adopted and had only lived in the
United States for six months, Artyom Savelyev did not understand or
respond to his native language when he arrived in Moscow after having
been sent there by his US adoptive mother (Savodnik 2010).

The myth of a shared whiteness that requires the erasure of adopted
children's national origins and linguistic particularities as potential
grounds for ethnic othering also works to hide the conditions that led to
the surge in relinquished children in the former USSR and their subsequent circulation in the international adoption market in the first place.
Reid ends her book by rejecting calls urging international adopters to
donate the money they spent on the process so that children can instead
stay with their birth families. She writes:

Would we have done a better thing if we had taken [their adopted daugh-
ter] from the orphanage and given her back to her birth mother, with

the thirty-five thousand dollars or so we spent in the adoption process?
. . . But a) we're not that noble; b) that one-time gift would not have al-
tered the *crushing cultural conditions* that had so harmed her birth parents and would harm their children; and c) even with such a gift, her
birth parents could never have given her the opportunities to fulfill her
potential that we have given her.(72–73, my italics).

Reid's attribution of the surge in institutionalized children to "crushing
cultural conditions" contradicts another of her brief asides that "[m]any
of the children in the orphanage are there only temporarily [because]
their parents can't feed them" (122). Hansen appears similarly (and
deliberately?) ignorant of the context surrounding child relinquishment
in post-Soviet countries. In his conversations with an orphanage director, Hansen thus cannot grasp why the birth mother of his adopted child
was labeled "indigent" because she did not leave an address when she
relinquished her child at the hospital. Applying US-based middle-class
notions of maturity, Hansen writes that under this definition, "half of
the twenty-year-olds I've known were indigent" (222).

Both authors ignore parental destitution as a major reason for child
relinquishment in the post-USSR, even though it is a widely accepted
explanation for child relinquishment in Latin America. Although some
of the children who reside in Russian and Ukrainian orphanages have
escaped parental abuse or neglect, the overwhelming majority are social
orphans with at least one living parent (McKinney 2009). The majority
of these parents are young, single, female migrants who have come to
urban centers. In the absence of adequate public child care services and
lacking the extended families they left behind, these women are unable
to hold a job and simultaneously take care of their children (Isupova
2004). Children can be lawfully relinquished, even for short periods of
time, but only if the parents have residence permits in the city of the
child's birth (Issoupova 2000, 82–83). When parents do not have such
permits or cannot afford housing (and thus cannot leave their addresses
with the orphanage where they relinquish their children), they lose their
parental rights.

Instead of acknowledging the global inequities that lead parents to
give up the right to their relinquished children, who then become available for transnational adoption, Reid justifies her ability to adopt from

the former USSR by reclaiming the sentimental birth mother discourse that has become especially important to adopters from Eastern Europe. As Heather Jacobson has found, while parents who adopt from China emphasize their desire to maintain their children's "birth culture," adoptive parents of children from Eastern Europe generally tend to limit the discourse about their adoptees' countries of origin to the absent birth mother. In these narratives, which are particularly strong in Schwartz's memoir, the adoptee is cast as a gift that the birth mother made directly to the adoptive parents, independently of the actual, often unknown conditions of relinquishment.[15] Reid also employs this narrative to openly reaffirm her own privilege as a (First World) adopter in comparison to the (Second World) birth mother without having to consider her moral responsibilities vis-à-vis the causes of this inequity. She writes: "I empathize with Natalie's birth mother, but my determination to parent is stronger than my empathy. I grieve for her loss, and I revere her for her gift to me. But I am thankful to the depths of my being that *I* am raising Natalie, and not she. . . . But that's life this time, and I thank all of the powers in the universe that I am the lucky one" (71–72, italics in original).

Adoption Trouble

The memoirists' affirmations of their adoption consumerism, which obscures the neoliberal conditions enabling large-scale adoptions from the former USSR and normalizes their rejections of adoptable children as mere obstacles on the path to adoptive invisibility, helps contextualize the large number of abuse cases of post-USSR adoptees in the United States. In fact, the connections between some of the memoirs examined here and the adoption failures that have dominated US media coverage of Eastern European adoptions are surprisingly explicit. Cathy Harris, the independent adoption provider Schwartz employed, facilitated the adoption of several children who ended up becoming high profile abuse cases in the United States around the same time that she was working with Schwartz. In 2001 and 2003, Harris mediated the adoptions of three children for John Krueger who had been accused of child molestation in the past. In 2007 Krueger was sentenced to seventy-five years in prison for sexually abusing his eight- to eleven-year-old adoptive charges as well as the adopted child of acquaintances ("Boys Adopted" 2006).[16] In response to his conviction, Ukraine tried to outlaw single-parent adoption. In addition, Harris facilitated the adoption of a Ukrainian child, Nataliya, for Peggy Sue Hilt. In 2006, Hilt, who according to her lawyer was an alcoholic and had mental problems, was sentenced to twenty-five years in prison for killing her other, two-year-old daughter who she had adopted from Russia six months earlier ("Adoptive Mother" 2006).

As the search for adoptive invisibility can lead parents to prioritize adoptees' physical, racial, and ethnic "fit" over other desirable attributes, these children may also suffer from unexpected health issues. These in turn increase the chance that they will have difficulty adapting to their new placements and the possibility of adoption failures. After rejecting the girl she had diagnosed with Fetal Alcohol Syndrome (FAS) in Ukraine, Schwartz ignored the recommendation of adoption providers and adopted two other unrelated children who had reported health conditions that she believed were minor compared to FAS. Upon returning home, Schwartz was thus wholly unprepared for the many doctor's visits and medical expenses as well as her children's developmental delays and the length of time it took them to understand and speak English. Schwartz was surprised that her twenty-month-old son, who appeared to just have a lazy eye, turned out to have Coats disease, which required two surgeries and left him blind in that eye. The second, two-year-old boy had hydrocephalus, a condition where fluid builds up inside the skull. Schwartz never indicates that she understands that this condition, like FAS, can lead to serious physical and mental disabilities, such as short-term memory loss, problems with physical and visual coordination, and epilepsy. Schwartz also never seems to grasp the highly problematic nature of adopting two unrelated children at the same time, which is a practice that Ukraine outlawed shortly after Schwartz's adoption.

Reid's second adoption of a Ukrainian child initially also appeared problematic. Sniezhana (renamed Lana) did not turn out to have any of the feared medical, neurological, or psychological disorders that initially predisposed Reid and her husband to consider terminating their parental rights. Instead, Lana exhibited excessive familiarity with strangers. Even though Reid does not remark on this parallel, probably because Lana's behavior was more pronounced, earlier in her memoir she had described how her older adopted daughter had similarly gone "easily to the other mothers" and showed an "apparent murkiness about who her mommy is" (50). These behaviors are typical of institutionalized children who are discouraged from attaching themselves to one particular caregiver and thus may fail to understand that affective responses to a specific person are expected from them after adoptive placement (Tunina and Stryker 2001). The mainstream treatment of such attachment issues focuses on changing the behavior of the caregivers, particularly stressing their responsiveness and sensitivity to the children. As Reid writes, Natalie's behavior improved when Reid stayed home with her, and she even realized that Lana's problems might similarly be mitigated if Reid spent more time with her rather than hiring babysitters.

In spite of this recognition, however, Reid prioritized her desire to finish her memoir over the needs of her newly adopted second child. Instead, Reid diagnosed Lana with reactive attachment disorder (RAD), a condition she had not assigned to her first adopted child. As Rachel Stryker has argued, the RAD diagnosis allows adoptive parents to define what they see as their child's problematic postplacement behaviors—especially their failure to reward parents with love and attachment—as pathology, thus locating the primary source of the problem within the children (Stryker 2010). As it marks the wish for a less troublesome road to attachment between adoptive parents and their children, the RAD diagnosis can mask adoptees' difficulties in adapting to their new placements and obscure their traumas of relinquishment and institutionalization, which are compounded by language barriers. Adopted children from Soviet successor nations not only do not speak English, but developmental delays may also make them less proficient in their own mother tongues. Reid even vaguely realized that Lana's behavior may have been symptomatic of her institutionalization and her difficulties in adjusting to her new placement, admitting that she had "no idea what this child has gone through—spending her first years the focus of no one's love, crossing the world with perfect strangers, working her way into our tight-knit little family" (267).

When they receive an RAD diagnosis for their adopted children, some parents subscribe to controversial attachment therapies that are directed at changing not their own but their adopted children's behavior.

In contrast to the most commonly practiced therapies that focus on improving parent-child relationships and teach positive parenting skills to aid attachment, more controversial techniques consist of confrontational therapies and therapeutic-parenting training. Promising that their children can be disciplined to attach themselves to adoptive parents, these techniques condition children to comply with parents' expectations and also train parents to turn their houses into "therapeutic homes" where they constantly discipline their children (Stryker 2010, 12–17).

Because some of the attachment techniques are physically coercive, the application of these methods led to several post-Soviet adoptee deaths at the hands of their parents. The mother of two-year-old David Polreis who beat the boy to death in 1996 was working with an attachment center and claimed in her legal defense that the boy had severe RAD, which brought public attention to this diagnosis (Stryker 2010, 24). Six-year-old Viktor Alexander Matthey (born Viktor Sergievich Tulimov) died in 2000 of cardiac arrhythmia due to hypothermia after his adoptive parents had engaged in the prolonged use of supposed "attachment parenting techniques," such as dehydration, whippings, and confinement in an unheated and unlit pump room (Reilly 2001). Viktor's case exemplifies another commonality in post-Soviet adoption failures: he had been adopted into what was already a large family with younger adopted twin brothers and four biological children ("Adopted Siberian Boy" 2000). Eight-year-old Dennis Merryman (born Denis Uritsky) was starved to death in 2005 as a form of attachment parenting. He had lost two pounds since his adoption five years earlier. His parents also already had three biological and five adopted children (Park 2008). In the narratives of child pathology that the adoptive parents used in their legal defense, they portrayed themselves as the long-suffering victims of children's abhorrent behavior, which could only be corrected by the application of controversial attachment therapies (Stryker 2010, 4). The majority of the documented cases of post-Soviet adoptees who died at the hands of their US adoptive parents did so within six months to a year of their placements in the United States—during their most intense adjustment phase (Miller et al. 2007, 379). Artyom Savelyev was also "returned" after six months in the United States. His adoptive mother was reported to have contacted an attachment specialist (Hall 2010) and to have considered adopting a second child.

Conclusion

In their search for adoptive invisibility, the three memoirists endorsed an unbridled adoption consumerism enabled by the myth of global whiteness, the then largely unregulated adoption market between the United States and several post-Soviet countries, and favorable US immigration policies for transnational adoptees. Moving beyond the early 1990s focus on anticommunist humanitarianism to explicit affirmations of parental consumerism, the authors completely ignored the neoliberal transformations in the former USSR as major factors that contributed to their children's relinquishment and their eventual transnational adoption. Reid's explicit affirmation of adoption consumerism has received widespread support in the US adoption community. In addition to the "usual suspects" like Harvard professor Elizabeth Bartholet (1993) who has consistently worked against efforts to regulate transnational adoption, the director of the Evan B. Donaldson Adoption Institute and associate editor of *Adoption Quarterly* Adam Pertman also wrote an endorsement of Reid's book. Pertman's support indicates that even more mainstream advocates of transnational adoption apparently find nothing objectionable in Reid's extended affirmations of neoliberal adoption consumerism in search of adoptive invisibility.[17]

Recommendations for ameliorating the neoliberal character of transnational adoption have included calls for tighter regulations. Under pressure from adoption advocates, adoptive parents, and the adoption industry, however, the US government has generally worked to *ease* legal restrictions guiding the entry of adopted children into the United States. This trend was manifested in the passage of new adoption regulations for Haitian children. A few weeks after the earthquake, the US Department of Homeland Security issued unprecedented regulation permitting Haitian children to enter the United States with special, humanitarian visas. Similarly, when Western European nations halted adoptions from Guatemala in the late 1990s and early 2000s in response to concerns about corruption, black market trading, and child trafficking, US agencies and individuals increased their adoptions from this country (Bunkers et al. 2009).

Reforms on an international level and by individual nations have focused on outlawing adoptions through unregulated agencies or facilitators, which are central to the existence of the neoliberal adoption market. The Hague Adoption Convention requires adoption service providers to be accredited in order to practice in a Convention country. Following the dissolution of Artyom Savelyev's adoption, Russia and the United States negotiated an agreement that limited adoptions to US accredited agencies working in compliance with the Hague Convention, required adopters to undergo mental health tests, and mandated that all adopted children keep their Russian citizenship until they turn eighteen. Long desired by Russia but resisted by the United States, the agreement was signed in 2011 and required adoption agencies and adoptive parents to continue reporting on the adopted child's health and living conditions after their adoption (Weir 2010). But in 2013 Russia completely banned adoptions to the United States. At the same time, however, adoptions from Ukraine increased.

Romania, Ghana, Bhutan, Kyrgyzstan, and Rwanda have also ended transnational adoption, while Guatemala and Kazakhstan have halted new adoptions until a Hague Convention-compliant system is implemented. Colombia only allows applications by non-Colombian parents if they adopt children with special needs or older than six years and eleven months. In South Korea, which has the lowest fertility rate in Asia but still ranked as the sixth-largest source of adopted infants in the world in 2012, the government passed the so-called Korean Adoption Law. The law follows the Hague Convention on Intercountry Adoption in recommending that adoptable children remain in the country of their birth and only be adopted internationally if no foster home is found. The new legislation also mandates that parents get court approval before adopting children, and it requires adoption agencies to declassify information on birth parents. Since the enactment of the legislation, the number of transnational adoptees has declined (Ji-sook 2012). One of the driving forces behind the legislation was the Truth & Reconciliation for the Adoption Community of Korea organization, which is led by Jane Jeong Trenka, a prominent Korean American adoptee who returned to Korea and has brought attention to Korean transnational adoption to a wider global public.

A more tightly regulated adoption market may not only help prevent more cases of disrupted placements and adoptee abuse. It may also correct some US parents' view of adoptable children as consumer items to be plucked selectively—in accordance with parental criteria of desirability—from the former Second World and reinserted into First World economies as members of US middle- and upper-middle-class families. Coupled with the US myth of a shared whiteness, such consumerist attitudes have allowed parents to abdicate responsibility for understanding the neoliberal conditions that have enabled their children's relinquishment and to ignore their children's national, cultural, and linguistic differences from the majority US culture.

The view of Eastern European children as simply white undoubtedly provides them with immense and immediate racial privilege by severing possible associations with the historical vestiges of an older "in-between" racialized identity that was assigned to turn of the twentieth century eastern European immigrants. But the three adoption memoirs examined in this chapter also highlight the downside of such efforts to seamlessly incorporate post-Soviet children into neoliberal versions of US whiteness. The assumption that recent post-USSR arrivals share a common racial identity with their US parents of European descent can cause substantial harm. Adoptive children are expected to fully assimilate to the majority white US society and to conform to the needs of their US families for adoptive invisibility that include reciprocal attachment. When these expectations are not met, some adoptees, like Artyom Savelyev, evidently become rejectable and even "returnable," and such decisions provoke an outpouring of sympathy rather than criticism from major parts of the adoption community. In addition to the adoption failures, adoptee abuses, and deaths that have dominated US media accounts, we have yet to see how Eastern European adoptees, once they find their public and artistic voices, will react to their collective commodification through the US parental quest for adoptive invisibility.

4

Fictions of Irregular Post-Soviet Migration

Indian American author Bharati Mukherjee recently theorized a new form of US immigrant writing, which she calls the "Literature of New Arrival." Her list of authors who participate in this new form of writing includes five first- or 1.5 generation immigrant writers from the former Soviet Union and Yugoslavia, namely Gary Shteyngart, Olga Grushin, David Bezmozgis, Aleksandar Hemon, and Téa Obreht. But Mukherjee completely eclipsed these writers' backgrounds when she asserted that the "Literature of New Arrival" encompasses a new "generation of *non-European* immigrant American authors" (683, my italics) and then proceeded to discuss only the work by contemporary authors of Caribbean, Asian, and Latin American descent.

Mukherjee emphasizes the non-Europeanness of the "Literature of New Arrival" so she can contrast this writing with literary productions by descendants of early twentieth-century European immigrants, particularly Jewish American authors, such as the work by her friend Philip Roth whose grandfather arrived in the early twentieth century from the Austro-Hungarian empire. Mukherjee argues that Jewish immigrants who are generally viewed as religious refugees from European pogroms "embraced America as they understood it, totally, without reservation or evasion" since for them "there was no going back to the homeland that had failed them . . . and assimilation was the goal they desired for their US born offspring" (Mukherjee 2011, 684). Compared to the Jewish American literature which partially modeled itself after traditional Anglo-American writing, Mukherjee posits that the "Literature of New Arrival" employs transnational aesthetics, such as fused languages, proliferating plots, and overcrowded casts, to represent disrupted lives and neglected histories of the authors' homelands.

Mukherjee's half-hearted inclusion of (post)-Soviet and post-Yugoslav authors in the category of contemporary US immigrant writing is an improvement on the reality TV shows and immigration scholarship that associate the post-Soviet diaspora with the entire US majority population of European descent and place it in explicit contrast with other contemporary immigrants constituted as nonwhite. While some Slavic studies scholars have examined the English-language writing of post-USSR authors, this work has so far received the most attention from critics of Jewish American literature.[1] In addition to Shteyngart, critics have generally placed the work of authors like Ellen Litman, Lara Vapnyar, Sana Krasikov, Anya Ulinich, Yelena Akhtiorskaya, and David Bezmozgis (a post-Soviet migrant who moved to Canada) in the Jewish American canon. This canon includes cultural productions by second-and third-generation Jewish migrants such as Philip Roth, Bernard Malamud, and Saul Bellow, as well as by twentieth-century eastern European first- or 1.5-generation immigrant writers like Mary Antin, Abraham Cahan, and Anzia Yezierska who came from the Pale of Settlement in the Russian empire. Mary Antin arrived in 1894 at the age of thirteen from Plotzk, today's Belarus; Abraham Cahan emigrated in 1882 at twenty-two from Vilnius, today's Lithuania; and Anzia Yezierska came in the 1890s from Plinks, now Poland. The cultural productions of these immigrants laid the foundation for a literature of assimilation to a white US racial identity that only became fully available to eastern (and southern) European immigrants by the mid-twentieth century.

Andrew Furman has argued that the work by post-USSR authors of Jewish background reintroduces Jewish American writing into the territory of immigrant literature that had been ceded "to writers of other ethnicities" (2008). Other critics have suggested that post-Soviet fiction continues the focus of twentieth-century Jewish American literature on family migration and immigrant adaptation.[2] Donald Weber (2004) has posited that the new literature highlights the ordeals of immigrant families in accommodating to a new environment, while Alvin H. Rosenfeld (2008) writes that the emphasis on the protagonists' "coming of age meld[s] with immigrant families' awkwardness of adaptation to a new culture, a new language, a somewhat alien way of life."

While these assertions adequately describe *some* of the contemporary post-USSR literature, they do not hold for all of this work. In particular, Sana Krasikov's debut short story collection *One More Year* (2008) and Anya Ulinich's novel *Petropolis* (2007b) significantly differ from canonical Jewish American literature. The two works deliberately move away from the themes of family-based migration and upward assimilation that characterized much of twentieth-century Jewish American writing.[3] Krasikov and Ulinich instead fictionalize the lives of unauthorized and temporary post-Soviet migrants in the United States. Unlike the majority of twentieth-century eastern European and early post-USSR emigrants (including the authors themselves) who came with their families, many of the fictional migrants who inhabit Krasikov's and Ulinich's work arrive by themselves on nonimmigrant visas and overstay them to become unauthorized. Krasikov's and Ulinich's characters find themselves in situations similar to other contemporary US arrivals who often plan to stay for short periods of time to save money and return home, all the while sending remittances to their families (McNevin 2011, 6), which is a phenomenon now theorized as being part of return migration.[4] Some are transnational mothers who are forced to leave their children and families behind. Most are not Jewish.

While attention to undocumented movement in the United States has focused on cross-border migration from Mexico and more recently Central America, Krasikov and Ulinich fictionalize another significant portion of the unauthorized population, the so-called visa overstayers. Except for Saltanat Liebert's (2009) ethnographic study of irregular immigrants from Kazakhstan, there is no scholarship on post-Soviet irregular migration, even though undocumented status is not unknown among members of the post-USSR diaspora. Three of the twenty-seven post-Soviet migrants I interviewed mentioned that they personally knew immigrants from Russia who had overstayed their temporary visas. Available official figures from 2012 collapsed undocumented migrants from Canada and Europe and estimated their number at 600,000. This figure exceeded the undocumented population from the Caribbean (550,000) and from "the Middle East, Africa, and Other" (400,000), and was slightly below that of migrants from South America (700,000) (Passel and Cohn 2014).

Besides associating post-USSR migrant writing with the Jewish American literary tradition, critics have also placed this work in a diasporic framework. Adrian Wanner has emphasized that, because many of the post-USSR authors are marketed and self-identify as "Russian" and often downplay their Jewish identities, their writing should be considered "translingual and transcultural Russian Jewish fiction written in American English" (Wanner 2012, 171). In his book *Out of Russia*, Wanner (2011) has compared post-Soviet literatures in the United States, Germany, and Israel.[5]

While such a diasporic approach usefully moves beyond the focus on continuities between contemporary and early twentieth-century Jewish American writing, the literature by Krasikov and Ulinich also bears specific US characteristics that point to larger shifts in the enforcement of US immigration policy. Since the early 1990s the United States has restricted access to refugee status for post-Soviet Jewish immigrants and tightened the procedures for all those claiming persecution. Many migrants thus employ the only available legal options for migration to the United States—family unification or temporary visas.

Several of the protagonists in Krasikov's and Ulinich's fiction overstay their temporary visas or engage in (sham) marriages with US citizens in order to obtain legal status in the United States. Because of their status, these fictionalized migrants have limited access to US citizenship rights and to the US labor market. They turn to the kinds of low-wage unskilled or service sector jobs—mainly in construction, cleaning, and domestic work—that are typically held by undocumented immigrants. Krasikov has coined the term "postmigration" to describe the status of these migrants for whom it is often not clear if life in their countries of origin or in the United States is the better choice (Norris 2008).

Krasikov and Ulinich also complicate the tendency to associate post-USSR immigrants with a system of whiteness, where an assigned white racial identity is assumed to provide access to a more extensive network of citizenship rights. Their work is peopled with diverse post-Soviet migrants who were marked as "ethnic" in the USSR and who are assigned nonwhite identities in the United States. While Krasikov fictionalizes members of the Tajik minority in Uzbekistan as well as immigrants from the Eurasian countries of Russia and Georgia, Ulinich presents a mixed-race protagonist from Russia who is of African descent and is perceived as either black or of an uncertain ethnicity based on her appearance or alternatively, as Jewish based on her last name. In their emphasis on racially and ethnically diverse protagonists who arrived with irregular status, the two works thus complicate assumptions about the exceptionality of post-Soviet migrants when compared to the majority of other contemporary US immigrants.

Migrant Arrival

Even though they themselves are of Jewish descent, Krasikov and Ulinich have both rejected their association with US definitions of Jewish identity and have also critiqued efforts to classify their fiction as Jewish writing. Ulinich has said that the literature by post-Soviet authors emerged in response to the demise of the USSR, which spurred large-scale out-migration and thus created a new generation of immigrant writers. She has posited that

> the reason all of us appeared at more or less the same time has more to do with Russian politics than with literary trends. During the Soviet times, before Gorbachev came to power in Russia in 1986, it was fairly difficult to emigrate, and fewer people came to the U.S. Starting in the late 1980s, it became easier to leave, and people began to arrive in droves. I suppose, statistically, more people mean more potential writers. All of the writers . . . , with the exception of Gary [Shteyngart], came to the U.S. in the early 1990s. It took us a while to grow up and learn English, and so here we are now. (Kinsella 2007)

As Ulinich indicates, unlike Shteyngart, the best known of the post-USSR authors whose family came as religious refugees in 1979, Krasikov and Ulinich (as well as Vapnyar and Litman) participated in the much more numerous out-migration during the last years of the USSR and after the country's dissolution. Born in Ukraine and raised as a Russian speaker in the former Soviet republic of Georgia, Krasikov came to the United States in 1987 with her parents when she was eight, while Ulinich emigrated with her family from Russia in 1990 when she was seventeen.

Krasikov and Ulinich have also dissociated their work from the categories of "Jewish American" or "New Jewish" writing, unlike the few post-Soviet authors of Jewish descent who have linked themselves with this tradition.[6] Krasikov strongly disagreed when asked if her work belongs to the "genre of Jewish-American-Russian fiction" (Ford 2008), and Ulinich has marked her difference from New Jewish writing in a short story entitled "The Nurse and the Novelist." The story is an open attack on the work of Jewish American writer Safran Foer, which she calls "atrocity kitsch" because it attempts to make "sense of the past as part of a contemporary character's self-exploration" (Ulinich 2008). Nor do Krasikov and Ulinich identify with US notions of Jewish identity. Ulinich has said that when "I came to America, I . . . was expected to pick up Jewish religious traditions that were interrupted, in my family's case, nearly one hundred years before. Here, my cultural identity—that of a secular person who wants nothing to do with, say, religious holidays, is frequently considered almost a tragedy perpetrated upon my people by the Soviet regime" (Penguin Books, n.d.). Krasikov has similarly stated that "[c]oming from a Soviet background where so much of the identity is being a group that hasn't been treated well, that's an identity I don't relate to well. Like any old and deep tradition, there's so much more to it than that. To approach it the way a lot of Russian immigrants do, I find kind of unpalatable. That we're Jews because we were oppressed" (Ford 2008).

As they disassociate themselves from Jewish American definitions of identity, these novelists also do not chronicle the emergence of a collective (white) "Russian" identity, which is the subject of the reality TV shows discussed in the first chapter. In fact, Ulinich (like other post-Soviet authors, including Vapnyar and Shteyngart) has portrayed Brighton Beach, the setting of Lifetime's *Russian Dolls* in a rather unflattering manner (Wanner, forthcoming), and Vapnyar (2011a) has devoted an entire *Wall Street Journal* opinion piece to dismissing *Russian Dolls*. Instead of emphasizing issues of Jewish American identity or an emerging "Russian" ethnic identity, Krasikov's and Ulinich's work explores the difficult circumstances under which recent post-USSR immigrants arrive in the United States, circumstances shaped by limited options for legal entry. The protagonist of Ulinich's *Petropolis* comes to the United States on a fake student visa through an agency that arranges the emigration of Russian women for transnational marriages. While in Krasikov's *One More Year* some characters arrive as Jewish refugees and one on a visa for highly skilled workers, many more come on nonimmigrant work, J-1 work travel, or student visas. They overstay these visas or enter into marriages with US citizens for the sole purpose of acquiring legal status.

Written in a realistic style, *One More Year* is peopled with migrants from various USSR successor nations, including today's Russia, Georgia, and Uzbekistan. The collection won a National Book Foundation's "5 under 35" Award and the 2009 Sami Rohr Prize for Jewish Literature.

While a few of the collection's migrants are well-to-do, most have fallen from their former intelligentsia status, which was considered middle class in the Soviet Union's classless society.

Only one of Krasikov's characters, Grisha Arsenyev, came to the United States in the mid-1990s and, like earlier immigrants from eastern Europe, was able to bring his family with him. Arsenyev arrives as a skilled migrant with his wife to work in the US IT industry, probably on an H-1B visa. At the time, Russia had become one of several post-socialist countries that, alongside Asian nations, sent large numbers of skilled professionals to the United States, including many who would end up working in the IT sector. As Krasikov writes, Grisha's visa "had been processed not by the staffs of refugee committees, but by a covey of lawyers working for IBM, assigned to skim the cream of Eastern brainpower" (131). Unlike other migrants, Grisha was also able to keep his Russian citizenship. But Grisha's situation at IBM is similar to that of many IT workers from India, who, as Payal Banerjee has shown, are dependent on their companies for their legal status and income, which makes them highly exploitable (Banerjee 2006). After IBM provides him with the promised green card, which allows him to pursue other employment opportunities, Grisha takes another high-powered bank job building market models for mortgage traders. But he feels unappreciated there, passed over for promotions, and, at the age of forty-six, becomes one of the few post-Soviet migrants who return. In Russia, he participates in new business opportunities, particularly the emerging real estate market that he wants to model after that in the United States. Another of Krasikov's stories, called "Debt," juxtaposes a migrant who entered the United States claiming religious persecution, was offered free English classes, used clothes, and a job by a Jewish assistance organization with a non-Jewish Eastern European migrant who could only find menial work and needed six years to start his concession business. This required him to travel on weekends and leave his infant daughter in the care of an acquaintance.

In contrast to characters who arrive in the United States with their families on highly skilled or refugee visas, many more of Krasikov's protagonists in *One More Year* come to the United States alone and on a temporary nonimmigrant visa. They often plan on a short sojourn, during which they intend to generate sufficient funds to send remittances back to their families and eventually return home. In Krasikov's story "Maia in Yonkers," which was originally published in the *New Yorker*, the protagonist leaves Georgia after her husband dies and the state-owned company where she worked as an accountant is privatized and closed. She sees no other way to support herself and her son than through emigration. A labor recruitment agency provides her with a temporary work visa and airfare to New York City, and hires her out to its US counterpart. Ranging from one-person to large-scale networks, these employment agencies are unregulated or operate illegally; they often have counterparts in the United States that supply letters of invitation to potential migrants (Liebert 2009, 68). Some businesses, especially in Georgia, even establish connections with smugglers who transport migrants without US visas across the US-Mexico border. They arrive in Mexico on tourist visas to that country, are met at the airport by Mexican intermediaries, and are then smuggled across the border desert into Phoenix, Arizona. From here they are transported to locations on the East Coast where jobs for Russian speakers are easier to find (Liebert 2009, 69). Once Maia arrives in New York City, the recruitment agency continues to exploit her. The company confiscates her passport until she repays the cost of her airfare, thus further limiting her travel and employment opportunities in the United States.

While Maia's story highlights the fact that many migrants need to employ labor recruiters to navigate the complicated US immigration system in order to obtain visas, her account also points to the new phenomenon of transnational motherhood that has become increasingly common among migrants from postsocialist countries. The practice was relatively rare a century ago. The term transnational motherhood was coined in the late 1990s with regard to migrants from Latin America (Hondagneu-Sotela and Avila 1997). But a significant number of Eastern European women now also find themselves in similar positions as they emigrate for work opportunities that are often well below their educational levels and are forced to leave their families behind (Tolstokorova 2010b, 190). Like many other Eastern European mothers who accept positions abroad in order to provide for their families through remittances, Maia leaves her teenage son in the care of her sister. She sends remittances home to support her family and plans to return to her son after just "one more year." In fact, Maia's responsibilities to her son represent the main push factor for her emigration, which she sees as one of very few ways to provide for him, while also giving her a reason to tolerate their separation and to endure the difficulties of her life in the United States. Transferring her childrearing tasks to a female relative enables her to later perform similar caretaking duties for another woman in exchange for remuneration. Krasikov has said that her prior journalistic research on "multiple nanny chains," in which women watch other women's children, and which is the basis for the remittance industry, provided the inspiration for this story (Lopate 2008).

Anya, the protagonist of another of Krasikov's stories, "Better Half," similarly uses the services of labor recruiters in Russia to enter the United States on a temporary work travel visa. This J-1 Summer Work and Travel visa enables hotels, restaurants, and other businesses to exploit the cheap seasonal labor of foreign college students, who are mostly from Eastern Europe and whose numbers have increased from about 20,000 in 1996 to more than 150,000 in 2008. The hiring businesses are exempt from paying Medicare, Social Security, unemployment or health insurance costs, and often dispense very low wages to the students while also charging exorbitant rents for substandard housing (Mohr et al. 2010). The fictionalized restaurant owners in the Maine fishing village where Anya works as a waitress make a substantial profit from hiring her: they pay Anya slightly more than they charge for the small place that she shares with other women.

At the end of the summer, Anya overstays her visa and finds a waitressing job in a nearby commuter town, where the manager is not interested in verifying her legal status. But because it prevents her from traveling to visit her sick father in Russia and gain readmission to the United States, her undocumented status eventually becomes a liability. Anya defaults to marriage to a US citizen for the sole purpose of obtaining lawful residency. But her husband recognizes the power the US state has granted him in denying legal status to Anya; he abuses her and confiscates her passport. With the help of a sympathetic lawyer, Anya eventually receives legal status and work eligibility under a visa program for undocumented immigrants who are victims of domestic violence and sexual assault.

Anya Ulinich's debut novel *Petropolis*, which won the National Book Foundation's "5 under 35" Award in 2007, was a finalist for the Sami

Rohr Prize, and received the Goldberg Prize for Emerging Writers of Jewish Fiction in 2008, similarly focuses on a post-USSR transnational mother who arrives in the United States on a temporary visa with the help of another assisted migration network. This is a mail-order bridal company that abuses the student visa loophole in US immigration law to enable women entry into the United States.

Petropolis is the story of Sasha Goldberg, a mixed-race woman of Russian and African descent, who Ulinich has said is not meant to represent the "experience of any specific demographic," but to function as the "perfect satirical hero who can best showcase the American and Russian social and cultural wackiness" (Stromberg n.d.). This protagonist helps satirize attempts to associate post-USSR migrants with one racial identity. Sasha's father Victor Goldberg is the product of a sexual encounter between a Russian woman and an African man during a 1950s youth festival, when Russians were first allowed to meet visitors from Western countries. Because raising a mixed-race child in the USSR would have been very difficult, Victor, along with many of these children, is relinquished to an orphanage. But he is soon adopted by a Jewish couple of intelligentsia status who select him from the other available children because he was "the lightest" (19), as his mother later tells him. Physically, Sasha takes after her father more than her mother, an "archetypical Russian beauty." Sasha has "yellow freckled skin, frizzy auburn hair, and eyes like chocolate eggs" (12). Ulinich has said that she made Sasha a racially ambiguous character who would be perceived differently in different national contexts in order to examine the workings of race and racism in both the USSR and the United States. As the author has stated, if Sasha had been "simply" Jewish, her representation would have raised the issue of Soviet anti-Semitism but missed the fact that in contemporary Russia racism is primarily directed against migrant workers from successor nations in Central Asia.[7]

Sasha grows up during the early post-Soviet years in a dilapidated Siberian town that had originally been founded as the administrative center of a Stalinist gulag. She faces exclusion in school because of her appearance. And because she has been given her father's adopted last name, a Jewish identity—that ironically has no basis in either her biology or her adherence to a specific religious practice—is also imposed on her. Ulinich here satirizes the strength of anti-Semitism in the former

USSR and post-Soviet Russia; as she has said, "having the name Gold-berg makes you a Jew in Russia."[8] At some point, Sasha realizes that "[p]erhaps . . . her parents gave her a Jewish name to take the focus off *black-skinned*" (31, italics in original).

Even after the dissolution of the USSR, Sasha's mother holds on to the idea that her membership in the former intelligentsia, which, as Ulinich has said elsewhere, was "defined not so much by material wealth but by a person's place of residence and education level," positions her above oth-ers in the town (Stromberg n.d.). She tries to mold Sasha's mixed-raced body into that of the ideal "Russian" woman of the intelligentsia by plac-ing her on a strict diet and insisting on an appropriate gait and posture. These attempts predictably backfire. When Sasha becomes pregnant at sixteen, her mother informally adopts her grandchild and sends Sasha to a well-known art school in Moscow. Instead of attending the school, however, Sasha locates a mail-order bride agency that acknowledges her potential as a "Passionate Dark Beauty" (110) and issues her a fake birth certificate claiming she is in her twenties. The agency also provides Sasha with a one-year student visa to a fake US university. This scheme is designed to allow the agency's customers a longer "courtship period" with their "fiancés" (110), while promising the women eventual legal sta-tus in the United States through marriage to a US citizen.

Like Krasikov's protagonist Maia, whose emigration is motivated by the need to take care of her child, Sasha becomes a transnational mother, and like Krasikov's character Anya, she also tries to gain legal status in the United States through marriage to a US citizen. Sasha yearns to cre-ate a stable economic environment for her daughter, and, as soon as she can, she sends remittances to her family in Siberia. After a year of living in Phoenix, Arizona, with a much older man who locks away her pass-port to maintain his investment in his "bride," Sasha sets out to search for her father, who had abandoned the family in the last years of the USSR for the United States where he was able to obtain political asylum.

Undocumented and Irregular Migrant Life

After escaping from her "fiancé" on her by now expired student visa, Sasha takes a job as live-in help for a wealthy Jewish family in Chicago. The Tarakans (Russian for "cockroach") are involved in an organization that helps post-Soviet Jews migrate to the United States, but have no qualms exploiting the same migrants when they are undocumented. Here the novel likely satirizes the motivations of assistance organizations such as HIAS, the Hebrew Immigrant Aid Society, that center on issues of religious identity. The Tarakans simply assume that Sasha is Jewish and teach her about the Jewish faith, while using her as a trophy during fund-raisers for their organization. At the same time, they confiscate her passport and fail to compensate her for the domestic work she completes alongside the (paid) Mexican help. While they include Sasha in the family's Friday Sabbath ceremonies, on the other days of the week she is reduced to scrounging for food.

In addition to satirizing the marriage migration business that transforms post-USSR women into dependent wives and sex objects in exchange for the promise of legal status, Ulinich thus also critiques their abuse as domestic workers by wealthy elites in the United States. Sasha's employment illustrates how Eastern European women have joined Caribbean, Latin American, and Filipina immigrants—documented and undocumented—to become the domestic workers of choice for an occupation that was, until World War I, dominated by African Americans and eastern and southern European immigrants (Labadie-Jackson 2008). Sasha's uncertain status somewhere between that of an employee and a family member, tied to the family through a supposedly shared religious and ethnic identity, combines the most burdensome aspects of domestic work with the vulnerability of being an undocumented and low-status worker. In fact, Sasha's tenuous ethnic and religious ties with the family function to hide the awkwardness of her position as not-quite-family member and unpaid help, and open her up to experiences of dependence, isolation, and abuse. She nevertheless makes friends with the family's eighteen-year-old disabled son Jake, who has cerebral palsy and with whom she shares a special bond based on their common outsider status, which eventually turns into affection. Jake helps her regain her passport and escape from the Tarakans to New York City.

Here Sasha begins to work unauthorized as a house cleaner and also locates her father whose citizenship helps her to eventually obtain permanent residency. In the city, she is often identified as African American, both by other post-Soviet immigrants and by US Americans. This association is always tied to her being racially profiled as a potential criminal. When she visits a friend's Russian relatives in an assisted living home on Coney Island, for example, they lock the door as soon as they see her and only soften when they hear her speak Russian. Similarly, her father's second wife Heidi, a college professor of Russian history, is afraid of "getting mugged" by Sasha, whom she at first perceives to be "a big black girl . . . with a halo of frizz around the forehead" (242). After she gets to know her, Heidi is tempted to exploit Sasha as free live-in babysitter and domestic help, as the Tarakans did. The professor is also unable to fathom why women would become transnational mothers, why these "foreigners [Sasha and a Jamaican nanny she meets on the playground] abandon their children so easily" (246).

Throughout her stay in the United States—one year on a bogus student visa and the second as an undocumented immigrant—Sasha makes sure her mother and child receive remittances, while working toward her GED, taking college courses, and starting her own cleaning business. By the end of the novel, however, even after she has received legal status, Sasha still pursues this kind of work. While she may enjoy the flexibility the job offers since it enables her to pursue her vocation as an artist and teacher, the fact that she stays in this occupation also exemplifies the difficulties of moving into a different labor segment even after immigrants legalize their status, improve their English, or have resided in the country for longer periods of time. When her mother dies, Sasha moves her daughter to the United States and creates a family with Jake. Now Sasha's home and any reason for return or a visit have disappeared and her identity has become even more muddled. She muses, "As long as Mama and Nadia live there, Asbestos 2 is still a place I can go return to. . . . Soon, it will all be contained within me, slowly disappearing. . . . What am I? Homo Post-Sovieticus? Homo Nowhere?" (311).

The novel draws on some of Ulinich's own experiences as an unauthorized migrant in the United States, which she has described in interviews and in an essay published in the *New York Times* (Ulinich 2007a). Unlike the migrants she fictionalizes in her work who arrive on their own, Ulinich came to the United States in 1990 with her family. Yet, just like her characters (and unlike the majority of post-Soviet authors), her family arrived "on a tourist visa without English, money or legal immigration status," after refugee status was no longer available even for those, like her family, who were of Jewish background. Lacking work permits, the family labored as house cleaners and accepted the only jobs available to those not authorized to work, namely "dismal 'cash under the table' jobs." Even though the family was used to material poverty in the former USSR, where most people lived in small apartments and no one had nannies or domestic help, their undocumented status represented a significant fall from their position as members of the Russian intelligentsia to "the absolute bottom of the [US] social hierarchy. . . . [where they were] doing menial labor for cash and eating donated food." In a desperate attempt to escape this situation and to legalize her own status, Ulinich entered into marriage with a US citizen. Even though the relationship soon became highly abusive, with her husband threatening to report her to immigration authorities, Ulinich felt that she could not leave for fear of endangering her legal status. In her *New York Times* essay, Ulinich writes that because of this experience, "[t]o this day, I struggle to think of love outside the context of power dynamics" (Ulinich 2007a). Ulinich's status was eventually legalized through a US government program for victims of domestic abuse, the same program that helped the fictional character Anya in Krasikov's story "Better Half."[9]

Like Ulinich's autobiographical account, two of Krasikov's stories show that diminished legal options for admission to the United States leave post-Soviet migrants, particularly women and even those who have professional qualifications and skills, with few choices for employment. In "Maia in Yonkers," Krasikov's protagonist Maia, who had been an accountant in the Soviet Union, initially works for a cleaning company and then, to escape the associated health hazards, takes a job with another agency that specializes in domestic care. The story ends by showing that Maia has no alternatives to her existence as a transnational mother and as a live-in caregiver: her low pay delays her plans for unification with her son, which would put an end to the remittances, and she lacks the financial resources to pursue other avenues to legalize her or her son's status, such as paying a US citizen to marry her or sponsoring her son's immigration. Even though she had originally planned only on a temporary sojourn during which she would send remittances and hope to save enough money for an eventual return, Maia's migrant experience threatens to become permanent.

Another of Krasikov's stories from *One More Year*, "Companion," also features two post-Soviet migrants who end up working in menial jobs in the United States. The story focuses on a forty-five-year-old Russian immigrant, a former nurse, who has settled for the informal position as a live-in household aid and caregiver for an elderly US American man. While she originally took the job of "companion" as a temporary solution to save money toward her own apartment, at the beginning of the story she had already been staying with this man for over a year. The hopelessness of her situation becomes clear when she meets the younger Thomaz, a surgeon from Georgia who came to the United States with the sole intention of generating remittances to send to his family.

Thomaz emigrated after serving in the 1992 War in Abkhazia, which resulted in the mass exodus and ethnic cleansing of the Georgian population. After returning from the war, Thomaz was unable to find paid work as a physician because "people don't go to doctors at all. . . . They die at home" (18). He comes to the United States, where he works unauthorized on an expiring tourist visa, laying carpets during the day and cleaning supermarkets at night. He is so lonely and anxious about his legal status that he engages in a relationship with the protagonist, perhaps with the intention of legalizing his situation through marriage. The ending of the story leaves that option open. That workers like Thomaz are ubiquitous in the United States was illustrated in the well-publicized series of workplace raids in 2003 that yielded around 250 undocumented migrants from Mexico and Eastern Europe who had worked for subcontractors who provided cleaning services for Wal-Mart. Some of the workers had been recruited by Russian middlemen for a contractor called National Floor Management, which employed migrants from Georgia, Russia, Hungary, Ukraine, Poland, Lithuania, Mongolia, and the Czech Republic (Shinkle 2006).

Immigration Law and Enforcement

In addition to representing the difficulties of temporary and undocumented migrant life in the United States, Krasikov and Ulinich also address the assignation of US ethnic and racial categories to their post-Soviet migrant characters and thus participate in discussions about immigration that have focused on the practice of racial profiling that targets undocumented immigrants from Mexico and Central America.

Krasikov's protagonist Anya who works unauthorized as a waitress observes significant differences between her situation and that of her colleagues who are from Ecuador, Guatemala, and El Salvador. These unauthorized migrants have fewer interactions with English speakers, probably to avoid the risk of discovery and deportation. In contrast, Anya seems to think she is exempt from suspicions about being undocumented because she is considered white.

Perhaps because *Petropolis*'s Sasha Goldberg is considered either ethnically ambiguous or black in the United States, she too is spared by immigration officials conducting a surprise check on a bus from Phoenix to Chicago, even though she is traveling on an expired student visa. When making such checks, which are legal within one hundred miles of the US-Mexico border, officers are allowed to consider "heritage" as a justification for selectively asking passengers about their citizenship and immigration status (Mirandé 2003, 365–366). When Sasha acts as though she is related to a little girl with black hair "braided in cornrows" (131), an immigration official ignores them without inquiring into their immigration status. At the same time, a Spanish-speaking family with a baby is pulled off the bus. But even though Sasha is spared discovery of her undocumented status in Arizona, the novel shows that she is later profiled as "black" and associated with criminality when she moves to New York City, an area with a much larger population of African Americans.

Like racial profiling, the surge in deportations under the Obama administration that often led to the separation of families also disproportionately targeted Mexican and Central American nationals (Preston 2012). More than half of all deportations in the history of US immigration controls have taken place since 1990. Even though deportability was first established in nineteenth- and twentieth-century immigration law, only a few thousand people were deported between 1882 and 1924, at the virtual end of European mass migration. By the end of the 1920s, however, tens and then hundreds of thousands of people were deported each year, mostly from eastern and southern Europe (Hester 2015, 143). But beginning in the 1930s, the Border Patrol prioritized the deportation of Mexicans, and their portion of the overall deportable population increased from 29 percent in 1931 to 96 percent in 1945 (Hester 2015, 143).

Under the so-called Operation Wetback initiative in 1954, the US government removed over 1 million Mexicans, while deporting only 6,000 other immigrants, half of them from Canada. Most of these were so-called voluntary removals—immigrants who agree to voluntarily return to their country to avoid formal deportation hearings (Hester 2015, 144). Under the Obama administration, voluntary removals were formally documented and included in the overall numbers of deportations. Because of these changes, immigrants who agree to voluntary removal and then try to reenter undocumented can be prosecuted in federal court. Between 2009 and 2011, the US government deported 2.5 million immigrants, half of whom were voluntary removals (Hester 2015, 150), a number that surpassed those removed in any other year in US history (Goodman 2011).

Contemporary immigrants from countries other than Mexico are also deported, though in much smaller numbers. In 2011, over 4,000 Ukrainians and 3,500 Russians who were considered inadmissible or deportable returned to their homes, as compared to 200,000 Mexicans and 28,000 Canadians, the second-largest group to be removed. These numbers decreased to 2,600 Ukrainians and 2,000 Russians in 2013, which is significantly smaller than the 88,000 Mexicans and 24,000 Canadians removed during that same time period (Simanski 2014). US Immigration and Customs Enforcement removal figures for 2014 list 170,000 Mexicans as opposed to 112 Russians, 96 Ukrainians, and 2 persons from the "USSR" (Department of Homeland Security 2014).

One case of deportation to the territory of the former East Bloc is highlighted in a recent documentary by Ruth Leitman, titled *Tony and Janina's American Wedding* (2010). The film chronicles the deportation of a mother and her six-year-old US-born son to Poland, while her husband is able to remain in the United States because of the couple's differential legal status at entry. Tony came in the late 1980s on a temporary work visa and eventually received permanent status through work sponsorship, while his wife Janina applied for political asylum in 1989. Her application was denied in 1995, by which time Poland had long transitioned to capitalism, thus removing the grounds for granting her asylum. Janina agrees to voluntary departure, but stays undocumented in the United States after giving birth to her son and helping her husband launch his cleaning business. When her status is discovered after she applies for a green card, authorities initiate deportation proceedings against her. Her deportation in 2007 triggered a ten-year ban from the United States under a 1996 law meant to discourage violations of voluntary departure rulings. The documentary chronicles how the family repeatedly fails to get the ban on her return lifted, even after Tony becomes eligible for naturalization and after he starts suffering severe medical problems. This strict interpretation of US legislation by the Vienna consulate in charge of European migration was in direct contrast to the loosening of similar rules for Mexican migrants who have violated US immigration law. Consulate workers in Mexico regularly filed electronic waiver applications for work visa applicants with prior unauthorized histories in the United States that would make them subject to three- or ten-year bans depending on the length of their stay. About 85 percent of these waivers were approved, so that in 2010 the majority of Mexican workers with work visas had histories of undocumented residence in the United States (Cave 2011).

Leitman's documentary shows how Janina's deportation transforms her Polish American family, whose lives in the United States initially appeared to follow in the footsteps of earlier European permanent family immigration with the promise of upward mobility, into an economically unstable postimmigrant family like those fictionalized by Krasikov and Ulinich. Tony is reduced to sending remittances to his family in Poland, because his own return is not economically viable. His housecleaning business suffers and he loses his house. A supporter of the Republican Party and an admirer of Ronald Reagan, Tony begins to work with Latina/o immigrant rights groups, joining in their events and rallies, and eventually testifying at a congressional hearing of the proposed Strive Act, an immigration reform bill that failed to pass Congress in 2007. The most recent, 2013 comprehensive immigration legislation bill that included a path to citizenship for unauthorized immigrants similarly failed in Congress and was never approved by the House.

In these public appearances, Tony is always called a small business owner, even though, like many other contemporary migrants, such as the ones fictionalized by Krasikov and Ulinich, he works in a menial service occupation—housecleaning—but happens to be self-employed. According to Littman, the documentary filmmaker, Tony feels a deeper kinship with Latina/o immigrant rights groups than with the Polish community, whose members have largely forgotten their immigrant roots and identify with a largely symbolic white ethnic identity.[10] While Polish Americans have remained Chicago's second-largest ethnic minority (after Mexican Americans) ("Chicago Metro Area" 2004), they rarely vote as a bloc and have little political representation. A community leader at the Northwest Neighborhood Federation and the Polish American Association, Tony also becomes involved with the Polish Initiative of Chicago (PIC), which seeks to revitalize the Polish American community and advocates for more expansive migrant rights by supporting an Illinois initiative to grant drivers' certificates to undocumented immigrants as well as comprehensive immigration reform on the federal level.

While his activism was directed at helping resolve his wife's case, Tony also reached out to immigrant rights groups and initiatives that did not view him as their primary constituency. His involvement belies the perception that their perceived whiteness wholly protects migrants from tightened immigration legislation and enforcement. His activism also highlights the potential for solidarity among migrants of diverse national backgrounds, independently of their racialization in this country, on the basis of their shared undocumented status. In 2011, after four years of separation, Janina was granted a waiver in recognition of a documented unexceptional hardship for a family member in the United States and was allowed to return. These kinds of waivers are rarely if ever approved. Janina's ability to return can be attributed to the publicity created by the documentary and the support her case received from several local politicians involved in immigrant rights struggles.

Conclusion

Leitman's documentary evokes the cross-national impetus of the immigrant rights activism that emerged in the early 2000s around efforts to pass federal comprehensive immigration legislation, which culminated in the Strive Act. Mass rallies for immigration reform in many US cities, such as San Francisco and Chicago in 2006 and 2007, highlighted fledgling coalitions among immigrants from Mexico, Central America, Eastern Europe, Ireland, Asia, and Africa (Hendricks 2006; "Chicago Rally" 2007; Tucker 2007).

Likewise, the work by Krasikov and Ulinich points to the potential for cross-ethnic and comparative approaches to the study of immigration literature and of unauthorized immigration more generally. Their fiction inserts temporary and undocumented movement from the former USSR into discussions about immigration to the United States that have focused on the largest human movement from Mexico and Central America. Such discussions have stressed that unauthorized migrants from these countries are singled out from the larger immigrant population for profiling and deportations because they are racialized as nonwhite. In contrast, the undocumented migrants in the fiction by Krasikov and Ulinich that are racialized as white, black, or Jewish are exempted from racial profiling as potential "illegals." Because these migrants are not even *recognized* as unauthorized, even if they are actually missing the documentation necessary for lawful admission, residency, or work, their risk of detection in encounters with authorities is minimized, though Janina's case and that of several other Eastern European deportees shows that they can be discovered and deported.

While the emphasis on the racial profiling of undocumented Latina/o immigrants can serve to create empathy, a point I will examine in more detail in the next chapter, Krasikov's and Ulinich's work offers another approach that highlights structural similarities among diverse immigrant populations based on their shared undocumented status and potential exposure to deportation. The two authors fictionalize protagonists who have to negotiate extremely limited options for legal entry, rely on unscrupulous labor recruiters, become transnational mothers, and accept low-wage jobs once they get to the United States. These fictional characters are exposed to dependency and abuse by employers and spouses, and are unable to leave the United States to visit their families for fear of being denied readmission. While the participants I interviewed who came on J-1 visas generally ended up in more permanent academic positions and marriage migrants worked in low-skilled jobs or were self-employed, the temporary and undocumented fictional post-USSR migrants in Krasikov's and Ulinich's work are confined to low-wage jobs in the service industry. Despite their often high educational level, they work in housecleaning, waitressing, childrearing, or construction, positions that are also taken by other recent undocumented migrants and from which it is hard to transition to middle-class status.

Krasikov's and Ulinich's work also questions the uncritical assignation of a white privileged racial identity to all post-USSR migrants by presenting an ethnically and racially diverse range of protagonists from different Soviet successor nations, one of whom is racially profiled because she is considered black. Even the fictionalized post-Soviet immigrants who could be considered white and who, like the marriage and postdoc immigrants I interviewed, are exempt from racialization as "illegals" or "criminals," trouble the idea that this racial identity wholly protects them from institutionalized inequities in accessing residency, citizenship, and the labor market.

The cultural productions by Krasikov and Ulinich underscore the fragility of idealized assimilationist narratives to a privileged network of whiteness for undocumented or temporary immigrants, even those who are racialized as white. In the absence of putative phenotypical or biological differences from the majority US population, it is their undocumented status that justifies their limited access to segmented citizenship rights and increasingly scarce resources. The protagonists in the work of Krasikov and Ulinich thus live lives similar to the majority of immigrants in the United States today who arrive on a temporary, irregular, or undocumented basis and are inserted into low-skilled service jobs that offer little hope of upward mobility or a path to eventual legalization (McNevin 2011, 6).

Krasikov's and Ulinich's representations of temporary and irregular migrants from post-Soviet countries also complicate attempts to continue placing contemporary literary and cultural productions about migration into separate canons that were established on the basis of US racial and ethnic identities, depending on the authors' background. The work by Krasikov and Ulinich highlights the fact that post-USSR authors are indeed part of the contemporary "Literature of New Arrival," but in more complex ways than Bharati Mukherjee may have imagined. These writers employ similar transnational aesthetics and themes as other contemporary immigrant authors who belong to the "Literature of Arrival," as they address how the increasingly limited legal options for entry into the United States that remain available today shape migrant lives in this country.

The Post-Soviet Diaspora in Comparative Perspective

In 2010, my home state of Arizona made history by passing Senate Bill 1070, the first in a series of similar laws that declared undocumented status a state crime. As amended by House Bill 2162, SB 1070 requires Arizona state and local police to investigate the immigration status of those who are arrested or detained when there is "reasonable suspicion" that they lack legal status. The law was challenged for allowing racial profiling by targeting those from Mexico and Central America, who make up the largest proportion of undocumented immigrants in the country.[1] While portions of the bill were immediately enjoined, in 2015 a US district court judge found that SB 1070 was not enacted with discriminatory intent and will likely not be enforced in a racially discriminatory manner.

Co-written by Kris Kobach, a lawyer for the legislative branch of the Federation of American Immigration Reform (FAIR), SB 1070 moved the issue of immigrant profiling into the national limelight and created a blueprint for laws in states like Alabama, Georgia, and South Carolina. In addition to state legislation, racial profiling has also been mobilized in the service of the more restrictive enforcement of US *federal* immigration legislation, as manifested in the criminalization of immigration violations, the speeding up of deportation proceedings, and the growing number of incarcerations and family separations (Bennett 2016; Chacón 2007; Miller 2005; Provine and Doty 2011; Chin et al. 2010).[2]

In a 2003 article that questioned the legality of the rise in racial profiling, immigration scholar Alfredo Mirandé described his encounter with a young, blonde, well-dressed worker at a discount motel in Florida. Based on his appearance, Mirandé initially assumed that the man was the motel manager. But when Mirandé realized that the employee only spoke Russian or "another Slavic language" and toiled in housecleaning or maintenance, he noted his shock at having witnessed what he identified as a "White" man "performing the low paying, minimum wage jobs that Latinas and Black women normally assumed" (Mirandé 2003, 356).

These motel workers resemble the fictionalized unauthorized migrants in the works of Anya Ulinich and Sana Krasikov discussed in the previous chapter. They are also likely from the former Soviet Union, since post-USSR migrants constitute the majority of Eastern Europeans in the United States.[3] In his article, Mirandé associates these men with racial profiling, stating that they are exempt from being targeted as "illegals" because they are "phenotypically indistinguishable from other White men" (365–366). Mirandé here characterizes the whiteness ascribed to Eastern European immigrants as an especially protective quality that may outweigh their undocumented status or their position at the bottom of the US socioeconomic hierarchy, and he places them in opposition to immigrants from Mexico who have dominated human movement to the United States.

Mirandé's emphasis on the privilege of exemption from racialized exclusion granted to those constituted as white expands upon a central tenet in whiteness historiography, which has also influenced immigration studies. Work on whiteness emerged in response to assertions that the marginalization experienced by turn of the twentieth century European immigrants was similar to the adversities facing contemporary nonwhite immigrants in order to absolve the descendants of European immigrants from their association with white privilege and white supremacy. But historians have shown that early European immigrants were largely exempt from systemic racial violence and strove to obtain the full economic and social privileges of whiteness by embracing tenets of white supremacy as they set themselves apart from or engaged in hostilities with their nonwhite contemporaries, particularly African Americans and Chinese immigrants. While entire fields, such as Afro-Asian studies or comparative approaches to Latina/o and African American studies, have emerged to interrogate intersections between different groups, contemporary immigrant communities regarded as white are generally treated separately or remain understudied because their privilege is assumed to render them utterly different from those racialized as nonwhite.[4] Studies of intersectionality that stress how social and cultural categories of identity, such as gender, race, class, sexual orientation, religion, and nationality, interact to create multiple systemic forms of social inequality also position these inquiries in explicit contrast to a privileged whiteness.

This chapter draws on additional data from my interviews with post-Soviet immigrants and examines speculative literary fiction to place post-USSR immigrants in conversation with scholarship on populations racialized as nonwhite, while also acknowledging that the privileges associated with whiteness are still central to an evolving US ethnoracial hierarchy. In the contemporary version of this hierarchy, racialized privilege is assigned to the beneficiaries of neoliberalism, those groups or individual members of collectivities who are upwardly mobile, while racialized stigma is attributed to its dispossessed (Melamed 2011, 44). Between 2010 and 2011, I queried post-Soviet immigrants about their attitudes toward the anti-immigrant discourses that targeted Latina/os and culminated in the passage of Arizona's Senate Bill 1070. The results of my interviews complicate (largely speculative) popular and scholarly discourses about the relationship between the two groups. Participants mostly stressed their ambivalence toward the bill from which they expected exemption because of their own modes of entry as documented or highly skilled migrants (but rarely their whiteness) or they expressed empathy with Mexican immigrants as the group most targeted by SB 1070. This empathy was often based on interviewees' status as immigrants or on their experience with state surveillance in the former USSR and in contemporary Russia.

My findings are reminiscent of the attitudes of turn of the twentieth century European immigrants who set themselves apart from contemporaries who were subjected to institutionalized racial discrimination in order to be considered white. But the views of my interviewees also resembled the ways in which eastern European Jews in particular expressed their ambivalence or opposition to manifestations of white supremacy by empathizing with African Americans in order to express their own racial distinctiveness. Their empathy was based on comparisons with their own marginalization in the Russian empire (Goldstein 2006). It is important to remember that most of the post-Soviet migrants I interviewed were not Jewish and, for the most part, were securely associated with a white racial identity. Their ambivalence or opposition to immigration restrictions thus largely underscores that they are collectively positioned at a social distance from Latina/os in the US socioeconomic and racial hierarchy, a distance that seemingly can only be bridged through expressions of empathy.

Set in a near-future, dystopian United States, Russian American writer Gary Shteyngart's novel *Super Sad True Love Story* (2010) speculatively explores how the construction of Soviet immigrants, particularly those who are Jewish and who left the former Soviet Union shortly before its neoliberal transition, resembles that of Asian Americans who in the last few decades have come to be included in notions of whiteness through the concept of the model minority. While turn of the twentieth century Chinese immigrants were regarded as Asian "coolies" and Europeans as model immigrants who lifted themselves up by their bootstraps to achieve the American Dream (Ngai 2004; Jung 2005), today both groups are linked to the myth of upward mobility, which has allowed Asian Americans to enter into an expanded whiteness to which Jewish Americans already (though ambivalently) belong. In contrast to the work by Krasikov and Ulinich, which fictionalizes the situation of undocumented post-Soviet migrants, Shteyngart's novel offers a more explicitly comparative cross-ethnic lens on Soviet Jews. *Super Sad True Love Story* explores similarities between second-generation lower- and middle-class Korean and Russian Jewish immigrants in a context where African American and Latina/o populations continue to be marginalized and associated with economic and racial notions of nonwhiteness. In the novel, the fictionalized United States is undergoing developments similar to the neoliberal shock therapies that took their deepest form in the former Soviet Union, which resulted in its demise and created large diasporic out-migration. The United States similarly collapses, immigrants and their children start returning to their homelands, and the divisive US racist and anti-immigrant rhetoric and politics that masked racially inflected forms of economic inequality give way to attacks on ever larger portions of the population who are characterized as dispossessed losers of neoliberalism.

Cross-Racial Comparisons and the Question of Empathy

A major tenet of whiteness historiography is its emphasis on the ways in which European immigrants actively participated in the construction of their whiteness by supporting manifestations of white supremacy. While new European immigrants often abstained from or condemned racial violence and institutionalized racism such as slavery or lynchings, over time they increasingly distanced themselves from or were hostile toward nonwhite communities in order to gain access to all facets of white privilege, including upward mobility.[5] Some work has qualified the nexus between immigrants' desire for assimilation, upward mobility, and support of white supremacy. Jewish immigrants and their organizations largely stayed away from race riots and anti-immigration politics (Roediger 2005, 15; Barrett and Roediger 1997; Goldstein 2006, 31). While Italians limited their protest of the Quota Laws, which they considered anti-Semitic, to contesting their characterization as an "inferior race" (T. Guglielmo 2003, 69–70), Jewish organizations more consistently opposed immigration restrictions (Satzewich 2000, 279; Barrett and Roediger 1997, 31).[6] Jewish newspapers unanimously condemned the Chinese Exclusion Act (MacDonald 1998, 313), and Jewish groups systematically fought efforts to pass literacy requirements in the 1910s, even though they would not have affected migration from the Pale, which was already slowing down at the time (MacDonald 1998, 301).

In addition to opposing immigration restrictions, including those targeting other groups, Jewish immigrants overwhelming resisted participating in or embracing expressions of white supremacy because of their own experience of suppression in Russia and their social exclusion from US society, even as they began to strive for inclusion in whiteness (Goldstein 2006, 59). Many newly arriving eastern European Jewish immigrants compared emancipation from slavery to struggles against Russian tyranny, and lynchings and race riots to Russian pogroms, while immigrant publications indicted the police for failing to protect African Americans and for inciting white rioters (Goldstein 2006, 64–81).

These feelings persisted in attenuated form even when Jewish immigrants began to be affected by growing anti-Semitism and later, when they entered more fully into whiteness. When their own racial status became increasingly uncertain in the early years of the twentieth century, Jews in the north in particular began to employ more indirect comparisons between lynchings and Jewish suffering (Goldstein 2006, 65). Jewish blackface minstrel shows emerged to stress the whiteness of Jews in direct contrast to African Americans. When eastern European Jewish immigrants became upwardly mobile after World War II, they were even more torn between their desire to enter white society and their feelings of empathy for African Americans based on comparisons with their own experience of racial persecution and their belief in their own racial distinctiveness (Goldstein 2006, 85). In the 1960s, some Jewish Americans found an outlet for these feelings by expressing their empathy for African American civil right struggles or by becoming directly involved in civil rights causes (Goldstein 2006, 6).

Just as twentieth-century eastern European Jewish immigrants were often compared to and understood their own racial distinctiveness as Jews through analogy with the experience of African Americans, the small body of comparative scholarship on second-generation immigrant populations in New York City that includes Soviet Jewish migrants has nominally explored their relationship to African American populations. One study found that, unlike turn of the twentieth century eastern Jewish immigrants who often worked and lived in close proximity to African Americans as merchants or peddlers, second-generation Soviet Jewish respondents usually lived in Jewish-dominant ethnic enclaves and only came into contact with African Americans in more diverse public educational institutions, where the two groups nevertheless often remained separate (Zeltzer-Zubida and Kasinitz 2005). This finding hints at the fact that first-generation (post)-Soviet Jews appear to believe in the myth of immigrant bootstrapism, which keeps them at a social and physical distance from economically underprivileged minorities and other immigrant groups (Senderovich 2016). Russian-speaking Jews tend to be both less religious and more conservative than their US counterparts. According to a recent survey, between 60 and 70 percent of Russian-speaking Jews wanted to vote Republican in the 2016 presidential election, often because of the GOP's support for Israel, where many have friends and relatives. Russian-speaking Jews also tended to be suspicious of Syrian refugees because of their suspected ties to terrorism (Khazan 2016). In addition, (post)-Soviet Jewish immigrants appear to maintain the anti-"black" prejudices that were pervasive in the former USSR and pejorative views toward populations in Asia and the Caucasus, as fictionalized in Anya Ulinich's novel discussed in the previous chapter. Compared to the generally more conservative politics of first-generation (post)-Soviet Jewish immigrants, however, most second-generation Russian-speaking Jews are more progressive and identify with the multiethnic culture of New York City (Kasinitz et al. 2008). Participants in a recent survey of Russian-speaking Jews on the West Coast also mentioned that they personally knew more politically progressive than conservative Soviet Jews (Khazan 2016).

In addition to the politically conservative attitudes associated with Soviet Jewish immigrants, Mirandé's article with which I began the chapter, as well as the reality TV shows and scholarship on post-Soviet ballroom dancers discussed in chapter 1, also attribute anti-Latina/o sentiments to post-USSR immigrants (not just those of Jewish descent), including members of the 1.5 generation who, like the second-generation Russian-speaking Jewish participants in the study conducted in New York City, would have grown up in a multiethnic United States. These assertions are based on the fact that members of the post-Soviet diaspora are exempted from immigration enforcement directed at Latina/os.

To better understand the attitudes of post-Soviet immigrants, I interviewed twenty-seven post-USSR participants, most of them not Jewish, about their views of immigration debates in Arizona in addition to questioning them about their immigration experiences and return considerations, which I examined in chapter 2.[7] These interviews took place between November 2010 and December 2011, at a time when the Arizona legislature had just passed Senate Bill 1070 and before the US Supreme Court upheld the legality of immigration status checks while allowing for future hearings on the allegations of racial profiling in the summer of 2012. Arizona lent itself well to the collection of such data because in this state post-USSR migrants are very likely to interact with other migrants, reside or travel in proximity to the US-Mexico border, and experience public debates about immigration and racialized discourses that usually target Latina/os.

My participants had come to the United States as either marriage (K-1) migrants, on various nonimmigrant (J-1 and H-1) visa, with green cards, or under refugee provisions. The majority were women, and only two of my participants identified as Jewish. Most came from Russia and Ukraine, but some also hailed from post-Soviet nations in Asia. Three participants who identified as Buryet (a member of the largest aboriginal group in Siberia), Armenian, and Kazakh, respectively, reported that in the United States they were usually considered Chinese, "Middle Eastern," or either Korean or Japanese—rather than white—based on their accents and appearance. While a small minority of my interviewees (two) expressed their support for SB 1070, the vast majority of participants felt more ambivalent toward or rejected this legislation.

All my interviewees, including those racialized as nonwhite, expected that they would be exempt from the enforcement of Arizona's new law. The legislation stipulates that "[a] law enforcement official or agency of this state or a county, city, town or other political subdivision of this state may not solely consider race, color or national origin in implementing the requirements of this subsection *except to the extent permitted by the Unites States or Arizona constitution.*" The italicized exception, in fact, *allows* profiling because it refers to prior US and Arizona Supreme Court decisions that have authorized consideration of appearance in the enforcement of immigration law by Border Patrol agents. Both the 1982 *State v. Graciano* decision in the Arizona Supreme Court and the 1975 US Supreme Court case *United States v. Brignoni-Ponce* affirm that it is constitutional for Border Patrol agents to take into account the appearance of occupants when deciding to stop vehicles near the US-Mexico border as long as it is not the only factor under consideration (Chin et al. 2011).

Participants said, for example, that they were not "targeted or affected in a personal way by the bill" (24m) or that it did not touch them personally (25f). These expectations were largely based on their status as either documented or highly skilled immigrants, and rarely on the white racial identity that was ascribed to most of them. For example, one interviewee said, "I usually think of these [immigration] debates as related to low-skilled workers, which I don't consider myself being" (16f). Marriage migrants in particular employed the rhetoric surrounding the passage of SB 1070 that pitted undocumented against documented immigrants to draw sharp distinctions between themselves—migrants who had come lawfully—and unauthorized immigrants. One interviewee said, "Since I came legally I don't have those problems and I just think everybody should come legally" (8f). Another claimed, "I know that I came [the] right way, I'm here legally. I did and my husband paid a lot of money for me to be here. All the paperwork. For the first five years you had to go through renewal of all your paperwork every year, pay fees, pay money, do paperwork. So I mean I paid for that to be here" (9f).

Only a small number of interviewees expected to be exempt from the enforcement of SB 1070 because of their ascribed whiteness. One participant stated that she thought her white identity and her ability to speak English like a native speaker would protect her from even being considered an immigrant (10f). Another participant said, "Arpaio [the Arizona sheriff involved in immigration enforcement] would not stop white people" (4m).

The participants' focus on how their skill level, visa status, or (more rarely) their racial identity set them apart from unskilled and undocumented Mexican migrants reaffirms their privilege and points to their distance from populations targeted by immigration enforcement. While this point is reminiscent of the ways in which turn of the twentieth century European migrants distanced themselves from African Americans in order to be included in whiteness, my interviewees' statements also simply showed that they had internalized and were repeating the dominant discourses surrounding SB 1070, which stressed that their forms of entry, skill level, and white identities would exempt them from the effects of anti-immigrant discourses and legislation.

Interviewees' expectations of exemption from immigration enforcement were supported by several participants' encounters with *federal* authorities—at US-Mexico border crossings, internal traffic checkpoints, and surprise checkpoints on a bus—which Arizona residents are more likely to experience because of their geographical proximity to the national border. At the checkpoints, which are located along major highways at least thirty-five to one hundred miles from the national border, officers have an even smaller threshold than agents at the border when it comes to probable cause for stopping vehicles to ask for citizenship and immigration status. Here individuals are essentially detained for the duration of the questioning. Racial profiling at border crossings and checkpoints has long been practiced and is legally sanctioned. Heightened border enforcement after 9/11 has resulted in increased racial profiling for Latina/os who are often automatically questioned about their immigration status because of their presumptive "foreignness" (Johnson 2003, 852–853). This normative use of racial profiling leads to the exemption of people considered white. Thus, one of my interviewees was not even required to show her documentation at a San Diego border crossing (2f). Two others were asked for documentation on a bus traveling from Phoenix or at an internal checkpoint in California, but were let go even though they were not able to produce the required documents (10f, 25f).

In contrast to these experiences with federal authorities, some participants reported negative encounters with *local* US law enforcement or with expressions of xenophobia by members of the US public that highlighted their noncitizenship status. Bill Ong Hing (2002) has coined the term "de-Americanization" to describe instances where individuals or entire groups are marked as "foreign," irrespective of their community's history in the country or individuals' residency or citizenship status. Ming H. Chen has noted that noncitizenship status can also be ascribed to individuals who may be considered white and appear phenotypically similar to the majority US population. As Chen posits, for example, members of the newly established "Arab/Muslim" category have come to be constructed as "alien outsiders" to US citizenship, even though the category cuts across several racial groups and includes those defined as white by the US government (Chen 2009, 421). Thus, even a white racialized identity does not always protect from de-Americanization; as one participant said, "People can be very, very rude. They still look at you, they see your accent as [if] you don't belong" (11f).

Two interviewees recounted negative encounters with local immigration enforcement by Arizona police prior to the passage of SB 1070. Participants reported that when they were stopped for traffic violations and the law enforcement official heard their accents, they were asked for additional documentation of their residency or citizenship status (11f, 3f)—in violation of Arizona law which only allows officials to ask for a person's name (not even his or her driver's license or identification). Several interviewees also reported speech acts by members of the US public that negatively marked them as "foreigners." One participant recounted that his family was called "foreigners" in a grocery store because of his wife's accent (17m), another reported that her son was told to "go back to Russia" in his charter school (12f), and a third noted that her neighbor assumed she was a non-Western visitor rather than a resident of the United States. The interviewee said: "I felt like even if we had citizenship at this point, she would always think of us as, 'You are just visitors.' Or, 'You're not Westerners' or something like that" (7f). Participants also reported being stereotyped as communists (12f) and mail-order brides (7f) or of being associated with overwhelmingly negative media depictions of Russia (12f).

Interviewees did not cite their occasional de-Americanization by local police or by members of the public to support their ambivalence or opposition toward SB 1070. Their refusal to compare their own experiences with anti-immigrant sentiment and policy to the systemic racialized targeting of Latina/os can be read as a politically more progressive gesture than the insistence by some white ethnics that the marginalization of their turn of the twentieth century immigrant forebears absolves them from white privilege and from the history of white supremacy in the United States.

But because the interviewees did not see their experiences with de-Americanization as part of a larger pattern of xenophobia or realized that the enforcement of laws like SB 1070 could also be expanded to other groups or larger numbers of immigrants, they could only express their opposition or ambivalence toward the law as empathy for those targeted. In its original form, SB 1070 contained language that would have made the new legislation easily applicable to much larger numbers of immigrants, but attention to this issue was completely overshadowed by the focus on the law's relationship with racial profiling. A provision included in the original bill—which was struck down by the Supreme Court in 2012—made failure to carry "an alien registration document" a state crime and would have allowed the arrest of individuals thought to be in Arizona "illegally" until their immigration status was verified. While requirements for the registration of noncitizens were inscribed in immigration law as early as the 1798 Naturalization Act and the 1880s Chinese Exclusion Acts, the language used in SB 1070 was drawn from the 1940s Alien Registration Act, which has remained in the US Code. The Alien Registration Act was originally designed to identify and expel political "subversives," mainly European immigrants considered "socialists" or "anarchists," during the war years. Even though the comprehensive registration efforts required under the Act were largely disbanded after World War II, language from the legislation was incorporated into special registration procedures, which were authorized by the Bush administration in 2002 and 2003, and required male noncitizens of twenty-five predominantly Muslim-majority countries to register with US immigration authorities (Morawetz and Fernández-Silber 2014, 143–144). In late 2016, the Obama administration deleted the published rules for this National Security Entry-Exit Registration System in order to prevent the incoming Trump government from simply renewing or expanding this framework.

Because the noncitizen registration requirement originally included in SB 1070 would have legalized the profiling of those suspected to be noncitizens based on assumptions of their "foreignness," legal scholars at the time advised that "it may be prudent for everyone to carry identification so status can be proven on the street rather than waiting in jail while records are checked" (Chin et al. 2011, 53). After I informed them that this provision could potentially have affected them, several of my interviewees took a more explicit stance against SB 1070 (1f, 2f, 9f). One did so because she thought she could be mistakenly profiled, saying, "I don't like people checking my papers every time they stop me. Simply because I know I have an accent and I know my skin color, sometimes people think that I'm Hispanic. Because my skin is dark for Russians" (9f).

Interviewees' ambivalence toward a law from which they thought they would be exempted could also become the basis for expressions of empathy. One marriage migrant, for example, stated that all immigrants needed to come legally, but also expressed empathy with migrants who arrived undocumented by emphasizing the difficulties of immigration under the current system, which she herself had experienced. The interviewee said:

> I think that everybody needs to be here legally and they need to go through whatever the process is at that time. And if they have to pay fees, they have to do that. Maybe they need to think about making it easier because it's a really hard process and not everybody can really do it. And maybe that's the main reason why a lot of people are here illegally, because it is really expensive, it is really hard. . . . So I mean I think maybe they can change it and make it a little bit easier, maybe then they would have less undocumented people this way. (12f)

Other participants articulated their empathy with Latina/os as the main targets of SB 1070 and of the racist discourses surrounding the law more explicitly. One interviewee said about SB 1070: "It's horrible, it's inhuman, it's fascist in some ways, but I think it's most obviously racial profiling. To me it's an outcry. To me it's simply a reaction, it's a sign that [the] federal government is not addressing the problem because . . . states have to go with laws that extreme" (10f). Another participant stated, "I definitely don't like that people who have been living here for a few years, doing something good for the society, are thrown away. So . . . I don't support this kind of politics" (27f). Yet another interviewee thought that SB 1070 was leading to the destruction of families (19f), and a third characterized the debate surrounding the law as hypocritical and self-serving on the part of politicians. He said:

> I consider most of them being totally hypocritical because they start close to the election, when they get into issues of the Mexican border, terror crime, social problems. But then immediately after [the] election all that disappear[s] because honestly they recognize that no matter what they say it's beneficial for you as a candidate. Because illegal immigrants don't have any real rights and all this, so they abuse the social system. Forget it! It's just not true. It's absolutely not true. . . . And [the US benefits] maybe even more from illegal than from legal migration! (26m)

When they expressed a specific reason for their empathy, several participants highlighted their shared identities as immigrants or their experience with undemocratic forms of state surveillance in the new Russia or in the former USSR. These expressions are reminiscent of the ways in which turn of the twentieth century Jewish immigrants rejected manifestations of white supremacy by establishing comparisons between African American marginalization and their own histories of exclusion in their regions of origin. It is important to state that these parallels cannot be attributed to any assumed geographical, racial, or ethnic continuity between the predominantly Jewish immigrants from Russia's Pale of Settlement and today's immigration from post-Soviet nations in Europe and Asia, which is no longer dominated by those who come as Jewish refugees. In the absence of comparative work with other groups, however, it is unclear if other groups or individuals also use empathy and comparative analogies to developments in their countries or regions of origin in order to understand the situation of Latina/o migrants.

One interviewee said, "You're still an immigrant even if you are white" (12f), another noted, "I will be still kind of an immigrant inside. . . . Because I've been there, done that, I can understand what other people go through" (1f), and a third stated, "I just try to be understanding, see that to be in somebody else's shoes who is you know having this hard time. I try to think, 'What if I'm in this people's shoes, how would I feel?'" (12f). Another participant compared the profiling of Latina/os to similar practices in post-Soviet Russia, where members of other nationalities are racially targeted by law enforcement, which she did not condone. She said:

> I see an example in Russia, there is a lot of immigrants as well. And how we deal with them at the level of police. If you see it's a homeless person, if you think he is special nationality because he has a lot of business in Kazakhstan, Uzbekistan and those Asian looking people. . . . They would take those people and they would put them in cells to find out if they have documents. And if they do, they would release them if they can prove. But if they have fake documents, they have to deport them. And that's what happens. . . . Who is going to decide how you look right? (1f)

The opposition of many of my interviewees to racial exclusion and profiling also manifested in comparisons to their own experience with the Soviet government that, among other things, relied on the practice of constant surveillance. One respondent commented, "I don't like to be carrying my documentation every time. I've been doing that for my whole life in Moscow" (17m), and another said that the bill reminded him of the USSR where one needed permits to move to certain cities (20m). He explained that SB 1070

> reminded me of some of the police regime we had in my own country. . . . You travel to a big city like Kiev and then very often if there is some suspicion that you don't live there, they would ask for your passport. And essentially I think that was completely inappropriate, violating the rights of people. Even if they come there for a visit, they don't live there, but it's not like they have to carry their passport all the time with them. So you kind of presume them guilty of something, even though there is really nothing necessarily behind it. So this whole thing with checking the identity and checking the legal status under any kind of legitimate reason—or you find some reason for asking that. I think this is a bit overboard, it's a bit too much. So I could imagine that there are a lot of naturalized Americans who would be speaking with a strong accent and that immediately targets that population no matter what. (20m)

Another interviewee noted: "I'm completely negative about [SB 1070] because all the Russians profile. It is so much against the nature of this country. . . . [If they did] that would basically, that would change America, like 9/11 changed the mentality of the country and the basic rights of this country" (23m).

Neoliberalism and Race

These expressions of empathy by post-USSR immigrants highlight their social distance from Latina/os. Both groups are differently subjected to immigration enforcement and positioned differently in the US socio-economic hierarchy where notions of inequality are overlaid onto racial categories. Compared to Latina/os and African Americans who continue to be associated with a marginalized racialized status and notions of economic distress, post-Soviet migrants are collectively placed in a position similar to that of Asian Americans, who have entered into expanded notions of whiteness.

In the absence of a body of comparative work on contemporary Asian American and (post-)Soviet immigrant populations, I examine Gary Shteyngart's novel *Super Sad True Love Story* (2010), which imaginatively portrays parallels between second-generation Korean and Russian Jewish immigrants in a dystopian, near future New York City against the backdrop of the ongoing racial and economic marginalization of African Americans and Latina/os. While Shteyngart—and his protagonist—represents the numerically smaller migration from the former USSR before its dissolution in 1991, his work is often discussed together with that of the post-Soviet writers examined in the previous chapter as it includes attention to developments in Soviet successor nations. Shteyngart is widely known for his novel *The Russian Debutante's Handbook* (2002), which was the first to address the contemporary Russian Jewish immigration experience in the United States and was published with the support of his mentor, Korean American author Chang-rae Lee, and for *Absurdistan* (2006), a novel depicting a Jewish Russian immigrant's temporary return to a fictional post-Soviet nation in Asia. Shteyngart's most recent *Super Sad True Love Story* was a *New York Times* bestseller and "Notable Book of the Year" in 2010, and won the Salon Book Award for Fiction in 2010 and the British Bollinger Everyman Wodehouse Prize in 2011. The novel's protagonist, second-generation Russian American Lenny Abramov, works for a multinational company that sells the promise of indefinite life extension to superwealthy customers and also deals in homeland security. Critics have called the novel a work of "speculative realism" because it fictionalizes advances in medical technologies geared at reversing aging (Kriebernegg 2013) and the kind of "omnipresent mobile networked technology" that is recognizably similar to the I-Phone and social media available today (Bellin 2016; Fan 2016).

But the novel also portrays the realities of a "postracial" United States (Saldívar 2013), particularly the ways in which whiteness, understood as upward mobility, has expanded to include not just those historically, if ambivalently, associated with a white racial identity but also Asian Americans, while the collective economic marginalization of other populations continues to be associated with nonwhiteness. *Super Sad True Love Story* is set forty years after the protagonist's parents emigrated from Moscow, which if Shteyngart is referencing his own parents' arrival in the United States in 1979, is some time in 2019. When the novel opens, the United States is "a barely governable country presenting grave risk to the international system of corporate governance and exchange mechanisms" (179). The country is run by the "Bipartisan Party," its infrastructure has severely deteriorated, members of its decimated middle class predominantly work in "Credit" or "Media," and the "American Restoration Authority" oversees the ever-present state surveillance and manipulative rhetoric made famous by the novel *1984*. At war with Argentina, the United States also freely employs explicitly racist and anti-immigrant discourses to justify its use of force toward members of its own population, first targeting the largely nonwhite urban poor, then attacking protesters, and eventually marginalizing all impoverished immigrants and US-born citizens.

The story of the relationship between middle-aged Russian Jewish protagonist Lenny Abramov and his significantly younger Korean American girlfriend, Eunice Park, is told through Lenny's diary entries and Eunice's postings on her social media "Globalteens" account. While Jewish Americans' insistence on their racial specificity has historically manifested in the tendency to avoid interracial marriages, Jewish-Asian relationships have become relatively common today. Lenny's pattern of dating East Asian Americans can be traced back to his attendance at a prestigious math-and-science high school in New York City, where another Korean American woman named Eunice defended him from his classmates' taunts for his relatively weak academic performance compared with theirs.

The novel's focus on Lenny and Eunice's relationship illustrates similarities in the immigration experiences of Koreans and Soviet Jews. They came from countries undergoing significant transformations in the late 1970s and early 1980s; their cultural, political, and religious conservativism emphasizes family cohesion over a commitment to the larger society; and their acceptance of and inclusion in US narratives of (white) immigrant success encourages them to stress the importance of education and upwardly mobile careers for their children.

Lenny's family exemplifies the Soviet Jewish immigrant experience in the United States that is also briefly fictionalized in Sana Krasikov's short story collection, as discussed in the previous chapter and referenced in depictions of post-Soviet immigrants in reality TV shows examined in chapter 1. His parents emigrated to be able to offer him a better life and to escape religious persecution and material deprivation in the former USSR. As Lenny writes in his diary, his parents arrived "with one pair of underwear between them" in "search of dollars and God" (10–11) "just so the fetus inside my mother, that future-Lenny, could have a better life" (324). Discriminated against as Jews in the Soviet Union, which particularly manifested in their inability to attend prestigious universities, upon their arrival as Jewish refugees the Abramovs received assistance from the Jewish community and were provided with English lessons and used furniture.

But despite his university degree and his occupation as an engineer in the Soviet Union, Lenny's father experienced severe downward mobility working as a janitor in the United States. With a mother who is a stay-at-home wife, the Abramovs hovered at the lower end of the middle-class spectrum. Presumably because they "never had a good word to say about HolyPetroRussia" (136), the Abramovs are not shown to have considered returning to their changed homeland. While the country is never discussed in detail, its new name hints at its overreliance on natural resources and the government's newfound alliance with the formerly marginalized Russian Orthodox Church.

Lenny has been socialized as Jewish American, and he freely admits that he has built a close relationship with his boss Joshie Goldstein by evoking shared "Jewish feelings of terror and injustice" (51). Because Lenny is also deeply invested in emphasizing similarities between his girlfriend and himself, he employs his parents' immigration story to weave a similar account of Eunice's family out of publicly available on-line data (Palumbo-Liu 2012, 38). While Koreans arrived in the United States in the early twentieth century and after the Korean War, a third wave came after the passage of the 1965 Immigration and Naturalization Act. The Parks were part of the even larger numbers who arrived in the United States throughout the 1980s following the rise of several US-backed dictatorships. The declaration of martial law, the closing of universities, and the arrest of political opponents culminated in the 1980 massacre of Kwangju residents as the city rose to support student protestors. Like post-Soviet immigrants, who generally come with advanced levels of education, the Parks were part of the high proportion of post-1980s Korean immigrants who were well educated and arrived in the United States in search of educational opportunities, a better life, or to join family (Zong and Batalova 2014).

Eunice's family initially followed the model minority trajectory of up-ward mobility. The father worked as a podiatrist and the mother was a housewife. But the family's economic status worsened after Medicare disappeared and the father's mostly poor Mexican immigrant clients could no longer afford his services. As their "immigrant nest egg [was] steadily declining" and their two daughters continued to furiously par-ticipate in the "idiotic consumer culture" (38), the family was becoming "your average American immigrant with bad Credit" (296).

The Parks develop serious doubts that their immigration to the United States was the right choice. In her postings to her daughter, Eunice's mother compares the country's increasing militarization to the 1980 conflicts in South Korea and states that "we never [should] leave Korea which is now richer country than America, and also not have so much political problem, but how we were to know that when we leave?" (41). While Korean immigration stagnated in the 1990s and then de-clined following economic and political improvements in South Korea, the Parks' financial problems prevent them from joining the small but growing numbers of "A-level Koreans" (183) and their US-born children who are returning. Toward the end of the novel, the parents receive a "Chinese 'Lao Wai' foreigner passport" because of Joshie's political connections. This allows them to move to New York City where the father is incorporated into the residence quota for the highly skilled.[8]

Both families push their children toward economic success, and they are also politically conservative. The Parks are Christian fundamentalists whose experience with South Korean dictatorships has taught them to refrain from getting involved in politics. Because of their "inbred Soviet Jewish conservatism" (11), the Abramovs openly support an increasingly undemocratic US government, mainly, it seems, because it is headed by a Jewish defense minister with close ties to "SecurityStateIsrael." The Abramovs exemplify first-generation Soviet Jews who consider Republicans to be more supportive of Israel's conservative ethnonationalist policies, and often have relatives on the political right there (Senderovich 2016). The Abramovs watch "FoxLiberty-Prime and FoxLiberty-Ultra" (11) and fly the US and Israeli flags outside their house. Buying into the US and Israeli rhetoric that constructs those who are culturally or religiously different as enemies, the father tells Lenny that "SecurityStateIsrael should use the nuclear option against the Arabs and the Persians, fallouts in direction of Teheran and Baghdad as opposed to Jerusalem and Tel Aviv" (135–136).

But the novel also acknowledges important differences between the two immigrant communities. Eunice emphasizes that her family, in which her father's physical abuse of his wife and children is sanctioned by their fundamentalist religious beliefs, is "no comparison to Lenny's" (145). She also highlights the white male privilege underlying Lenny's fixation on East Asian women, writing that he is "one of those white guys who can't tell a good-looking Asian girl from an ugly one. We all look the same to them" (301).

By focusing on intersections between Jewish Russian and Korean immigrants, the novel points to the fact that, as Susan Koshy (2001) and Richard Alba (2009) have argued, Asian Americans are now regarded as an assimilable ethnicity in ways that move beyond their historical association with nonwhiteness and marginalization.[9] As they find themselves among the more prosperous groups in the United States, East and South Asian Americans are in the process of becoming "honorary whites." Like the post-Soviet migrant cast on reality TV discussed in chapter 1, they are also often associated with the myth of an immigrant America, which is based on idealized accounts of the post–World War II upward mobility of European immigrants. These ideas of immigrant success and assimilation are expanded to include Asian Americans through the "model minority" label that associates them with the bootstrapism of earlier European immigrants. Like them, the new arrivals tend to move to urban centers with viable ethnic enclave economies where they use ethnic networks to establish themselves in economic niches (Liu 2000, 177). The commitment of Asian migrants and their descendants to work, self-sufficiency, family, and education has supposedly enabled them to do better than other racialized groups of immigrants (Kibria 1998, 952).

While Shteyngart's novel highlights similarities in the Korean and Soviet Jewish immigrant experiences, particularly their association with and internalization of the myth of immigrant upward mobility, it also shows how the two communities differ from other groups who continue to suffer disproportionately from the country's economic decline and the rise in undemocratic practices. The "Boat Is Full" campaign targets Mexican immigrants. It relies on the symbol of a "Mexican Otter" with a "red-white-and-blue bandana . . . perched upon a goofy-looking horse, the two of them galloping toward a fiercely rising and presumably Asian sun" (7–8). At one of the internal security checkpoints strategically placed throughout the city, Lenny witnesses how National Guardsmen pick on his company's Dominican driver, forcing him to sing the national anthem and parade in front of Credit Poles, only to tell him that "[s]oon the time'll come . . . for us to send your *chulo* ass home" (179, emphasis in original). The ever-present Poles that display the credit scores of passersby are marked with racially charged language and symbolism that pit Asian and Latina/o (immigrant) populations against each other by evoking their differing economic group status. A "miserly ant happily running toward a mountain of wrapped Christmas presents" urges onlookers, in Chinese and English, to spend more, while a cartoon of a "frowning grasshopper in a zoot suit showing us his empty pockets" declares in English and Spanish "Save It for a Rainy Day, *Huevón*" (54). These images indicate that Asian (Americans) remain the target of racist discourses despite their association with upward mobility. They are collectively called "Chinese" and are urged to spend rather than save. The novel here references the fact that even Asians and Asian Americans with a high occupational status and class privilege encounter cultural stigma as they continue to be ascriptively racialized as quintessential nonwhite "foreigners"—those from "Asia" (Lowe 1996; Murti 2010).

Just as discourses targeting Latina/s as "illegals" today are reiterated by other immigrants, the differently racialized imagery of Asian Americans and Latina/os is also internalized by members of the communities themselves. Eunice's friend, a second-generation middle-class Korean immigrant, describes a Latina as a "gross illegal immigrant fuck-tard who probably rates 300 on a Credit Pole. I hope they deport her ass soon" (147). Just as anti-immigration discourses and laws can always be expanded to include groups beyond the ones targeted, immigrants in the novel are also constantly reminded that *all* of them are potentially deportable if they are poor (11). Thus, Lenny's parents avoid Credit Poles because they are afraid that their low credit scores will expose them to the possibility of deportation.

In a thinly veiled reference to the displacement of less well-to-do residents from their communities through processes of urban renewal, the predominately African American and Latina/o urban poor are unceremoniously removed from their homes, supposedly to prepare for the visit of the Central Chinese Banker on whose investment policies the country's survival now depends. When the newly homeless people build ramshackle housing in Central Park, the National Guard use deadly force to disburse them. As Lenny and his friends watch the live streamed coverage of these confrontations in which several people are killed, their initial feelings of fear and their "empathy for those who were nominally our fellow New Yorkers" are quickly replaced by the knowledge "that it wouldn't happen to us" because "[o]ur lives are worth more than the lives of others" (157, 165). This scenario highlights the potentially short-lived effects of empathy for those the novel calls "low networth individuals" (LNWIs) constituted as different, in this case mainly in terms of racialized class status.

But the subsequent all-out military assault on Tompkins Park, where former National Guardsmen prepare for an uprising because they failed to receive their promised bonus and health care benefits upon their return from Argentina, makes clear that ideological opponents have also entered the category of undesirables whose lives have become worthless. The creation of tent cities under the leadership of "Aziz's Army" is a thinly veiled reference to the 2011 Occupy Wall Street movement, which arose in New York's Zuccotti Park in protest against social and economic inequality. When the fictionalized protesters in Tompkins Park are killed during an apocalyptic event that comes to be called "the Rupture," Lenny becomes as concerned for Eunice, whose low credit scores makes her vulnerable to being "shot just like the LNWI protesters" (242), as for his middle-class Indian and Korean American friends who live in Staten Island and whose survival, he is told, entirely "depends . . . on their assets" (242). As he is trying to leave Staten Island to return to the city, a ferry with two of his Jewish friends, one of whom streams a show slightly critical of the Bipartisan Party, is intentionally destroyed by military assault helicopters.

After the violent suppression of dissent during "the Rupture," all communication technologies cease to function, driving several people to commit suicide because they cannot live without their electronic devices. Schools are closed, and as work and food become scarce, formerly middle- and upper-middle-class men are forced to perform the kind of underpaid manual labor in public works that, in the north, was historically completed by turn of the twentieth century European immigrants. Naomi Klein has theorized that what she calls "disaster capitalism" employs the chaos following major disasters such as uprisings, wars, or weather events to implement neoliberal reforms that favor elites at the expense of a country's majority population. The practices of disaster capitalism, which are largely enabled by the lending policies of global financial institutions such as the World Bank and the International Monetary Fund (IMF), historically moved from Latin America in the 1970s and Eastern Europe in the 1990s, to the United States and West Asia after 9/11.

In Shteyngart's novel, the post-Rupture chaos is used to implement shock therapies of the kind formerly experienced by the Soviet Union, which led to its dissolution and the emergence of various successor nations. The IMF similarly devises a "recovery plan for America, [that] divide[s] the country into concessions, and hand[s] them over to the sovereign wealth funds. Norway, China, Saudi Arabia" (257). "Riffraff with No Credit" (257) is removed from the city, and only those with specialized and highly skilled occupations are allowed to enter, which is reminiscent of practices in the Soviet Union where residence permits were required to live in certain cities. Lenny points to similarities between the two countries' demise as he ponders his father's humiliation "of growing up a Jew in the Soviet Union, of cleaning piss-stained bathrooms in the States, of worshipping a country that would collapse as simply and inelegantly as the one he had abandoned" (321).

The implementation of shock therapies in order to liquidate as many assets as possible and provide handsome returns for foreign investors is accomplished with force to frighten into submission an even larger range of devalued populations. Lenny's rent-controlled building on the Lower East Side, which is largely inhabited by elderly Jewish women, is cleared out under the guise of "harm reduction" after it is declared to be "too close to the river" and thus susceptible to flooding due to global warming (309). The residents are given one day to move to "abandoned housing in New Rochelle" (309), which Lenny states condemns them to sure death. After the apartment building is torn down, it is replaced with triplexes reserved for "foreign residents." The acquisition of this overpriced real estate at a cost that equals fifty years of Lenny's annual salary affords "foreign residents" a host of other privileges, such as exemption from the all-pervasive security surveillance, including cavity, data, and property searches, as well as protections by a private security company. While similar privileges are currently associated with an ascribed white racial identity and upper class status, the novel predicts that they will only be available to members of a superwealthy global elite, particularly those residing in countries with stronger economies and more valuable currencies.

Lenny realizes that he and Eunice "won't survive together" in this "America 2.0 . . . New York: Lifestyle Hub, Trophy city" (374). As Eunice leaves him for his boss Joshie, whose connections and wealth allow her to study in London where she meets her next boyfriend, Lenny moves to "Toronto, Stability-Canada" where only those with valuable skills are allowed to reside. Here he not only exchanges his now worthless US citizenship for a Canadian passport but, after the death of his parents, he also changes his name to the more "North American" Larry Abraham in reference to the founder of Judaism. After residing in Canada for a decade, Lenny moves to the Tuscan Free State, "a place with less data, less youth, and where old people like myself were not despised simply for being old" (328). Lenny's leaked diary and Eunice's hacked Globalteens postings are simultaneously published in New York and Beijing, with critics accusing Lenny of slavishly emulating literary writers and lauding Eunice's entries for being "more alive than anything else . . . from that illiterate period" (322).

Conclusion

Although the second-generation middle-class Jewish immigrants in Shteyngart's novel initially express empathy with impoverished New Yorkers as they are literally condemned to death through state violence, these feelings quickly give way to affirmations of their racialized economic privilege which they think will protect them from similar forms of oppression. While the articulation of support for Latina/os by many of my post-Soviet interviewees similarly underscores their social distance from the group most targeted by anti-immigration policy from which they expect exemption, their empathy also highlights their ambivalence to and often outright rejection of immigration restrictions as one of the most recent manifestations of white supremacy. Unlike the twentieth-century European immigrants who needed to insist on their whiteness through contrast with African Americans or to compare themselves to this group to highlight their racial distinctiveness as Jews, most post-Soviet immigrants today are securely racialized as white. Even their struggles to create a new ethnicized cultural identity or to overcome the disadvantages of being foreign or, for some, the adversities associated with their legal status, do not appear to require that they set themselves apart from Latina/o immigrants.

But their (sometimes tentative expression of) support is politically more limited than the forms of alliance building available to members of groups who are not as securely associated with whiteness. Those racialized as "Arabs/Muslims" and African Americans who currently face collective profiling—as "terrorists" or "criminals"—or Asians and Asian Americans who can point to histories of exclusion in the United States, can evoke these parallels as grounds for cross-ethnic alliances. Asian immigrants in particular have used such similarities to join immigration rights movements of the early 2000s that were dominated by Latina/o immigrant rights groups. In contrast, by expressing empathy for Latina/os as the main targets of anti-immigration enforcement, post-Soviet migrants behave like the intended recipients of human rights representations, which aim to engage audience members' sense of ethics and justice so that they identify with causes distant or alien from their own experience and are mobilized into some kind of unspecified action (Smith and Schaffer 2004).

The only exceptions seem to be individual or smaller groups of migrants who are directly affected by a tightened immigration system. Undocumented Irish immigrants formed the Irish Lobby for Immigration Reform (ILIR) in 2005, which initially called for ethnically specific immigration reform under the slogan "Legalize the Irish," but then joined the Coalition for Comprehensive Immigration Reform (CCIR) to support a more comprehensive immigration agenda. In his 2007 testimony before the House Subcommittee on Immigration, Niall O'Dowd, the chairman of ILIR, supported legal provisions that would have primarily helped other immigrant groups, such as measures for easier family unification and temporary work visas.[10] Post-Soviet or Eastern European migrants do not (yet?) have similar organizations. The Polish American protagonist of Ruth Leitman's documentary *Tony and Janina's American Wedding*, discussed in the previous chapter, illustrates how an individual immigrant became involved in immigration rights movements. He did so primarily to fight for the reentry of his unauthorized wife, but his case took on cross-ethnic significance as he, like Niall O'Dowd, also testified before Congress in support of the 2007 Strive Act.

What would happen if contemporary post-Soviet (and other European) immigrants—as well as native-born whites—were to reclaim the selective exclusion of southern and eastern European immigrants as grounds for cross-ethnic alliances for immigrant rights? Instead of using this history—and other historical forms of European immigrant marginalization—to bolster denials that they enjoy white privilege, the descendants of turn of the twentieth century European immigration could employ it to understand how immigration legislation has racialized ever changing groups of immigrants in similar ways and can thus easily be expanded to include other immigrant groups. The 1920s Quota legislation extended the racialized logic of the 1880s Chinese Exclusion Acts, which declared all those of Chinese ethnic descent to be inadmissible. The Acts employed comparisons to (black) slavery to characterize the largest portion of Chinese migrants who came as unskilled laborers as "coolies." Discussions surrounding the passage of the 1885 Foran

Act extended this racialized rhetoric to eastern and southern European arrivals who came through organized migration networks to take low-skilled jobs, characterizing them as participants in coerced and temporary forms of labor migration (Sadowski-Smith 2008).

The Foran Act and the 1917 Literacy Act, both of which were passed to regulate eastern and southern European immigrants, were later also applied to immigrants from Mexico, who have become the most regulated group of immigrants in US history (Ngai 2004). But unlike European immigrants, who were gradually incorporated into all facets of whiteness, the racial identity of Mexicans was often questioned in legal decisions about citizenship, and they were subject to residential and educational segregation, racialized violence, and dispossession, even though Mexican migrants, like Europeans, were legally granted US citizenship under the 1848 Treaty of Guadalupe Hidalgo (Fox and Guglielmo 2012).[11]

A recognition of the historical expansion of racialized anti-immigrant legislation and discourses across an evolving white-nonwhite binary could shape contemporary post-Soviet immigrants' understanding of their place in the US racial hierarchy and their relationship to other arrivals. Such a lens would question the ways in which post-Soviet immigrants have become associated with a post–World War II whiteness that can apparently only be understood in contrast to nonwhite populations and thus does not allow for common ground between groups racialized as either white or nonwhite.

The historical parallels between the regulation of Chinese and new European immigration, which centered on the economic adversity faced by both groups' impoverished majorities, appear to have been inverted today as members of the post-Soviet diaspora, like Asian immigrants and their descendants, are collectively distanced from the socioeconomic bottom of US society, which is still occupied by African Americans and increasingly Latina/os. Shteyngart's novel highlights how structures of inequality are being complexly overlaid onto multiracial realities, in which assumed collective access to upward mobility places (post-)Soviet immigrants alongside Asian Americans, a population that has historically been considered nonwhite. His work thus emphasizes the increased flexibility of a supposedly pan-European whiteness that, at least in its association with economic success and upward mobility, can be equally attributed to (post-)Soviet immigrant and Asian populations.

Through its focus on increases in the number of US immigrants and their children who return to their countries of origin, particularly those from South Korea, *Super Sad True Love Story* also deconstructs the myth of an immigrant America being kept alive through association with Asian and (post-)Soviet immigrant populations. Because of their projected upward mobility, members of both groups are considered to be "good" immigrants and are contrasted with other, presumably less desirable migrants from Latin America and domestic US populations racialized as nonwhite. The division of populations through their association with either racialized value or racialized stigma prevents the formation of larger coalitions against neoliberal policies that, as fictionalized in Shteyngart's novel, eventually come to negatively affect nearly everyone but a tiny US and global elite.

Conclusion

Immigrant Whiteness Today

Among the vast field of contenders in the 2016 US presidential election, a record number were second-generation immigrants. Democratic candidate Bernie Sanders should have been the poster child for the American Dream of immigrant success. He was born into a working-class home with a Jewish father who had come to the United States from Galicia, then part of the Austro-Hungarian empire (today's Poland), during the last years of this mass migration, only to struggle through the Great Depression. His mother was the daughter of eastern European Jewish immigrants from today's Russia and Poland. After the war, Sanders's father discovered that most of his family had died in the European Holocaust. By the time Sanders graduated from college, both his parents were deceased. He held a variety of low-wage jobs and worked his way up the political ladder to become a successful US senator, having served the longest as an independent in US congressional history.

But Sanders's path toward a successful political career, despite his experiences with poverty as the son of a Jewish immigrant from Poland and his upbringing in an urban ethnic ghetto, was never framed as an example of upward immigrant mobility. Having been actively involved in African American civil rights struggles and labor movements, Sanders never assumed the right to represent immigrants and his campaign did not focus on issues of immigration. Many Russian-speaking Jewish immigrants did not consider him representative of their views or experiences or planned to vote for him because of his self-identification as a socialist, an ideology they associated with the former USSR (Khazan 2016).

Instead, several second-generation Latina/o and Asian American immigrants who ran on the Republic ticket reclaimed the myth of an immigrant America in the service of their campaigns. Ted Cruz, Marco Rubio, and Bobby Jindal made their immigrant families central to their biographies by reaffirming the conservative message that is at the center of the myth of an immigrant America, though they all, to differing degrees, opposed new legislation that would expand immigrant rights.

Their appropriation of the immigrant myth highlights the increasing flexibility of the turn of the twentieth century European immigrant story of bootstrapism, which was originally linked to the post–World War II ascendance of whiteness as a pan-European identity. The son of Indian parents, Jindal went furthest in stressing old-fashioned forms of assimilation that involve the loss of one's immigrant culture. He changed his first name, converted to Catholicism, downplayed his connections with India and its culture, and made Christianity and assimilation a centerpiece of his public life (Gown and Bridges 2015). As the children of Cuban immigrants, Ted Cruz and Marco Rubio represent what Maria de Los Angeles (1988) has termed the Latin Alger myth. The campaigns of these three candidates exemplified that the narrative of immigrant success can be expanded to other subgroups or to individuals of color who are supposedly pulling themselves up by their bootstraps.

The extension of recycled notions of post–World War II immigrant success to migrants who do not have roots in Europe points to the ways in which racial, cultural, economic, and social layers of whiteness are increasingly becoming disconnected from one another. While whiteness has remained a privileged racial identity that is regularly mobilized in the service of white supremacy and white nationalism, other aspects of whiteness are undergoing significant changes as they are being delinked from a specific racial identity. As Coleen Lye asks with regard to Asian Americans, does their upward mobility (in the face of their continued racialization as "foreign others") confirm the persistent power of white privilege, the fact that not much has changed since its consolidation after World War II, or does it reveal the evolution of whiteness toward a largely symbolic privilege devoid of actual material power (Lye 2008, 1734)?

The case of post-Soviet migrants examined in this book provides a partial response to this question. In the absence of other available models of cultural, ethnic, and racial identification, notions of a common pan-European whiteness or one of its ethnicized versions are pushed onto the new arrivals and many of the immigrants also identify with (portions of) this narrative. The reality TV shows I explored in chapter 1 portray post-Soviet migrants as following in the footsteps of idealized turn of the twentieth century European migration and set them in direct opposition to the largest group of contemporary migrants from Latin America. These narratives, in which members of the post-Soviet diaspora are expected to follow the same upwardly mobile and assimilationist trajectory as mythologized turn of the twentieth century European migrants, help perpetuate the fiction that the same opportunities are still available to at least the contemporary immigrants racialized as white. In fact, it appears that post-USSR immigrants fit the role of heirs to the idealized turn of the twentieth century European immigrant story of triumph over adversity even better than other immigrant groups, such as (South) Asians or Cuban Americans, because the physical appearance of many members renders them "unquestionably" white.

When individual migrants complicate this assumption, they are simply not represented as members of the post-USSR diaspora. Thus, media accounts of the 2013 Boston Marathon bombing have called the perpetrators, brothers Dzhokhar and Tamerlan Tsarnaev, simply "Chechens" or falsely, immigrants from Chechnya (Kaleem 2013), by extending the family's self-identification in terms of (post)-Soviet notions of ethnicity to the US context where it has different connotations, all the while overlooking the fact that the family was ethnically-mixed and resided in Russia before their emigration and that many members either carried or tried to acquire Russian citizenship. The father's grandparents had been displaced from Chechnya, but before their emigration the Tsarnaevs had resided predominantly in the Central Asian republic of Kyrgyzstan. They arrived in the United States in 2002 from Dagestan, a republic in Russia's Caucasus, where the mother grew up as an ethnic Avar.[1] When the US media called them "Chechen," this designation helped emphasize the Tsarnaevs' Muslim identity and the brothers' radicalization through the Salafist school of orthodox Sunni Islam, which is rooted in West Asia. This narrative reinforced the linkage between terrorism, Islam, and West Asia, which has expanded the historical links between communism as an ideological threat and the geography of East Bloc nations during the Cold War (Atanasoski 2013, 13, 207).[2] Terrorism simply cannot be associated with whiteness.[3] The May 2013 cover of the *Week* thus even darkened the Tsarnaevs' skin color to make the brothers appear more "Arab." In addition to highlighting their Muslim faith, the US media also emphasized the family's failure to achieve the American

Dream, which further dissociated them from the "white" post-Soviet diaspora and its presumed links to the myth of upward mobility. The economic deprivation of the Tsarnaevs was so severe that the parents returned to Dagestan after a decade in the United States, while leaving their grown children behind (Zirin 2013; "The Tsarnaev Family" 2013; Jacobs et al. 2013).[4]

Just as the Tsarnaev brothers could not be depicted as members of a "white" diaspora because of their links to terrorism inspired by radicalized versions of Islam, immigrant illegality can only be imagined in the context of the "brown" bodies of Latina/os (Cacho 2012). Undocumented post-Soviet migrants have remained absent from these discussions to such an extent that their presence surprises even immigration scholars, as discussed in chapter 5. The so-called "new Irish," a much smaller group, received far more media and scholarly attention in the 1980s than post-Soviet immigrants today, though Irish public activism and their emphasis on their unauthorized status did not succeed in complicating the association of undocumented migration with Latina/os.

Aside from the privileges of exemption from racial profiling and residential segregation, it appears that it is the increasingly mythologized racialization of members of the post-Soviet diaspora as white and their association with the fiction of an enduring and unchanging system of US whiteness that sets them apart most clearly from other contemporary arrivals or their descendants. When this notion of a privileged racial identity is expanded globally, it allows US-born individuals of European descent to assert mythical kinship with children and women who reside in countries of the former East Bloc. Their ascribed white racial identity supposedly makes them the perfect potential kin for US men or families. As during the white ethnic revival of the 1960s, this expanded notion of a symbolic white ethnicity again serves deeply conservative ends. The myth of a global whiteness promotes neoliberal forms of transnational adoption and marriage migration, all the while obscuring the growing global inequalities that enable these two types of human movement in the first place.

By devoting an entire book to the diverse and understudied post-USSR diaspora, I am hoping to offer a model that can be expanded to more explicitly comparative work on different US immigrant groups. Adoptions from Russia and Ukraine in particular point to intersections with the largest adoptee populations from China and Korea in ways that revise dominant narratives about race and family formation. Other approaches could examine the role of post-Soviet women as part of a larger movement of marriage migration, mainly from Asia. The emerging body of fiction by post-Soviet authors on post-USSR unauthorized immigration highlights intersections with other contemporary migrants as well as with the work of US immigrant authors from various other parts of the world. My interview data point to parallels between post-Soviet immigrants and contemporary migrant groups from Asia and Latin America that also open up comparative approaches to this population.

Such approaches would emphasize the diverse effects of neoliberalism on migration to the United States, and would also offer sites for more inclusive struggles for migrant citizenship rights that highlight connections—rather than stark divisions—between the post-Soviet diaspora and other migrant groups. Shteyngart's novel, discussed in chapter 5, takes this approach further by also imagining the inclusion of US-born minority populations in coalitions against increasing inequities in a "postracial" United States. While such a model recognizes the continued role of whiteness as a privileged racial category, it also places it alongside other racial formations in order to decenter its persistent status as a US founding mythology, even in the face of significant domestic and global changes.

The results of the 2016 US presidential election, which took place after the completion of this book, appear to have severely questioned the potential for coalitions across the white-nonwhite divide. Analyses of exit polls revealed deep divisions along the lines of race, gender, age, and education, as wide as and in some cases wider than in previous elections. A majority of white voters supported Republican nominee Donald Trump, while voters of color, especially African Americans and Latina/os, overwhelmingly preferred Hillary Clinton, the Democratic candidate. White men, in particular, voted for Trump, and did so in larger numbers than during the 2012 election. Whites without college degrees supported him by the largest margin in exit polls since 1980. To some extent, race also continued to outweigh educational attainment: while larger numbers of college graduates supported Clinton, a slightly higher percentage of white college graduates (4 percent) voted for Trump, though that percentage represented a decline from the numbers of white college graduates who had supported Mitt Romney during the last election. Younger people (18–29) overwhelmingly voted for Clinton, though larger numbers had supported Obama in 2012 (Tyson and Maniam 2016).

These results show that a small majority of white voters were more than willing to ignore the Trump campaign's sexism, racism, and its normalization of white nationalism and white supremacy, which included calls for the even more explicit racial profiling and exclusion of Muslims and Mexican immigrants and the inclusion of self-professed "alt-right" extremists into the administration, in favor of amorphous policies that would make "America great again." As the post–World War II economy and welfare state that delivered privileged access to those racialized as white has been replaced by neoliberal policies, a majority of white voters appears to feel the loss of these privileges very acutely, even though minority populations suffer more in actual social and economic terms. Rather than attributing these changes to economic transformations, which include the loss of manufacturing and advances in automation, as well as the decline of the welfare state, these white voters once again fell for the fiction of whiteness, which is centrally linked to the populist strategy of projecting blame on those constructed as other, namely racialized minorities and groups of "foreigners" and "terrorists," and which fuels white nationalism.

Because the analyses of exit polls did not consider immigration status, it is unclear what percentage of Trump supporters were first-, 1.5-, or second-generation immigrants. In addition, many immigrants cannot vote because they are not naturalized citizens. It is thus difficult to determine potential differences in attitudes between US- or foreign-born voters who self-identify and are identified as white. But Trump's election has already galvanized the formation of several protest movements around issues of immigrant, reproductive, and LGBTQ rights as well as struggles for environmental protection and legislative change. One of these movements has been the formation of a Facebook group called "Anti-Trump Soviet Immigrants." The group describes its members as stemming "from a giant and relatively wealthy and educated immigration population. . . . Many of us understand how we are connected to other refugees and immigrants and other oppressed groups in general.

Many of us reject Islamophobia. Many of us are queer. This group is a start and began from a conversation among Jewish refugees, Ukrainian Catholics, and other Soviet bloc immigrants wanting a place to share information and tools about how to build power together and talk to our relatives." Founded by a lawyer, this group may represent a very small portion of the overall diaspora and is only open to Soviet immigrants. But at the very least, its existence points to the recognition that immigrant status can work as a political and mobilizing tool across different populations.

Alongside other populations, immigrants of all backgrounds will need to mobilize against the policies and rhetoric of the current administration. Several influential figures in the administration are linked to a network of anti-immigration groups originally founded by John Tanton in the late 1970s to address concerns about how population growth, thought to be fueled by immigration, negatively affects the environment. The Federation for American Immigration Reform (FAIR), which co-sponsored Arizona's anti-immigrant SB 1070 in 2010, has long promoted a moratorium on immigration that would allow only the entry of spouses and minor children of US citizens. As its philosophies are based in eugenics, the discredited "science" of racial "hygiene" that fueled the 1920s Quota Laws and the Nazi ideology in Germany, one of FAIR's goals is to end the Immigration and Nationality Act of 1965, which supplanted the 1920s quota system.

Attorney General Jeff Sessions and his former communication director Stephen Miller, now a senior policy advisor to President Trump, are associated with FAIR. So is Kris Kobach, Kansas Secretary of State, a lawyer for FAIR's legal arm, and an advisor on President Trump's transition team who helped draft Arizona's Senate Bill 1070. Sessions has said that he supports the passage of legislation like the 1920s Quota Laws, which, according to him, ended the "indiscriminate acceptance of all races." Without acknowledging the eugenic and racist underpinnings of the laws, he asserted that similar legislation was necessary to stem the growth of the foreign-born population, which currently stands at 13 percent of the overall US population and thus approximates the percentages in the 1890 Census (14 percent) before the Quota Acts (1921 and 1924) were passed (Serwer 2017). Stephen Miller crafted the strategy that defeated a bipartisan immigration reform bill, which included a path to citizenship for unauthorized immigrants in 2013, and he also authored President Trump's 2017 executive order limiting the entry of citizens from several majority-Muslim nations.

The order temporarily barred the admission of those with valid US visas from several majority-Muslim nations and indefinitely banned the entry of refugees. Its enforcement galvanized widespread protests outside US airports. In Phoenix, Arizona, Masha Priest who had arrived in the United States in 1991 as a refugee from the former Soviet Union, protested the executive order based on her own migration experiences (Walker and Cervantes 2017). Sergey Brin, a Google cofounder who had similarly emigrated from the former Soviet Union when he was six, was among the protesters at San Francisco's International Airport. A few days after the travel ban, when thousands of Google employees around the world mobilized against the executive order, Sergey Brin, Marwan Fawaz, a Lebanese immigrant who leads the company's Nest subsidiary, and Google's CEO Sundar Pichai, an Indian immigrant, opposed the executive order at the company's headquarters. Brin said that, as a refugee, he was personally outraged by the ban. He shared: "I came here to the US with my family, at age six, from the Soviet Union, which was, at that time, the greatest enemy the U.S. had—maybe it still is in some form. The risks of, at the time, letting in these foreigners from a land that might spy on you, learn the nuclear secrets, and send them back—and there were many cases of espionage—those risks were far greater than the terrorism risks we face today. And, nevertheless, this country was brave and welcoming. . . . I wouldn't be where I am today or have any kind of the life that I have today" (Wallace-Wells 2017). While these immigrants empathized with those suddenly barred entry based on their own personal experience, larger portions of the US population also understood the ban as an unconstitutional attempt to revive US anti-refugee and immigration policies. As the Trump administration is working on legislation to curb forms of legal migration, including highly skilled movement, it will make more explicit the full intention and scale of anti-immigration policies, which have so far been hidden behind more selective attacks on one specific (undocumented) form of migration. These policies will need to galvanize protest from immigrants across national, ethnic, and legal differences.

ACKNOWLEDGMENTS

This book has been a long time in the making. It would never have been finished without the help and advice of many colleagues and the support of friends and family. I am deeply grateful to Claire Fox for her friendship and unwavering support over many years, as well as for reading and commenting on significant portions of this work. Thanks also to Cecilia Menjivar for reading several drafts of various chapters of this book and for her steady professional guidance, as well as to Wei Li who inspired me to expand my interview project to post-Soviet academics and who collaborated with me on a related research project. Thanks to Rachel Ida Buff for our conversations about immigration, her encouragement and support, and for bringing the manuscript to NYU Press. Takeyuki Tsuda also read parts of my work and provided valuable professional advice. The friendship and support of Marta Sánchez and her feedback on chapter 4 have been equally invaluable. I am also glad to have the opportunity to thank Anikó Imre for her insightful reading of chapter 1, and Heather Jacobson for her pioneering comparative scholarship on adoption from the former Soviet Union and for our discussions on this topic, her guidance on matters of interview method, and her reading of chapter 3. Thanks to Kevin Sandler for his careful reading of what became chapter 1. I also want to thank Erika Lee, whose work has continued to inspire and shape my comparative perspective on human movement to the United States, and for encouraging me to pursue my interest in working on post-Soviet migration. Thanks also to Adrian Wanner for his pioneering comparative work on literary productions by members of the post-Soviet diaspora and for our conversations about this work, and to Cinzia Solari for her comparative scholarship on the emigration of Ukrainian women. The insights I have drawn over the years it has taken me to complete this book from exchanges with Robert McKee Irwin, Sophia McClennen, Isis McElroy, Gabriele Schwab, and Silvia

Spitta have also animated many of my arguments. Joni Adamson has my deepest thanks for her friendship and professional guidance.

I want to extend a special thank you to my colleagues at Arizona State University (ASU) Anna Cichopek-Gajraj, Anna Holian, Julian Lim, and Laurie Manchester, who read large portions of this manuscript and supported me intellectually and emotionally through the final stretches of completing the book. Thanks also to members of ASU's Institute for Humanities Research (IHR) cluster on immigration, Evelyn Cruz, Jennifer Glick, Cecilia Menjivar, Doris Marie Provine, Takeyuki Tsuda, and Wei Li for their careful reading and support of my work. I also want to thank Mark Tebeau and Kristin Koptiuch who read parts of the manuscript and provided valuable guidance on its framing as participants on an ASU Provost fellowship. My thanks also go to members of the 2013 NEH Summer Institute at Columbia University on Russian-speaking immigrants and refugees, Vitaly Chernetsky, Elena Dubinets, Andrew Janco, Scott Kenworthy, Yasha Klots, Maggie Levantovskaya, Koby Oppenheim, Vladimir von Tsurikov, Roman Utkin, and Kristen Welsh, for helping me to conceptualize how my work could bridge the fields of migration, American studies, and Slavic studies. Members of the ASU IHR's fellowship program Leah M. Sarat, Françoise Mirguet, Andrea Ballestero, and Sujey Vega also supported me in the early stages of my work.

I have been fortunate to have had the support of many other former and current colleagues at Arizona State University, including Monica Varsanyi, Hava Samuelson, Angelita Reyes, Eileen Diaz McConnell, Karen Leong, Mary Margaret Fonow, Ayanna Thompson, Keith Miller, Mark Lussier, Eric Wertheimer, Joe Lockard, Ron Broglio, Dan Bivona, and Laura Tohe. Thanks also to the anonymous readers at NYU Press whose comments helped to immensely improve the framing and organization of the book. And thanks to Anna Epifanova, Crystine Miller, Wan Yu, and Byeongdon Oh for their research assistance, and to Anna Epifanova and Yan Mann for their translation assistance. Matthew Frye Jacobson, Alicia Nadkarni, and Eric Zinner also have my thanks for moving this book forward to publication. Thanks also to Usha Sanyal for her thorough reading and copyediting of the manuscript. Finally, thanks to my family without whom none of this would matter.

A 2016–2017 Arizona State University Provost Fellowship allowed me to complete revisions on the book. I conducted interviews with post-

Soviet immigrants in Arizona with the help of a 2011–2012 ASU IHR fellowship. My participation in the 2013 NEH Summer Fellowship on the Russian-speaking diaspora supported me in the analytical framing of this book. I was able to begin work on transnational adoption with my collaborators Karen Miller-Loessi and Brandon Yoo under the aegis of an ASU IHR Seed Grant in 2007–2008.

Parts of chapter 1 were published as "Global Migration Meets TV Format Adaptation: The Post-Soviet Diaspora, 'Whiteness,' and Return Migration in *Dancing with the Stars* (US) and Ukraine's *The Bachelor*," in *European Journal of Cultural Studies* 17(6): 753–768, reprinted with the permission of SAGE Publications. An earlier version of chapter 3 was published as "Neoliberalism, Global 'Whiteness,' and the Desire for Adoptive Invisibility in U.S. Parental Memoirs of Eastern European Adoption," *Journal of Transnational American Studies* 3.2 (November 2011), reprinted with the permission of the *Journal of Transnational American Studies*. Parts of chapter 5 were published as Claudia Sadowski-Smith and Wei Li, "The Profiling of Non-Citizens: Highly-Skilled BRIC Migrants in the Mexico-US Borderlands and Arizona's SB 1070," *Population, Space, and Place* 22.5 (2016): 487–500, reprinted with the permission of *Population, Space, and Place*.

NOTES

INTRODUCTION

1 The 2010 10% Census data is a combined dataset of the 2006–2010 American Community Survey (ACS). Figures from the 2011 annual American Community Survey (ACS) estimate the numbers of those born in the former Soviet Union to be at 1.2 million. The ACS is based on a 5 percent sample and is considered less accurate than the Census, which after 2010 no longer enumerated foreign-born populations.

2 Between 1995 and 1996, Soviet successor nations were the top senders of immigrants to New York City. The more than 20,000 immigrants who came annually outnumbered immigrants from the Dominican Republic, which had been the primary sending country prior to 1995 (Liu 2000, 171). The estimated number of 1.2 million post-USSR migrants in the 2011 ACS surpasses the 1.1 million Korean immigrants (overwhelmingly from South Korea) or close to 3 percent of the 41.3 million foreign-born population that lived in the United States in 2013 (Zong and Batalova 2014) and thus moves post-Soviet immigrants ahead of the Korean diaspora to the place of eighth-largest immigrant group in the United States. The 2011 and 2015 annual ACS did not show significant increases in the numbers of the two immigrant groups.

3 In 1990, the former Soviet Union was the eighth-largest source country of immigration to the United States; its mostly Jewish immigrants were the largest refugee group to enter the United States, numbering about 30,000 per year (Gold 1998, 115). Between 1990 and 2006, the largest successor nation, the Russian Federation, made it into the top immigrant-sending countries to the United States almost each year (Robila 2010, 27).

4 I capitalize the terms Eastern and Western Europe when referring to the Cold War–and post–Cold War division of Europe, but use small letters when referencing the geographical pre–Cold War precursors of what, after World War II, roughly became the First and Second World.

5 Differences between Ukraine's major social groups who identify ethnically as Russian or Ukrainian, were mobilized to the point of military conflict after Ukrainian president Viktor Yanukovych refused to sign an association agreement with the European Union in 2013. The subsequent Euromaidan protests in Kiev led to the election of a new Ukrainian president, Petro Poroshenko, in 2014. Russia used the political chaos of the transitional government to annex the Crimean Peninsula,

and pro-Russian separatists occupied eastern Ukrainian cities to demand greater regional self-control and Ukrainian federalization. The intrusion of the new Russia into Ukraine has expanded upon Soviet imperialism toward its former republics and various Eastern European nations, which has been theorized through the lens of postcolonial theory.

6 The term postsocialism (rather than postcommunism) is used to denote the common, yet heterogeneous histories of state socialism and its aftermath in the unevenly aligned (or non-aligned) countries of Central and Eastern Europe (CEE) and the USSR (Suchland 2011, 837). The term postcommunism has been employed to primarily focus on the transitions of formerly socialist nations to capitalism.

7 Diasporic forms of migration are particularly characteristic for those of Jewish descent because Israeli and German immigration law favored their entry based on their ethnic descent. The Law of Return in Israel qualifies new arrivals for citizenship if they have one Jewish grandparent, and it also enables the entry of non-Jewish relatives. Immigrants from the former Soviet Union with one Jewish parent are similarly allowed to enter Germany along with their immediate family, even though requirements have been tightened since 2005.

8 In 1990, 92.3 percent of all post-Soviet migrants came as refugees. In 1999, that percentage had declined to 43.9, and a quarter of the arriving post-USSR migrants came as family members of US citizens, some of whom had earlier arrived as refugees (Logan and Rivera 2011, 30).

9 Approximately 160,000 Soviet Jews were granted refugee visas for the United States between 1970 and 1989 (Cohen et al. 2011, 9). Researchers who incorporate arrivals since 1989 estimate that the number of Soviet Jews who came to the United States is between 300,000 and 750,000 (Berger 2011). Approximately half of Soviet Jewish immigrants in the United States have immigrated since 1990 (Zeltzer-Zubida and Kasinitz, 2005, 194). After 1989, most post-Soviet immigrants to the United States had to rely on family reunification to obtain visas, and only 50,000 persons annually have been allowed to enter as refugees from the former Soviet Union, most of them of Jewish descent (Cohen et al. 2011, 8, 10). Priority was given to applicants with sponsorship in the United States (Clymer 2013).

10 Unauthorized immigrants constituted 26.3 percent of the overall US foreign-born population in 2012, while naturalized immigrants made up 73.7 percent, legal permanent residents 27.4 percent, and temporary legal residents 4.5 percent (Passel and Cohn 2014). According to the Department of Homeland Security, of the more than 41 million foreign-born people living in the United States in 2013, about 30 million were naturalized citizens, permanent residents, and legal residents.

11 The Pew Research Center estimated that 600,000 undocumented immigrants from Canada and Europe lived in the United States in 2012. That number is larger than populations from the Caribbean (550,000), from "the Middle East, Africa, and Other" (400,000), and close to the number of migrants from South America (700,000) (Passel and Cohn 2014).

12 Dissidents of Vladimir Putin's increasingly undemocratic regime and LGBTQ migrants seeking asylum continue to come (Armitage 2014; Krupkin 2015). Russia's recent economic downturn following the drop in oil prices and armed conflicts in Ukraine may spur more out-migration.

13 Despite their high rates of education and participation in a wide variety of occupations, Soviet women were discriminated against in terms of pay and promotion and were expected to take on domestic and care giving responsibilities in addition to their full-time jobs (Logan and Rivera 2011, 26).

14 The literature of "white confession" by writers like Peggy McIntosh (2004) and Ruth Frankenberg (1993) represents the earliest forms of whiteness scholarship. This work argued that white feminists had overlooked the importance of race in connection with gender inequality because they were largely unaware of their own privileges as white (largely middle-class) women.

15 In comparison to the over 3 million immigrants from Ireland who arrived between 1840 and 1890, 18 million immigrants from eastern and southern Europe came between 1890 and 1920 (Barrett and Roediger 1997, 3).

16 Between 1908 and 1909, 10,455 ethnic Russian immigrants also came to the United States but many returned to Russia. Among the prerevolutionary immigrant peasants were Carpatho-Rusyns from the Austro-Hungarian empire who spoke a dialect of Great Russian and considered themselves Russian. The Russian Orthodox Church converted many of them away from the Greek Catholic Church (Manchester 2015).

17 The Chinese Exclusion Act prohibited the admission of new arrivals on the basis of their geographical origin and biological descent, which made them ineligible for naturalization. The extension of this law to immigrants from other parts of Asia in 1923 led to the determination that Indian immigrants were nonwhite and thus ineligible for US citizenship because their origin in Asia overrode their "Caucasian racial ancestry" (Koshy 2012). The identification of whiteness with European origin was also used to initially deny legalization to some immigrants from present-day Syria until the 1915 Supreme Court decision *Dow v. United States* that "inhabitants of a portion of Asia, including Syria, were to be classed as white persons."

18 Migrants from the Pale largely came with urban, commercial, craft, and manufacturing skills (Brodkin Sacks 2010), and the women were accomplished needle workers (Glenn 1990, 5, 9). They and other eastern European Jews received substantial support from their more established central European coreligionsts who provided newcomers with an avenue for economic mobility that was not available to any other immigrant group. Central European Jews had arrived in the 1840s and 1850s, mainly from Germany. Unlike their contemporaries, the Irish immigrants, they had been a small group who acculturated quickly (Gold 1999, 124–125), and by the time eastern Europeans arrived, they owned most of the garment industry on the East Coast. Because central European Jews considered themselves racially similar to the new arrivals from eastern Europe, they provided

them with economic support, hired them in their factories, and mobilized against the passage of immigration restrictions, while also engaging in attempts at Americanizing the new arrivals (Gold 1998, 26). Unlike Italians or non-Jewish eastern Europeans who tended to occupy positions in between their fellow black workers and white (often Irish or German) supervisors or union leaders, eastern European Jewish women labored alongside the smaller numbers of Italian women in the largely Jewish-owned garment industry or in apartment-based sweatshops, and the men worked as petty tradesmen and peddlers (Goldstein 2006; Diner 2015). They either did not live in the same neighborhoods as African Americans or resided there as merchants or peddlers rather than as fellow tenants (Diner 2015, 78). In the rural South, peddlers sold their wares on plantations and contributed to the emergence of an autonomous economy among slaves (Diner 2015, 102). Jewish peddlers were compared to their Yankee predecessors, while Irish and Italian immigrants tended to be depicted as similar to African Americans (Diner 2015, 77).

19 However, throughout the 1960s discrimination persisted toward Jewish Americans. Restrictive covenant clauses in real estate titles that limited the sale or transfer of property to members of certain groups were intended to bar Jews from some of New York City's most desirable suburban neighborhoods. They were prohibited from joining social and athletic clubs; excluded from white collar and professional jobs in law, insurance, and accounting; and they also suffered discrimination in employment as well as quota systems on admission to private colleges, universities, and medical schools (Foner 2005, 17–19; Gold 1998, 122–23).

20 Russians first came to Alaska, where they engaged in the fur trade, converted indigenous people to Orthodoxy, and transliterated indigenous languages. After the acquisition of Alaska in 1867 by the United States, some Russians went to California. All Slavic peoples within Czarist Russia were seen as "Russians" (Satzewich 288).

CHAPTER 1. THE POST-SOVIET DIASPORA ON TRANSNATIONAL REALITY TV

1 In a 2001 episode of *The Sopranos*, for example, members of the "family" encounter a mobster who turns out to be a former member of the Russian military and who seemingly cannot be killed.

2 The linkage between terrorism and the "Russian mafia" or the Russian government also recycles tropes that connected turn of the twentieth century migrants, primarily Irish, Italians, eastern European Jews and their descendants, to notions of organized crime. In the case of Jewish immigrants from eastern Europe, this association dates back to the flourishing of criminal activity in New York City in the late nineteenth and early twentieth centuries (Orleck 2001, 131). Crimes committed by a small group of immigrants from the Soviet Union in New York City during the 1970s and 1980s also came to be understood as the activities of a "Russian mafia," which was supposedly engaged in organized crime (Finckenauer and Waring 1998).

3 As late as season 8 (2010) of *24*, Jack Bauer was still fighting members of Russia's government and the "Russian mafia," which was now making common cause with Muslim Arabs in trying to transport nuclear arms to a fictional Islamic Republic. In the show's reprise as *24: Live Another Day* in 2014, Bauer was taken hostage by forces working for the Russian government.

4 The ease with which formats travel across national borders parallels the explicitly international roots of reality TV. Initially, most formats were developed in Western Europe and the United States and were then sold and adapted to other national contexts (Murray and Ouellette 2009; Moran 2009). While some scholars trace the inception of reality TV to the United States's 1990s series *The Real World*, others argue that the genre only arrived in the United States in 2000 with adaptations of the Dutch *Big Brother* and the Swedish *Survivor* (Madger 2004, 143).

5 For scholarship on *US DWTS* that focuses on issues of gender, ethnicity, and disability, see Quinlan and Bates 2008; Uba 2007; and McMains 2010.

6 In recent seasons, the BBC's original *Strictly Come Dancing* hired nine USSR-born professionals, including Oksana Platero (a Ukrainian-born dancer who lives in the United States and is married to a fellow Latina/o dancer), Katya Jones (an ethnically Korean, Russian-born dancer), Kristina Rihanoff, Aliona Vilani, Iveta Lukosiute, Anya Garnis, Artem Chigvintsev, Pasha Kovalev, Lilia Kopylova, and Gleb Savchenko. Taken as a group, these dancers have won the show more often than its thirteen British-born professionals (Creighton 2015).

7 Since Ukraine's independence, successive governments have attempted to displace the Russian language from its dominant position in large parts of Ukraine. In the 1996 constitution, Ukrainian is mentioned as the only state language (Kolstø 1999), and under Viktor Yushchenko (2004–2010) Ukrainian was declared the sole language in courts, state services, and universities. Viktor Yanukovych (2010–2014) had pledged to improve the status of Russian, but stopped short of elevating it to a second state language, and at his inauguration in 2014 the current president, Petro Poroshenko, insisted that Ukrainian remain the country's sole state language.

8 In 2011, during the airing of *Russian Dolls*, Levitis was sentenced to three years' probation for the felony charge of making false statements to federal officials in connection with the federal corruption probe of Brooklyn Senator Carl Kruger.

9 In her description of *Russian Dolls*, Dizik (2011) wrote, "Having the opportunity to mash up something as Russian as Brighton Beach with something as American as reality TV really drives home the fact that there's a place where KGB-era ways and Kim Kardashian can meet. And what's more American than that?" Dizik even moves beyond superficial stereotypes of a "Russian" identity by referring to other examples of "Russian American" culture, such as "Russian-speaking Mila Kunis" and Russian American novelist Gary Shteyngart's novel *Super Sad True Love Story* (2010).

10 In a twist that highlights how the show confuses domestic and global forms of race and racialization, *DWTS* announced the hiring of a black South African

dancer, Keoikantse (Keo) Motsepeas, as the show's first "professional of color," despite the fact that Cheryl Burke, a dancer with roots in the Philippines, had been a regular for eighteen seasons.

CHAPTER 2. HIGHLY SKILLED AND MARRIAGE MIGRANTS IN ARIZONA

1 For work on Protestant post-Soviet immigrants on the West Coast, see Hardwick (2001, 2002, 2008).

2 The Census probably undercounts small communities. The Russian-speaking immigrants in Arizona I interviewed believed that their numbers in the state are much higher.

3 I asked: "When did you arrive in the US? What were the legal circumstances that allowed you to migrate? What have been the main obstacles that you experienced as an international migrant? Have you experienced any kind of negativity toward you (or your family) because you are an international migrant or because you are from the former USSR? Has this background ever become an issue? Do you have any connections to other migrants from your home country? What percentage of your friends do you think is of the same national or ethnic background? How often do you travel back home? With whom do you keep in closest contact in your home country in addition to your family? How often do you contact them? How are you staying in touch with them? Are you following major events in your home country? Why or why not? Do you think your home country is doing well now? Does it have a bright future, especially compared with the US? Why/why not? As of now, are you considering returning to your home country to live or work at some point? Why or why not? If you plan to go back, what are the main reasons you would make this decision? Are you aware of your home country's policies and programs to recruit those who received a foreign education? Do you think they are effective? Why or why not?"

4 Recent work (Waters et al. 2010) has challenged segmentation theory by asserting that rather than the overall level of ethnic embeddedness or selective acculturation, it is the maintenance of coethnic ties within socioeconomically heterogeneous immigrant communities that is predictive of upward mobility for their members.

5 I audiotaped and coded the interviews according to the order of the interviews and the gender of the participant.

6 One of the interviewees from Russia had grown up in Kazakhstan until his early teens but was ethnically Russian.

7 The next largest group of my interviewees (five participants) had arrived on F-1 student visas to obtain graduate or undergraduate degrees at a US university, and hailed from Russia, Belarus, and Kazakhstan.

8 Three other participants also arrived on K-2 visas as dependent children of marriage migrants.

9 Another interviewee who had come as a dependent of a marriage migrant (on a K-2 visa) provided similar reasons for his family's emigration; his mother wanted

to ensure that he could avoid military service and study at a good US university. Like many marriage migrants, she had met her US husband via the Internet. One of the highly skilled participants I interviewed also mentioned that she had left the former USSR so her son could avoid the military draft.

10 Another participant who was trained as a chemist in the former USSR and then took several postdoctoral appointments, first in Western Europe and then in the United States, referred to the existence of a similar program. He worked at a private IT company that contracted with the US Department of Energy to help prevent Russian scientists from moving to countries considered to be US security risks, by assisting them in their search for nonmilitary jobs in Russia.

11 According to a 2010 Department of Education report, the latest of its kind, 51.6 percent of contingent faculty were women, and 81.9 percent of contingent faculty were white, that is, I presume US Americans who self-identify as white (Knapp et al. 2010).

12 This migration mirrors in reverse the gendered and racialized outsourcing of US service and IT jobs to call centers in India, which predominantly hire women. While call center workers enjoy relatively decent working conditions in terms of compensation and safety, they are paid significantly less than US workers in the same jobs, in part because of their racialized (non-Western) status (Bonacich et al. 2008, 350–351). In addition, these workers are subjected to the psychological stress of having to change their names and adopt fictional US identities in order to create the appearance of a (white) US work force for US customers (Bonacich et al. 2008, 351).

13 Their spouses are granted H-4 dependent status, which does not permit them to work, while a J-2 dependent visa status allows holders to apply for a work permit.

14 Figures for the category of "temporary workers," which was used in the US Census before 2006, however, were highest in 2002, with 9,500 Russians and 1,700 Ukrainians.

15 In comparison, in the same year, 13,000 Russians, 2,000 Ukrainians, and 3,500 Kazakhs entered the United States on F-1 student visas, which represented a significant increase from the 4,000 Russians who came on this type of visa in 2006.

16 Data are available at www.dhs.gov. The 2014 numbers invert the proportion of Russian and Ukrainian women who came as marriage migrants throughout the 1990s. In 1996, for example, 1,000 Russian and 733 Ukrainian women arrived on K-1 visas and a much smaller number, 228, came from other post-Soviet nations.

17 The contemporary "war on terrorism" has led to the further criminalization of transnational marriages and initiated their association with undocumented labor migration, human trafficking, and terrorism. Potential terrorists are suspected of using marriage migration to enter the United States (D'Aoust 2009, 21). The 2015 terrorist attacks in San Bernardino, California, illustrated how these fears led to calls for restrictions on marriage migration. Syed Rizwan Farook, a US-born second-generation immigrant of Pakistani descent, and his wife Tashfeen Malik, a Pakistani-born woman whom Farook met online and brought to the United

States on a fiancé visa, committed the deadliest terrorist attack since 9/11 until the June 2016 Orlando nightclub shooting. The couple had become radicalized several years prior to the attack, primarily through the Internet, and amassed large stockpiles of weapons, ammunition, and bomb-making equipment.

CHAPTER 3. THE DESIRE FOR ADOPTIVE INVISIBILITY

1 Few in the US press mentioned that the very public spectacle of his "return" repeated Artyom Savelyev's earlier experiences of relinquishment. In Artyom's adoptive home, where he was homeschooled, he was often punished and everything was prohibited, including raising his voice, playing, or leaving the house (Savodnik 2010).

2 The number of children adopted from Ukraine in 2013, 2014, 2015, and 2016 was 431, 521, 303, and 301 respectively, compared to 2,306, 2,040, 2,354, 2,231 from China, and 993, 716, 335, and 182 from Ethiopia (US Department of State, n.d.). In 2015 and 2014, 318 and 370 children respectively, were adopted from South Korea, a much larger number than the 138 and 182 children adopted in 2013 in 2016 (US Department of State, n.d.).

3 The focus on the problem behaviors of Eastern European adoptees often relies on questionable "adoption experts," such as Joyce Sterkel who runs the "Ranch for Kids" in Montana. A 2007 *Newsweek* article on the death of Russian adoptee Nina Hilt at the hands of her adoptive mother, quotes Sterkel as saying: "It's a horrible thing, but I understand how some people end up killing these kids. . . . They have no empathy, no affection, no love. My heart goes out to these parents because they don't know what to do" (Wingert 2007). Sterkel was also invited on a 2010 CBS Morning Show entitled "Adoption Outrage," which was devoted to the Artyom Savelyev case. Here she stated that adoptive parents of children with health and mental disorders have few ways of terminating their parental rights, thus justifying Torry Ann Hansen's actions. Psychological and medical scholarly research, however, has found only small differences between adopted and nonadopted individuals in terms of problem behaviors, mental health referrals, academic achievement, and cognitive performance (Bimmel et al. 2003; Juffer and van IJzendoorn 2005; van IJzendoorn et al. 2005; McCall et al. 2016).

4 For social sciences scholarship that has examined the identity formation of Eastern European adoptees in the United States (and Australia), see Jacobson 2008; Linville and Lyness 2007; and Scherman and Harré 2008).

5 For humanities work, see Eng 2003; Homans 2006; Novy 2005; Jerng 2006 and 2010. For social sciences work, see Lee 2003; Lee et al. 2006; and Yoon 2004.

6 Earlier US memoirs of Eastern European adoption include Dann 1998; Klose 1999; and Cooke Newman 2001. While the authors of these memoirs already eschew humanitarianism as a motivation for their adoptions from Eastern Europe, rely on independent adoption facilitators rather than agencies, and foreground the need for cultural proximity between parent and child through their own (often several generations-removed) immigrant backgrounds, they do not as clearly

employ the same consumerist logic of a global whiteness as the three adoption memoirs discussed in this chapter.

7 A 2015 article put the number of Russian adoptees killed by their adoptive parents at nineteen. According to a 2007 publication, between 1996 and 2007 eighteen internationally adopted children died at the hands of their adoptive parents, fourteen of whom were adopted from Russia, two from China, and two from Guatemala. Since the publication of the article, four more Russian children are documented to have died in the United States: fourteen-month-old Nikolai Emelyantsev, twenty-one-month-old Chase Harrison (born Dmitry Yakovlev), and seven-year-old Ivan Skorobogatov, renamed Nathaniel Craver (Craft n.d.), which would bring the number of post-USSR child victims to eighteen. The larger number of nineteen deaths cited in the 2015 article also includes the 2008 death of twenty-two-month-old Harrison Chase (Dimitry Yakolev) who was left in a hot car by his father, and the 2013 death of three-year-old Max Shatto (Maxim Kuzmin) whose passing was declared accidental by Texas authorities. The authors state that most of the killed children were boys under three years of age, had been in adoptive homes for short periods of time, and were thus unable to communicate well (Hegar et al. 2015). In addition to the documented child deaths, an unknown number of Eastern European adoptees in the United States have been (sexually) abused, with only some cases attracting media attention.

8 While Romania allowed only 30 intercountry adoptions in 1989, in 1990, the year after the execution of Nicolae Ceaușescu, it let more than 10,000 children leave the country (Kapstein 2003, 116). Until it ended adoption in 2001, Romania remained a significant source of children adopted to the United States; in 1999 and 2000 it ranked fifth after Russia, China, South Korea, and Guatemala with 611 and 1,119 adopted children, respectively (US Department of State, n.d.).

9 After Hansen and his wife rejected the possibility of adoption from Korea, they worked with an independent lawyer (of "Eastern European extraction") who falsely promised assistance with an adoption from Romania despite the country's 2001 moratorium on adoption. Here Hansen already revealed his preference for "unproblematic" white Eastern European identities that guided his later choice of Russian adoptees. Even though he knew it exemplifies "the last bastion of unapologetic prejudice," the couple decided not to adopt a Roma child so as to avoid having to "to pack all those crystal balls in your luggage. That, and you probably don't want your own kid trying to pick your pocket all the time" (99). When they did not advance in their quest to adopt from Romania, Hansen faulted the moratorium and the "virulent and xenophobic anti-international adoption lobby that exists in Romania, whose position seems to be that we foreigners want to use their children as sex toys" (101).

10 For example, Reid's adoption agency failed to communicate reports about the health status of some of the referred children and allowed a board member to circumvent Russian law requiring that both parents travel to the country to adopt.

11 Brooks Hansen, "The Boy in the Red Hat," *Brooks Hansen* (August 21, 2008), www.brookshansen.com.

12 Brooks Hansen, "Commencement Speech—May 27, 2012: 'The Trouble with Instinct,'" *Brooks Hansen* (May 27), www.brookshansen.com.

13 For work examining parents' efforts to maintain their adopted children's "birth culture," see Dorow 2006 and 2010; Howell 2007; and Jacobson 2008.

14 "Adopting Children from Ukraine," *Tryukraine.com: The Do-It-Yourself Guide to Ukraine* (n.d.), www.tryukraine.com. Copyright 2003–2017.

15 Schwartz writes, for example, "Tonight I will say a special prayer of thanks to the boys' birth parents who cared enough to surrender their children so that they could find their forever home. . . . [T]ell them that I will always be grateful for the gift they have given to me, and I will treasure their children until my dying day" (153).

16 On his website which was soon blocked, Krueger also highlighted his desire to adopt from Ukraine so he could have a white child, writing that "I chose the Ukraine because that is the only country in the world that would allow a single man to adopt a Caucasian child" ("John Krueger's Story" 2003).

17 The inside jacket features Pertman's blurb for the book: "A beautifully crafted, deeply insightful, painfully honest, and sometimes disturbing book. . . . I couldn't stop turning the pages." And Bartholet writes, "A moving, wise, and powerful account of the agony, joy, and moral complexity at the heart of parenting by choice that adoption is."

CHAPTER 4. FICTIONS OF IRREGULAR POST-SOVIET MIGRATION

1 For an exception, see the 2011 special issue of *Slavic and East European Journal*, which attempts to integrate post-USSR literature into the "study of the Russian literary canon in a transnational modernity" (Glaser 2011, 15).

2 Derek Parker Royal has explained in more detail that the fiction of what he calls "Russian émigrés" reasserts many concepts of Jewish American literature, such as a focus on "the in-between status of the immigrant, struggles between old world and new world mentality, guilt and shame generated by intergenerational conflicts, and ethno-religious marginalization" (2012, 239).

3 Other post-USSR literature explores both family migration and the arrival of single individuals from the former USSR. Lara Vapnyar's novel *Memoirs of a Muse* (2006), and her two story collections *There Are Jews in My House* (2003) and *Broccoli and Other Tales of Food and Love* (2008), for example, focus largely on family migration. But one of her stories, "Borscht," explores the lives of temporary migrants in New York City who came to the United States solely with the intention of sending remittances to their families in Russia. Like Krasikov's and Ulinich's protagonists, the male character works in construction, while the female protagonist is a transnational mother who works as a live-in nanny and housekeeper, and also makes money through prostitution. Asked about this story in an interview, Vapnyar has said that this "is a very common story, people come to

United States and stay there illegally, work very hard jobs. Lots of women come who work as babysitters and have to leave their families in Russia" (Vapnyar 2011b).

4 In 2005, Eastern Europe ranked third in receiving remittances, following Asia and Latin America/the Caribbean. The top five Eastern European recipients were the Russian Federation, Ukraine, Serbia, Poland, and Montenegro (Robila 2010, 15, 112).

5 For a similar diasporic perspective, see Gershenson and Shneer (2009); and Ryan (2011).

6 Yelena Akhtiorskaya, author of *Panic in a Suitcase* (2014), has set her work in the tradition of Jewish American immigrant novelists such as Henry Roth, a first-generation immigrant author who arrived in the early twentieth century from the Austro-Hungarian empire, and Charles Reznikoff, the US-born son of immigrants from Russia's Pale of Settlement. He was born a few years before Roth arrived in the United States (Fillar 2015).

7 Anya Ulinich, Public Reading from *Petropolis*, November 11, 2012, Arizona State University.

8 Ulinich, Public Reading.

9 Personal conversation with the author, November 11, 2012.

10 Post-Screening Q&A of Ruth Leitman's documentary film *Tony and Janina's American Wedding* (2010) with the filmmaker, April 12, 2011, Arizona State University.

CHAPTER 5. THE POST-SOVIET DIASPORA IN COMPARATIVE PERSPECTIVE

1 Fifty-eight percent of the estimated 11.2 million unauthorized immigrants in the United States are from Mexico, and just over half (51%) of all current Mexican immigrants are unauthorized (Passel et al. 2012, 12). In 2015, the Pew Research Center estimated that about half of the undocumented immigrant population was from Mexico (5.9 million), followed by Guatemala (675,000), India (450,000), Honduras (350,000), China (300,000), and the Philippines (200,000) (Passel and Cohn 2014). As the number of Mexicans leaving is now higher than those arriving, migrants from Central America account for a higher share of the new immigrants.

2 The criminalization of immigration violations is a result of changes in the treatment of migrants who are apprehended within a hundred miles of the US-Mexico border. They are now formally processed and their apprehensions are documented before they agree to "voluntary removals" so that they can potentially be prosecuted in federal court for reentry. This change was put in effect so as to counter criticism that the Obama administration was not sufficiently tough on immigration. In contrast, the number of deportations of migrants who are settled and working in the United States has fallen steadily since Obama took office, decreasing more than 40 percent since 2009 (Bennett 2016). Expedited US deportation proceedings in which incarcerated migrants can neither examine nor

confront evidence of their detention not only deprive them of US legal protections, but also deny them the human right of equal treatment and protections
before criminal courts. In addition, at the Mexico-US border, deaths have by far
surpassed the number of casualties recorded in the mid-1980s from drowning
(mostly in the Río Grande) or from homicide and auto-pedestrian accidents in
the late 1980s (Eschbach et al. 2003). While they have somewhat declined in the
context of overall decreases in Mexican migration (Gonzáles 2012), in the last
fifteen years at least 5,513 bodies were discovered, including 463 in 2012 (Spagat
2013). Between January and October 2015, 117 bodies were found along migration
routes in southern Arizona compared with 108 in 2014, 168 in 2013, 156 in 2012,
and 223 in 2010 (Duara 2015).

3 According to the 2010 Census, over 2 million immigrants have come from former
East Bloc nations, half of whom are from the former Soviet Union.

4 On recent comparative work in critical race theory, see Cacho 2012. On Afro-
Asian work, see Mullen 2004; Jung 2006; Koshy 2001; Lye 2008; and Raphael-
Hernandez and Steen 2006. On comparative work on Latina/os and African
Americans, see Milian 2013; and Dzidzienyo and Oboler 2005.

5 While Irish immigrants largely abstained from or condemned the mobbing of
free blacks and abolitionists in the 1820s, by the 1850s they supported proslavery
Democrats. Rather than competition in the job market, immigrants' attitudes
were fueled by fears stoked by Democrats that the emancipation of black slaves
would lead to a larger supply of unskilled laborers (Roediger 2008, 150, 278–
279). Similarly, politicians on the West Coast mobilized Irish leaders to support
Chinese exclusion, while on the East Coast Irish immigrants were largely indif-
ferent to the issue and did not contribute to the passage of the law (Gyory 1998,
14–15). Even though his work largely focuses on instances of racial hostility,
Thomas Guglielmo has also shown that Italians initially engaged in amicable
relations with African Americans and with the Mexican migrants who started
to arrive in Chicago in the mid-1930s, and that a large majority abstained from
joining the Chicago Color Riot of 1919 or identified with its African American
victims. The Italian language press condemned the killings of African Americans and the exclusion of Asian immigrants. Only when more sizable numbers
of African Americans arrived north at the onset of World War I and the 1924
passage of the Johnson-Reed Act virtually ended human movement from
Europe,did interactions between these two populations increase and turn more
negative (T. Guglielmo 2003).

6 Italians seemed to have deduced the idea that the Quota Laws were primarily
directed against Jews from the congressional debates of 1924, in which proponents
of restrictions targeted eastern European Jews, stressing that they were opposed to
intermarriages and participated in radical political movements (MacDonald 1998,
323).

7 I asked: "How do you see your situation as an international migrant in relationship to other immigrants in the United States, and specifically in Arizona? What

do you think about the current or proposed new immigration laws in Arizona,
e.g. SB 1070?"

8 However, the novel also attends to differences among Korean immigrant families
by portraying Lenny's friend Grace, a second-generation Korean immigrant, who
grew up in the Midwest with physician parents who "dispensed love and encouragement in the manner of the kindest, most progressive native-born" (163).

9 Among others, this association obscures the fact that Korean, Vietnamese, and
Filipina/o Americans have median incomes below the general population and
that Chinese Americans have above average poverty rates (Mahajan 2015).

10 The ILIR follows in the footsteps of the Irish Immigration Reform Movement
(IIRM), which was formed in 1987. IIRM originally set out to secure amnesty
for undocumented Irish immigrants in the United States, but achieved a more
influential position by coalescing with other initiatives to help immigrants from
all countries disadvantaged by the 1965 Immigration Act.

11 Mexican Americans in Dallas, Texas, for example, lived with de facto school segregation because of their racialization as nonwhite, which only changed when the
state superintendent of education in 1940 decreed that children of Latin American
extraction be classified as white and have the right to attend white schools (Phillips 2006, 126).

CONCLUSION

1 The Tsarnaevs never resided in Chechnya, but the father considered himself
to be of Chechen descent while growing up in Kyrgyzstan because his family
was relocated from Chechnya under the Stalin regime. In 1992, when Tamerlan
was six, the Tsarnaevs reportedly tried to move to Chechnya, but they returned
soon thereafter because the first war between Moscow and regional separatists
had broken out. Dzhokhar was born in 1993 in Kyrgyzstan. In 1999 the family
moved to neighboring Dagestan, his mother's home. In 2002 they immigrated to
the United States. The parents returned to Dagestan in 2012, but their two sons
and two daughters remained in the United States. When the US press used the
term "Chechen" to designate the Tsarnaevs, they initially borrowed the family's
self-identification, which is rooted in notions of ethnicity specific to Soviet and
post-Soviet immigrants that got lost in translation in the US media context. The
brothers' uncle was the first to identify the family as "Chechen." On Dzhokhar's
media page on the Russian-language social network Vkonte, which is popular
in the former USSR and among members of the post-Soviet diaspora, he posted
video messages sympathetic to the cause of Chechen independence and declared
that he spoke Chechen in addition to Russian and English. His brother Tamerlan
was identified as a "Chechen" boxer by photographer Johannes Hirn, who profiled
him as he was training for a boxing match in 2010 (Zirin 2013). While the US
press used the term "Chechen" to refer to the Tsarnaev brothers, in other national
contexts immigrants of similar background are more accurately identified as
"Russians of Chechen descent" (Marlowe 2015).

2 The brothers' designation as Chechen also hints at the history of Chechen sepa-
   ratism in post-Soviet Russia and its association with terrorist suicide attacks of
   the early 2000s, with which most US Americans are less familiar. This connection
   also explains the significant rise in the numbers of Russians who joined radical
   Islamist groups fighting in Iraq and Syria. Between 2014 and 2015, the numbers of
   those from areas of the Northern Caucasus, Chechnya, and Dagestan rose to third
   place after those from Tunisia and Saudi Arabia, and far surpassed the numbers of
   Western Europeans (Brannen 2015).
3 This is also true for discussions of right-wing acts of terrorism in the United
   States.
4 Before the bombings, Tamerlan visited Dagestan where his parents had returned
   around 2012, By this time the region was dominated by a low-level Islamist insur-
   gency led by groups who opposed the traditional Sufism of the Caucasus region.

BIBLIOGRAPHY

"Adopted Siberian Boy's Death Is Investigated in New Jersey." 2000. *New York Times* November 16. www.nytimes.com.

"Adoptive Mother Given 25 Years for Killing 2-Year-Old Daughter." *WRAL.com.* May 25, 2006. www.wral.com.

Akhtiorskaya, Yelena. 2014. *Panic in a Suitcase.* New York: Riverhead.

Alba, Richard. 2009. *Blurring the Color Line: The New Chance for a More Integrated America.* Cambridge: Harvard University Press.

Alba, Richard, and Victor Nee. 2003. *Remaking the American Mainstream: Assimilation and Contemporary Immigration.* Cambridge: Harvard University Press.

Alba, Richard, and Mary Waters, eds. 2011. *The Next Generation: Immigrant Youth in a Comparative Perspective.* New York: NYU Press.

Alexander, Reagan. 2011. "Maksim Chmerkovskiy Wants Hope Solo as His Next *DWTS* Partner." *People* July 17. www.people.com.

Alston, Joshua. 2010. "America's New Icons." *Newsweek* August 2: 51–57.

Angeles, Leonora, and Sirijit Sunanta. 2007. "'Exotic Love at Your Fingertips': Intermarriage Websites, Gendered Representation, and the Transnational Migration of Filipino and Thai Women." *Kasarinlan: Philippine Journal of Third World Studies* 22(1): 3–31.

Aranda, Elizabeth, and Elizabeth Vaquera. 2011. "Unwelcomed Immigrants: Experiences with Immigration Officials and Attachment to the United States." *Journal of Contemporary Criminal Justice* 27(3): 299–321.

Armitage, Susie. 2014. "Vladimir Putin's LGBT Refuseniks." *BuzzFeed News* April 13. www.buzzfeed.com.

Atanasoski, Neda. 2013. *Humanitarian Violence: The U.S. Deployment of Diversity.* Minneapolis: University of Minnesota Press.

The Bachelor [*Kholostiak*], Episode no. 2.13, March 31, 2012.

———. Episode no. 1, 6, 9, 13, June 9, March 17, April 21, and May 12, 2011.

Ball, Deborah Yarskike, and Theodore P. Gerber. 2005. "Russian Scientists and Rogue States: Does Western Assistance Reduce the Proliferation Threat?" *International Security* 29(4): 50–77.

Banerjee, Payal. 2006. "Indian Information Technology Workers in the United States: The H-1B Visa, Flexible Production, and the Racialization of Labor." *Critical Sociology* 32(2–3): 425–445.

Banerjee, Payal, and Frank Ridzi. 2008. "Indian IT Workers and Black TANF Clients in the New Economy: A Comparative Analysis of the Racialization of Immigration and Welfare Policies in the US." *Race, Gender & Class* 15(2): 98–114.

Barnes, Brooks. 2011. "Re-Alignment of Star Power." *New York Times* September 25. www.nytimes.com.

Barrett, James R., and David Roediger. 1997. "In between Peoples: Race, Nationality and the 'New Immigrant' Working Class." *Journal of American Ethnic History* 54(3): 3–44.

Bartholet, Elizabeth. 1993. *Family Bonds: Adoption and the Politics of Parenting.* Boston: Houghton Mifflin.

Bellin, Roger. 2016. "Techno-Anxiety as New Middlebrow." In *The Poetics of Genre in the Contemporary Novel*, ed. Tim Lanzendörfer, 115–126. London: Lexington Books.

Bennett, Brian. 2016. "High Deportation Figures Are Misleading." *Los Angeles Times* October 19. www.latimes.com.

Berger, Paul. 2013. "How Many Russian Speakers Are in the U.S.?" *Forward* November 25. forward.com.

Berger, Joseph. 2003. "The Russians Are Coming, Stepping Lightly." *New York Times* June 11. www.nytimes.com.

Bergquist, Kathleen Ja Sook. 2009. "Operation Babylift or Babyabduction? Implications of the Hague Convention on the Humanitarian Evacuation and 'Rescue' of Children." *International Social Work* 52(5): 621–633.

Bimmel, Nicole, Femmie Juffer, Marinus H. van IJzendoorn, and Marian J. Bakermans-Kranenburg. 2003. "Problem Behavior of Internationally Adopted Adolescents: A Review and Meta-Analysis." *Harvard Review of Psychiatry* 11(2): 64–77.

Biressi, Anita, and Heather Nunn. 2005. *Reality TV: Realism and Revelation.* New York: Columbia University Press.

Black, Grant C., and Paula E. Stephan. 2010. "The Economics of University Science and the Role of Foreign Graduate Students and Postdoctoral Scholars." In *American Universities in a Global Market*, ed. Charles T. Clotfelter, 129–161. Chicago: University of Chicago Press.

Bonacich, Edna, Sabrina Alimahomed, and Jake B. Wilson. 2008. "The Racialization of Global Labor." *American Behavioral Scientist* 52(3): 342–355.

Bonnett, Alastair, and Anoop Nayak. 2003. "Cultural Geographies of Racialization: The Territory of Race." In *Handbook of Cultural Geographies*, eds. Kay Anderson, Mona Domosh, Steve Pile, and Nigel Thrift, 300–312. London: Sage.

Borshay Liem, Deann, dir. 2000. *First Person Plural.* Film. National Asian American Telecommunications Association.

Bosniak, Linda. 2006. *The Citizen and the Alien: Dilemmas of Contemporary Membership.* Princeton: Princeton University Press.

"Boys Adopted by John Krueger." 2006. *Pound Pup Legacy* April 13. www.poundpuplegacy.org.

Brannen, Kate. 2015. "Russians Are Joining ISIS in Droves." *Daily Beast* December 7. www.thedailybeast.com.

Briggs, Laura. 2006. "Making American Families: Transnational Adoption and U.S. Latin American Policy." In *Haunted by Empire: Geographies of Intimacy in North American History*, ed. Ann Laura Stoler, 344–365. Durham: Duke University Press.

Briggs, Laura, and Diana Marre. 2009. "Introduction: The Circulation of Children." In *International Adoption: Global Inequalities and the Circulation of Children*, ed. Laura Briggs and Diana Marre, 2–28. New York: NYU Press.

Brodkin Sacks, Karen. 2010. "How Jews Became White." In *Privilege: A Reader*, ed. Michael S. Kimmel and Abbey L. Ferber, 87–106. 2nd ed. Boulder: Westview Press.

Brown, Marshall E. 2007. "Obsheena: A Communal Settlement in Central Arizona." *Past: Pioneer America Societal Transitions* 30: 24–34.

Bunkers, Kelley McCreery, Victor Groza, and Daniel P. Lauer. 2009. "International Adoption and Child Protection in Guatemala: A Case of the Tail Wagging the Dog." *International Social Work* 52(5): 649–660.

Cacho, Lisa Marie. 2012. *Social Death: Racialized Rightlessness and the Criminalization of the Unprotected*. New York: NYU Press.

Cantwell, Brendan. 2009. "International Postdocs: Education Migration and Academic Production in a Global Market." Ph.D. dissertation, University of Arizona.

———. 2011. "Academic In-Sourcing: International Postdoctoral Employment and New Modes of Academic Production." *Journal of Higher Education Policy and Management* 33(2): 101–114.

Carrión-Flores, Carmen E. 2006. "What Makes You Go Back Home? Determinants of the Duration of Migration of Mexican Immigrants in the United States." Society of Labor Economists Annual Meeting, Cambridge, Mass. www.aeaweb.org.

Carruthers, Susan L. 2009. *Cold War Captives: Imprisonment, Escape, and Brainwashing*. Berkeley: University of California Press.

Carter, Matt. 2012. "*Dancing with the Stars* Pro Maksim Chmerkovskiy: Intent on No Spray-Tanning." *Examiner* April 17. www.examiner.com.

Cartwright, Lisa. 2003. "Photographs of 'Waiting Children': The Transnational Adoption Market." *Social Text* 21(1): 83–109.

———. 2005. "Images of 'Waiting Children': Spectatorship and Pity in the Representation of the Global Social Orphan in the 1990s." In *Cultures of Transnational Adoption*, ed. Toby Alice Volkman, 185–212. Durham: Duke University Press.

Cassarino, Jean-Pierre. 2004. "Theorizing Return Migration: The Conceptual Approach to Return Migrants Revisited." *International Journal on Multicultural Societies* 6(2): 253–279.

Cave, Damien. 2011. "Better Lives for Mexicans Cut Allure of Going North." *New York Times* July 6. www.nytimes.com.

Chacón, Jennifer M. 2007. "Unsecured Borders: Immigration Restrictions, Crime Control and National Security." *Connecticut Law Review* 39: 1827–1832.

Chakravartty, Paula. 2006. "Symbolic Analysts or Indentured Servants? Indian High-Tech Migrants in America's Information Economy." *Knowledge, Technology & Policy* 19(3): 27–43.

Chen, Ming H. 2009. "Alienated: A Reworking of the Racialization Thesis after September 11." *American University Journal of Gender, Social Policy & Law* 18: 411–437.

"Chicago Metro Area Home to Nearly One Third of Polish Immigrants in the U.S." 2004. October 25. www.polish.org.

"Chicago Rally Country's Largest but Doesn't Top Last Year." 2007. *NBC5.com* May 2. www.nbc5.com.

Chin, Gabriel J., Carissa Byrne Hessick, Toni Massaro, and Marc L. Miller. 2011. "A Legal Labyrinth: Issues Raised by Arizona Senate Bill 1070." *Georgetown Immigration Law Journal* 25(1): 47–92.

Chmerkovskiy, Maksim. 2010a. "*Dancing's Maks*: Bruno Was 'Totally Out of Line.'" *TVGuide* October 3. www.tvguide.com.

———. 2010b. "*Dancing's Maks*: Carrie Ann Had No Right to Try to Spank Me." October 8. www.tvguide.com.

———. 2010c. "Don't Believe the Hype." December 16. www.maksimchmerkovskiy. blogspot.de.

Chozick, Amy. 2009. "Rippling Muscles on TV Dance Shows Are a Figment of Your Imagination." *Wall Street Journal* November 23. online.wsj.com.

Clymer, Adam. 2013. "Frank Lautenberg, New Jersey Senator in His 5th Term, Dies at 89." *New York Times* June 3. www.nytimes.com.

Cohen, Yinon, Yitchak Haberfeld, and Irena Kogan. 2011. "Who Went Where? Jewish Immigration from the Former Soviet Union to Israel, the USA and Germany, 1990–2000." *Israel Affairs* 17(1): 7–20.

Connolly, Kate. 2000. "Romania Lifts Lid on Babies for Sale Racket." *Guardian* October 30. www.guardian.co.uk.

Constable, Nicole. 2003. *Romance on a Global Stage: Pen Pals, Virtual Ethnography, and "Mail-Order" Marriages.* Berkeley: University of California Press.

Cooke Newman, Janis. 2001. *The Russian Word for Snow: A True Story of Adoption.* New York: St Martin's.

Cooper-Chen, Anne. 2005. "'A World of Millionaires': Global, Local, and 'Glocal' TV Game Shows." In *Global Entertainment Media: Content, Audiences, Issues*, ed. Anne Cooper-Chen, 237–251. London: Lawrence Erlbaum.

Craft, Carrie. n.d. "Several Russian Children Murder Cases Have Been by an Adoptive Parent." *About.com*. adoption.about.com.

Creighton, Sam. 2015. "*Strictly Come Dancing's* Russian Stars Reveal They Owe Their Success to the Soviet Union's Ruthless Regime That 'Groomed' Them to Be Champions." *Daily Mail* December 2. www.dailymail.co.uk.

Dancing with the Stars. 2011. ABC. Television. Episode no. 14,15, May 10.

Dann, Patty. 1998. *The Baby Boat: A Memoir of Adoption.* New York: Hyperion.

D'Aoust, Anne-Marie. 2009. "Love Stops at the Border: Marriage, Citizenship, and the Mail Order Brides Industry." Presentation at Penn Program on Democracy, Constitutionalism and Citizenship Workshop, Philadelphia, Pennsylvania. www. sas.upenn.edu.

Davis, Geoff. 2009. "Improving the Postdoctoral Experience: An Empirical Approach." In *Science and Engineering Careers in the United States: An Analysis of Markets and Employment*, ed. Richard B. Freeman and Daniel L. Goroff, 99–127. Chicago: University of Chicago Press.

de los Angeles Torres, Maria. 1988. "Working against the Miami Myth." *Nation* October 24.

Dell'Antonia, KJ. 2010. "I Did Not Love My Adopted Child: The Painful Truth about Adoption." *Slate* April 13. www.slate.com.

DeParle, Jason. 2010. "Arizona Is a Haven for Refugees." *New York Times* October 8. www.nytimes.com.

Department of Homeland Security. US Immigration and Customs Enforcement. 2014. "FY 2014 ICE Immigration Removals: Removals by Citizenship." www.ice.gov.

Dickens, Jonathan. 2002. "The Paradox of Inter-Country Adoption: Analysing Romania's Experience as a Sending Country." *International Journal of Social Welfare* 11(1): 77–83.

Diner, Hasia R. 2015. *Roads Taken: The Great Jewish Migrations to the New World and the Peddlers That Forged the Way*. New Haven: Yale University Press.

Dizik, Alina. 2011. "'Russian Dolls': I Really Can See Russia from My House." *Wall Street Journal* August 9. blogs.wsj.com.

Doane, Woody. 2003. "Rethinking Whiteness Studies." In *White Out: The Continuing Significance of Racism*, ed. Ashley W. Doane and Eduardo Bonilla-Silva, 3–18. New York: Routledge.

Dorow, Sarah K. 2006. *Transnational Adoption: A Cultural Economy of Race, Gender, and Kinship*. New York: NYU Press.

———. 2010. "Producing Kinship through the Marketplaces of Transnational Adoption." In *Baby Markets: Money and the New Politics of Creating Families*, ed. Michele Bratcher Goodwin, 69–83. Cambridge: Cambridge University Press.

Duara, Nigel. 2015. "Why Border Crossings Are Down but Deaths Are Up in Brutal Arizona Desert," *Los Angeles Times* October 21, www.latimes.com.

Dubinets, Elena. 2013. "'Other' Russianness as Hard Currency: Post-Soviet Russian Music Abroad." Presentation at the NEH Summer Seminar, America's Russian-Speaking Immigrants & Refugees: 20th Century Migration and Memory. Columbia University, New York, N.Y., June 28.

Dubrofsky, Rachel E. 2006. "*The Bachelor*: Whiteness in the Harem." *Critical Studies in Media Communication* 23(1): 39–56.

Duggan, Lisa. 2014. "Neoliberalism." In *Keywords for American Cultural Studies*, ed. Bruce Burgett and Glenn Handler, 181–183. New York: NYU Press.

Dzidzienyo, Anani, and Suzanne Oboler, eds. 2005. *Neither Enemies nor Friends: Latinos, Blacks, Afro-Latinos*. New York: Palgrave.

Eng, David L. 2003. "Transnational Adoption and Queer Diasporas: Two Mothers." *Social Text* 21(3): 1–37.

Eschbach, Karl, Jacqueline Hagan, and Nestor Rodriguez. 2003. "Deaths during Undocumented Migration: Trends and Policy Implications in the New Era of Homeland Security." *Defense of the Alien* 26: 37–52.

Fan, Lai-Tze. 2016. "The Digital Intensification of Postmodern Poetics." In *The Poetics of Genre in the Contemporary Novel*, ed. Tim Lanzendörfer, 35–56. London: Lexington Books.

Fillar, Diana. 2015. "An Interview with Yelena Akhtiorskaya." *Blue Mesa Review* www.bluemesareview.org.

Finckenauer, James O., and Elin J. Waring. 1998. *The Russian Mafia in America: Immigration, Culture, and Crime*. Ann Arbor: Northeastern University Press.

Follis, Karolina S. 2012. *Building Fortress Europe: The Polish-Ukrainian Frontier*. Philadelphia: University of Pennsylvania Press.

Foner, Nancy. 1997. "What's New about Transnationalism? New York Immigrants Today and at the Turn of the Century." *Diaspora* 6.3: 355–375.

———. 2005. *In a New Land: A Comparative View of Immigration*. New York: NYU Press.

Ford, Luke. 2008. "Russian Emigré Writer Sana Krasikov on Good & Evil." *lukeford.net* April 27. www.lukeford.net.

Fox, Cybelle, and Thomas A. Guglielmo. 2012. "Defining America's Racial Boundaries: Blacks, Mexicans, and European Immigrants, 1890–1945." *American Journal of Sociology* 118(2): 327–379.

Fox, Jon E., Laura Moroşanu, and Eszter Szilassy. 2012. "The Racialization of New European Migration to the UK." *Sociology* 46(4): 680–695.

Frankenberg, Ruth. 1993. *White Women, Race Matters: The Social Construction of Whiteness*. Minneapolis: University of Minnesota Press.

Fredrickson, Caroline. 2015. "There Is No Excuse for How Universities Treat Adjuncts." *Atlantic* September 15. www.theatlantic.com.

Freund, Daniel. 2012. *American Sunshine: Diseases of Darkness and the Quest for Natural Light*. Chicago: University of Chicago Press.

Friedman, James, ed. 2002. *Reality Squared: Televisual Discourses on the Real*. Newark: Rutgers University Press.

Furman, Andrew. 2008. "The Russification of Jewish-American Fiction." *Zeek* April 8. www.zeek.net.

Ganguli, Ina. 2013. "Saving Soviet Science: The Impact of Grants When Government R&D Funding Disappears." Unpublished paper.

———. 2015. "Immigration and Ideas: What Did Russian Scientists 'Bring' to the US?" *Journal of Labor Economics* 33(1): S257–288.

Gans, Herbert J. 2000. "Filling in Some Holes: Six Areas of Needed Immigration Research." In *Immigration Research for a New Century: Multidisciplinary Perspectives*, ed. Nancy Foner, Ruben G. Rumbaut, and Steven J. Gold, 76–92. New York: Russell Sage Foundation.

Garner, Steve. 2006. "The Uses of Whiteness: What Sociologists Working on Europe Can Draw from US Research on Whiteness." *Sociology* 40 (2): 257–275.

Gershenson, Olga, and David Shneer. 2009. "From Russia with Lessons in Transnational Jewish Identity-Building." *Jewish Daily Forward* March 11. www.forward.com.

Gilmore, Leigh. 2001. "Limit-Cases: Trauma, Self-Representation, and the Jurisdictions of Identity." *Biography* 24(1): 128–139.

———. 2010. "American Neoconfessional: Memoir, Self-Help, and Redemption on Oprah's Couch." *Biography* 33(4): 657–679.

Glaser, Amelia. 2011. "Introduction: Russian-American Fiction." *Slavic and East European Journal* 55(1): 15–18.

Glenn, Susan A. 1990. *Daughters of the Shtetl: Life and Labor in the Immigrant Generation*. Ithaca: Cornell University Press.

Gokhberg, Leonid, and Elena Nekipelova. 2001. "International Migration of Scientists and Engineers in Russia." In *International Mobility of the Highly Skilled*, ed. OECD, 177–188. Paris: OECD.

Gold, Steven J. 1999. "From Jazz Singer to What a Country! A Comparison of Jewish Migration to the United States, 1880–1930 and 1965–1998." *Journal of American Ethnic History* 18 (3): 114–132.

———. 2013. "The Socialization and Accommodation of the Russophone Immigrants." Presentation at the NEH Summer Seminar, America's Russian-Speaking Immigrants & Refugees: 20th Century Migration and Memory, Columbia University, New York, June 17.

Goldstein, Eric L. 2006. *The Price of Whiteness: Jews, Race, and American Identity*. Princeton: Princeton University Press.

Gonzáles, Daniel. 2012. "Arizona's Illegal-Immigration Population Plunges." *Arizona Republic* March 23. www.azcentral.com.

Goodman, Adam. 2011. "A Nation of (Deported) Immigrants." *Dissent* 58(2) (Spring): 64–68.

Gown, Annie, and Tyler Bridges. 2015. "From Piyush to Bobby: How Does Jindal Feel about His Family's Past?" *Washington Post* June 23. www.washingtonpost.com.

Grove, Casey. 2011 "'Dr. Phil' Appearance Nets Abuse Charges." *Alaska Dispatch News* January 27. www.adn.com.

Guglielmo, Jennifer. 2003. "Introduction: White Lies, Dark Truths," *Are Italians White? How Race Is Made in America*, ed. Jennifer Guglielmo and Salvatore Salerno, 1–16. New York: Routledge.

Guglielmo, Thomas A. 2003. *White on Arrival: Italians, Race, Color, and Power in Chicago, 1890–1945*. Oxford: Oxford University Press.

———. 2004. "Encountering the Color Line in the Everyday: Italians in Interwar Chicago." *Journal of American Ethnic History* 23(4): 45–77.

———. 2015. "Affirmative Action for Immigrant Whites." *Oxford University Press Blog* March 27. blog.oup.com.

Guterl, Matthew Pratt. 2001. *The Color of Race in America, 1900–1940*. Cambridge: Harvard University Press.

Gyory, Andrew. 1998. *Closing the Gate: Race, Politics, and the Chinese Exclusion Act*. Chapel Hill: University of North Carolina Press.

Hagopian, Elaine C., ed. 2004. *Civil Rights in Peril: The Targeting of Arabs and Muslims*. Ann Arbor: Pluto Press.

Hale, Mike. 2012. "The Children of Old Tehran Go Hollywood." *New York Times* March 9. tv.nytimes.com.

Hall, Ceridwen Leith. 2012. "Consuming Culture, Creating Memory: How American Parents Relate to Russian Adoptees." M.A. thesis, University of California, San Diego. www.escholarship.org.

Hall, Kristin M. 2010. "Russian Boy Terrified Family, Adopted Grandmother Says." *TheStar.com* April 10. www.thestar.com.

Hall, Peter A., and David Soskice. 2001. *Varieties of Capitalism: The Institutional Foundations of Comparative Advantage.* Oxford: Oxford University Press.

Hansen, Brooks. 2008. *The Brotherhood of Joseph: A Father's Memoir of Infertility and Adoption in the 21st Century.* New York: Modern Times.

Hardwick, Susan W. 2001. "Russian Acculturation in Sacramento." In *Geographical Identities of Ethnic America: Race, Space, and Place*, ed. Kate A. Berry and Martha. L. Henderson, 255–278. Reno: University of Nevada Press.

———. 2002. "California's Emerging Russian Homeland." In *Homelands: A Geography of Culture and Place across America*, ed. R. Nostrand and Lawrence Estaville, 210–224. Baltimore: Johns Hopkins University Press.

———. 2008. "Slavic Dreams: Post-Soviet Refugee Identity and Adaptation in Portland, Oregon." In *Immigrants Outside Megalopolis: Ethnic Transformation in the Heartland*, ed. Richard C. Jones, 25–42. London: Lexington Books.

Harnick, Chris. 2010. "Republicans Love 'Modern Family,' Democrats Favor 'Dexter,' New Study Shows." *HuffPost TV* November 10. www.aoltv.com.

Harvey, David. 2007. *A Brief History of Neoliberalism.* Oxford: Oxford University Press.

Hazen, Helen D., and Heike C. Alberts. 2006. "Visitors or Immigrants? International Students in the United States." *Population, Space and Place* 12(3): 201–216.

Hegar, Rebecca L., Olga Verbovaya, and Larry D. Watson. 2015. "Child Fatality in Intercountry Adoption: What Media Reports Suggest about Deaths of Russian Children in the U.S." *Children and Youth Services Review* 55: 182–192.

Hendricks, Tyche. 2006. "Irish Join Battle over Illegal Immigration, St. Patrick's Day Vehicle for Activists Seeking Reform." *San Francisco Chronicle* March 15.

Herman, Ellen. 2008. *Kinship by Design: A History of Adoption in the Modern United States.* Chicago: University of Chicago Press.

Hester, Torrie. 2015. "Deportability and the Carceral State." *Journal of American History* 102(1): 141–151.

Heyns, Barbara. 2005. "Emerging Inequalities in Central and Eastern Europe." *Annual Review of Sociology* 31: 163–197.

Hing, Bill Ong. 2002. "Vigilante Racism: The De-Americanization of Immigrant America." *Michigan Journal of Race and Law* 7: 441–456.

Hoffman, Allison. 2011. "Mother Russia." *Tablet* August 11. www.tabletmag.com.

Homans, Margaret. 2006. "Adoption Narratives, Trauma, and Origins." *Narrative* 14(1): 4–26.

Hondagneu-Sotelo, Pierrette, and Ernestine Avila. 1997. "'I'm Here, but I'm There': The Meanings of Latina Transnational Motherhood." *Gender & Society* 11(5): 548–571.

Howell, Signe. 2007. *The Kinning of Foreigners: Transnational Adoption in a Global Perspective*. New York: Berghahn Books.

Hübinette, Tobias. 2005. "Reconciling the Past/Imagining the Future: The Korean Adoption Issue and Representations of Adopted Koreans in Korean Popular Culture." *Asian Cinema* 16(2): 110–121.

Hughes, Donna M. 2000. "The 'Natasha' Trade: The Transnational Shadow Market of Trafficking in Women." *Journal of International Affairs* 53(2): 625–651.

Hunt, Bonnie, producer. 2010. *The Bonnie Hunt Show*. Television. Episode 2.131, March 26.

Hyatt, Susan Brin. 2011. "What Was Neoliberalism and What Comes Next? The Transformation of Citizenship in the Law-and-Order State," In *Policy Worlds: Anthropology and the Analysis of Contemporary Power*, ed. Cris Shore, Susan Wright, and Davide Però, 106–123. New York: Berghahn Books.

Idov, Michael. 2011. "Considering Lifetime's Wan New Reality Series, *Russian Dolls*." *Vulture* August 10. www.vulture.com.

———. 2014. "Stars in the East: Hollywood's Love-Hate Relationship with Russia." *Calvert Journal* January 28. www.calvertjournal.com.

Ignatiev, Noel. 1995. *How the Irish Became White*. Milton Park: Routledge.

Issoupova, Olga. 2000. "Problematic Motherhood: Child Abandonment, Abortion, Adoption, and Single Motherhood in Russia in the 1990s." *Slavonica* 6(2): 68–87.

Isupova, Olga. 2004. "The Relinquishment of Newborns and Women's Reproductive Rights." *Russian Social Science Review* 45(3): 40–57.

Jacobs, Sallie, David Filipov, and Patricia Wen. 2013. "The Fall of the House of Tsarnaev." *Boston Globe* December 15. www.bostonglobe.com.

Jacobson, Heather. 2008. *Culture Keeping: White Mothers, International Adoption, and the Negotiation of Family Difference*. Nashville: Vanderbilt University Press.

———. 2014. "Framing Adoption: The Media and Parental Decision Making." *Journal of Family Issues* 35(5): 654–676.

Jacobson, Matthew Frye. 1998. *Whiteness of a Different Color: European Immigrants and the Alchemy of Race*. Cambridge: Harvard University Press.

———. 2006. *Roots Too: White Ethnic Revival in Post-Civil Rights America*. Cambridge: Harvard University Press.

Jasso, Guillermina, Vivek Wadhwa, Gary Gereffi, Ben Rissing, and Richard Freeman. 2010. "How Many Highly Skilled Foreign-Born Are Waiting in Line for U.S. Legal Permanent Residence?" *International Migration Review* 44(2): 477–498.

Jerng, Mark C. 2006. "Recognizing the Transracial Adoptee: Adoption Life Stories and Chang-rae Lee's *A Gesture Life*." *MELUS: Multiethnic Literatures of the US* 31(2): 41–67.

———. 2010. *Claiming Others: Transracial Adoption and National Belonging*. Minneapolis: University of Minnesota Press.

Ji-sook, Bae. 2012. "Adoption Law Revision Draws Fire." *Korea Herald* March 18. www.koreaherald.com.

"John Krueger's Story." 2003. *Pound Pup Legacy* February 12. www.poundpuplegacy.org.

Johnson, Ericka. 2007. *Dreaming of a Mail-Order Husband: Russian-American Internet Romance.* Durham: Duke University Press.

Johnson, Kevin R. 2003. "September 11 and Mexican Immigrants: Collateral Damage Comes Home." *DePaul Law Review* 52(3): 849–870.

Juffer, Femmie, and Marinus H. van IJzendoorn. 2005. "Behavior Problems and Mental Health Referrals of International Adoptees: A Meta-Analysis." *Journal of the American Medical Association* 293(20): 2501–2515.

Jung, Moon-Ho. 2005. "Outlawing 'Coolies': Race, Nation, and Empire in the Age of Emancipation." *American Quarterly* 57(3): 677–701.

———. 2006. *Coolies and Cane: Race, Labor, and Sugar in the Age of Emancipation.* Baltimore: Johns Hopkins University Press.

Kaleem, Jaweed. 2013. "Tamerlan Tsarnaev, Suspected Boston Bomber, May Not Get Islamic Funeral from Wary Muslims." *Huffpost* 20 April. www.huffingtonpost.com.

Kapstein, Ethan B. 2003. "The Baby Trade." *Foreign Affairs–New York* 82(6): 115–125.

Kasatkina, Natalia. 2010. "Analyzing Language Choice among Russian-Speaking Migrants to the United States." Ph.D. dissertation, University of Arizona.

Kasinitz, Philip. 2013. "Situating America's Russian-Speaking Refugees and Immigrants: Transnational and National Disciplinary Contexts," Presentation at the NEH Summer Seminar, America's Russian-Speaking Immigrants & Refugees: 20th Century Migration and Memory. Columbia University, New York, June 10.

Kasinitz, Philip, John H. Mollenkopf, and Mary C. Waters, eds. 2004. *Becoming New Yorkers: Ethnographies of the New Second Generation.* New York: Russell Sage Foundation.

Kasinitz, Philip, John H. Mollenkopf, Mary C. Waters, and Jennifer Holdaway, eds. 2008. *Inheriting the City: The Children of Immigrants Come of Age.* New York: Russell Sage Foundation.

Katchanovski, Ivan. 2007. "Politically Correct Incorrectness: Kazakhstan, Russia, and Ukraine in Hollywood Films." Presentation at the Annual Meeting of the American Political Science Association, Chicago, Ill., August 30–September 2, uottawa. academia.edu.

Keough, Leyla J. 2006. "Globalizing 'Postsocialism': Mobile Mothers and Neoliberalism on the Margins of Europe." *Anthropological Quarterly* 79(3): 431–461.

Kershaw, Sarah. 2010. "In Some Adoptions Love Doesn't Conquer All." *New York Times* April 16, sec. 1.

Khazan, Olga. 2016. "Why Soviet Refugees Aren't Buying Sanders's Socialism." *Atlantic* April 12. www.theatlantic.com.

Khinkulova, Kateryna. 2012. "Hello, Lenin? Nostalgia on Post-Soviet Television in Russia and Ukraine." *View: Journal of European Television History and Culture* 1(2): 94–104.

Kibler, M. Alison. 2015. *Censoring Racial Ridicule: Irish, Jewish, and African American Struggles over Race and Representation, 1890–1930.* Chapel Hill: University of North Carolina Press.

Kibria, Nazli. 1998. "The Contested Meanings of 'Asian American': Racial Dilemmas in the Contemporary US." *Ethnic and Racial Studies* 21(5): 939–958.

Kimmel, Jimmy, producer. 2011a. *Jimmy Kimmel Live.* Television. Episode no. 9.115. April 20.

———. 2011b. *Jimmy Kimmel Live.* Television. Episode no. 10.15. September 27.

Kinsella, Kevin. 2007. "Kevin Kinsella Interviews Anya Ulinich." *MaudNewton.com* September 18. www.maudnewton.com.

Kivisto, Peter, and Thomas Faist. 2007. *Citizenship: Discourse, Theory, and Transnational Prospects.* Malden: Blackwell.

Klein, Naomi. 2007. *The Shock Doctrine: The Rise of Disaster Capitalism.* New York: Picador.

Kliger, Samuel. 2013. "Russian-Speaking Immigrants in the US: Identity, Integration, and Politics." Presentation at the NEH Summer Seminar, America's Russian-Speaking Immigrants & Refugees: 20th Century Migration and Memory. Columbia University, New York, June 14.

Klose, Robert. 1999. *Adopting Aloysha: A Single Man Finds a Son in Russia.* Jackson: University Press of Mississippi.

Knapp, Laura G., Janice E. Kelly-Reid, and Scott A. Gindler. 2010. "Employees in Postsecondary Institutions, Fall 2009, and Salaries of Full-Time Instructional Staff, 2009–10." US Department of Education. nces.ed.gov.

Kolossov, Vladimir. 2005. "Border Studies: Changing Perspectives and Theoretical Approaches." *Geopolitics* 10(4): 606–632.

Kolstø, Pål. 1999. "Territorializing Diasporas: The Case of the Russians in the Former Soviet Republics." *Millenium: Journal of International Studies* 8(3): 607–631.

Koniaev, Andrei. 2011. "'Russian Dolls' Glamor [Matreshkin glamur]." *Lenta.ru* August 16. www.lenta.ru.

Korobkov, Andrei V., and Zhanna A. Zaionchkovskaia. 2012. "Russian Brain Drain: Myths v. Reality." *Communist and Post-Communist Studies* 45: 327–241.

Koshy, Susan. 2001. "Morphing Race into Ethnicity: Asian Americans and Critical Transformations of Whiteness." *Boundary 2* 28: 153–194.

———. 2012. "Historicizing Racial Identity and Minority Status for South Asian Americans." *Asian Pacific American Collective History Project.* www.sscnet.ucla.edu.

Kostenko, Maksim Aleksandrovic. 2014. "Research of Main Factors of Newborn Children Abandonment in a Provincial Region of Russia." *Life Science Journal* 11 (2014): 347–350. www.lifesciencesite.com.

Kotkin, Stephen. 2015. "Russian-American Relations in the 21st Century." Presentation at Arizona State University, Tempe, Arizona, February 6.

Krasikov, Sana. 2008. *One More Year.* New York: Spiegel and Grau.

Kriebernegg, Ulla. 2013. "Ending Aging in the Shteyngart of Eden: Biogerontological Discourse in a *Super Sad True Love Story.*" *Journal of Aging Studies* 27(1): 61–70.

Krupkin, Taly. 2015. "U.S. Jews Helping Gay Russian Asylum Seekers Feel at Home." *Haaretz* February 18. www.haaretz.com.

Kushner, Tony. 2005. "Racialisation and 'White European' Immigration." In *Racialisation: Studies in Theory and Practice*. Ed. Karim Murji and John Solomos, 207–225. Oxford: Oxford University Press.

Labadie-Jackson, Glenda. 2008. "Reflections on Domestic Work and the Feminization of Migration." *Campbell Law Review* 31(1): 67–90.

Larson, Thomas. 2007. *Memoir and the Memoirist: Reading and Writing Personal Narrative*. Athens: Swallow Press.

Lee, Ellen, Marilyn Lammert, and Mary Anne Hess. 2008. *Once They Hear My Name; Korean Adoptees and Their Journeys toward Identity*. Silver Spring: Tamarisk Books.

Lee, Rachel. 2002. "Asian Americans' Performing Blackface and Yellowface: Costly Performances or Coalitional Enactments." In *Literature on the Move: Comparing Diasporic Ethnicities in Europe and the Americas*, ed. Dominique Marçais, Mark Niemeyer, Bernard Vincent, and Cathy Waegner, 147–158. Heidelberg: Universitätsverlag Winter.

Lee, Richard M. 2003. "The Transracial Adoption Paradox: History, Research, and Counseling Implications of Cultural Socialization." *Counseling Psychologist* 31(6): 711–744.

Lee, Richard M., Harold D. Grotevant, Wendy L. Hellerstedt, Megan R. Gunnar, and the Minnesota International Adoption Project Team. 2006. "Cultural Socialization in Families with Internationally Adopted Children." *Journal of Family Psychology* 20(4): 571–580.

Leitman, Ruth. 2010. *Tony and Janina's American Wedding*. Kartemquin Films. tonyandjanina.com

Levchenko, Polina, and Catherine Solheim. 2013. "International Marriages between Eastern European-Born Women and US-Born Men." *Family Relations* 62(1): 30–41.

Liebert, Saltanat. 2009. *Irregular Migration from the Former Soviet Union to the United States*. New York: Routledge.

Linville, Deanne, and Anne Prouty Lyness. 2007. "Twenty American Families' Stories of Adaptation: Adoption of Children from Russian and Romanian Institutions." *Journal of Marital and Family Therapy* 33(1): 77–93.

Lipsitz, George.1998. *The Possessive Investment in Whiteness: How White People Profit from Identity Politics*. Philadelphia: Temple University Press.

Litskevich, Ol'ga. 2011a. "Maksim Chmerkovskiy: 'I Regret Participating in *The Bachelor*." [Maksim Chmerkovskiy: "Ia zhaleiu, chto uchastvoval v *Kholostiake*"]. *Komsomol's'ka Pravda v Ukraine* June 8. www.kp.ua.

———. 2011b. "Maksim Chmerkovskiy: My Brother Told Me: 'Return Nadia!'" ["Maksim Chmerkovskiy: Brat skazal mne: 'Verni Nadiu!'"]. *Komsomol's'ka Pravda v Ukraine* June 9. www.kp.ua.

Liu, Laura Y. 2000. "The Place of Immigration in Studies of Geography and Race." *Social & Cultural Geography* 1(2): 169–182.

Logan, John R., and Julia A. Rivera. 2011. "Human Capital, Gender, and Labor Force Incorporation: The Case of Immigrants from the Former Soviet Union." *International Journal of Comparative Sociology* 52(1–2): 25–44.

Lopate, Leonard. 2008. "Post-Soviet Stories." *Leonard Lopate Show.* September 3. www. wnyc.org.

Lott, Eric. 1993. *Love and Theft: Blackface Minstrelsy and the American Working Class.* New York: Oxford University Press.

Lovelock, Kirsten. 2000. "Intercountry Adoption as a Migratory Practice: A Comparative Analysis of Intercountry Adoption and Immigration Policy and Practice in the United States, Canada and New Zealand in the Post W.W. II Period." *International Migration Review* 34(3): 907–949.

Lowe, Lisa. 1996. *Immigrant Acts: On Asian American Cultural Politics.* Durham: Duke University Press.

Lye, Coleen. 2008. "The Afro-Asian Analogy." *PMLA* 123(5): 1732–1736.

MacDonald, Kevin. 1998. "Jewish Involvement in Shaping American Immigration Policy, 1881–1965: A Historical Review." *Population and Environment* 19(4): 295–356.

Mahajan, Karan. 2105. "The Two Asian Americas." *New Yorker* October 21. www. newyorker.com.

Manchester, Laurie. 2015. "How Statelessness Can Force Refugees to Redefine Their Ethnicity: What Can Be Learned from Russian Emigres Dispersed to Six Continents in the Inter-War Period?" *Immigrants & Minorities.* dx.doi.org.

Marlowe, Lara. 2015. "Chechens Arrested as Alleged Paris Accomplices Charged." *Irish Times* January 21. www.irishtimes.com.

Massey, Douglas S., and Ilana Redstone Akresh. 2006. "Immigrant Intentions and Mobility in a Global Economy: The Attitudes and Behavior of Recently Arrived U.S. Immigrants." *Social Science Quarterly* 87(5): 954–971.

McCall, Robert B., Christina J. Groark, Larry Fish, Rifkat J. Muhamedrahimov, Oleg I Palmov, and Natalia V Nikiforova. 2016. "Characteristics of Children Transitioned to Intercountry Adoption, Domestic Adoption, Foster Care, and Biological Families from Institutions in St. Petersburg, Russian Federation." *International Social Work* 59(6): 778–790.

McIntosh, Peggy. 2004. "White Privilege: Unpacking the Invisible Knapsack," In *Race, Class, and Gender in the United States: An Integrated Study*, ed. Paula S. Rothenberg, 199–192. New York: St. Martin's Press.

McKinney, Judith Record. 2009. "Russian Babies, Russian Babes: Economic and Demographic Implications of International Adoption and International Trafficking for Russia." *Demokratizatsiya* 17(1): 19–39.

McMains, Juliet E. 2001. "Brownface: Representations of Latin-ness in Dance Sport." *Dance Research Journal* 33(2): 54–71.

———. 2006. *Glamour Addiction: Inside the American Ballroom Dance Industry.* Middletown: Wesleyan.

———. 2010. "Reality Check: *Dancing with the Stars* and the American Dream." In *The Routledge Dance Studies Reader*, ed. Alexandra Carter and Janet O'Shea, 261–272. 2nd ed. London: Routledge.

McNevin, Anne. 2011. *Contesting Citizenship: Irregular Migrants and New Frontiers of the Political.* New York: Columbia University Press.

Melamed, Jodi. 2011. *Represent and Destroy: Rationalizing Violence in the New Racial Capitalism*. Minneapolis: University of Minnesota Press.

Menjívar, Cecilia. 2006. "Liminal Legality: Salvadoran and Guatemalan Immigrants' Lives in the United States." *American Journal of Sociology* 111(4): 999–1037.

Men'shikova, Irina. 2011. "Show *The Bachelor*: Personal Tragedy of Social Success." [Shou *Kholostiak*: lichnaia tragediia sotsial'nogo uspekha]. *Khaivei*, April 2. www.h.ua.

Mignot, Jean-François. 2015. "Why Is Intercountry Adoption Declining Worldwide?" *Population & Societies* 519 (February): 1–4.

"Mikhail Levitis in the Encyclopedia of Russian Americans." 2011. [Mikhail Levitis v Entsiklopedii Russkoi Ameriki]. *RUNYWeb.com* August 12. www.youtube.com.

Milian, Claudia. 2013. *Latinizing America: Black-Brown Passage and the Coloring of Latina/o Studies*. Athens: University of Georgia Press.

Miller, Laurie C., Wilma Chan, Robert A. Reece, Linda Grey Tirella, and Adam Pertman. 2007. "Child Abuse Fatalities among Internationally Adopted Children." *Child Maltreatment* 12(4): 378–380.

Miller, Teresa A. 2005. "Blurring the Boundaries between Immigration and Crime Control after September 11th." *Boston College Third World Law Journal* 25(1): 83–123.

Milord, Johnny, dir. 2010. *Chelsea Lately Show*. Television. Episode 4.60, April 15.

Mirandé, Alfredo. 2003. "Is There a 'Mexican Exception' to the Fourth Amendment?" *Florida Law Review* 55(1): 365–389.

Mirskaya, Elena Z., and Yakov M Rabkin. 2004. "Russian Academic Scientists in the First Post-Soviet Decade: Empirical Study." *Science and Public Policy* 31(1): 2–14.

Mohr, Holbrook, Mitch Weiss, and Mike Baker. 2010. "J-1 Student Visa Abuse: Foreign Students Forced to Work in Strip Clubs, Eat on Floor." *Huffington Post* December 6. www.huffingtonpost.com.

"Mommy Confessions." 2010. *Dr. Phil Show*, Episode no. 1017, November 17. www.drphil.com.

Moorhead, M. V. 2012. "From Russia, with Milk." *Phoenix Magazine*. www.phoenix-mag.com.

Moran, Albert. 2009. "When TV Formats Are Translated." In *TV Formats Worldwide: Localizing Global Programs*, ed. Albert Moran, 39–54. Bristol: Intellect.

Morawetz, Nancy, and Natasha Fernandez-Silber. 2014. "Immigration Law and the Myth of Comprehensive Registration." *University of California Davis Law Review* 48: 141–205.

Morawska, Eva. 2004. "Exploring Diversity in Immigrant Assimilation and Transnationalism: Poles and Russian Jews in Philadelphia." *International Migration Review* 38(4): 1372–1412. www.jstor.org.

Morgan, Edmund Sears. 1975. *American Slavery, American Freedom: The Ordeal of Colonial Virginia*. New York: Norton.

Morokvasic, Mirjana. 2004. "'Settler Mobility': Engendering Post-Wall Migration in Europe." *Feminist Review* 77: 7–25.

Muir, David. 2014. "Maks Chmerkovskiy's Road to Mirror Ball Victory on *Dancing with the Stars*." *ABC News* May 23. abcnews.go.com.

Mukherjee, Bharati. 2011. "Immigrant Writing: Changing the Contours of a National Literature." *American Literary History* 23(3): 680–696.

Mullen, Bill V. 2004. *Afro-Orientalism*. Minneapolis: University of Minnesota Press.

Murray, Susan, and Laurie Ouellette. 2009. "Introduction." In *Reality TV: Remaking Television Culture*, ed. Susan Murray and Laurie Ouellette, 1–22. New York: NYU Press.

Murti, Lata. 2010. "With and Without the White Coat: The Racialization of Southern California's Indian Physicians." Ph.D. dissertation, University of Southern California.

Ngai, Mae M. 2004. *Impossible Subjects: Illegal Aliens and the Making of Modern America*. Princeton: Princeton University Press.

Norris, Sarah. 2008. "Sana Krasikov's Immigrant Song." *Village Voice* August 12. www.villagevoice.com.

Novy, Marianne. 2005. *Reading Adoption: Family and Difference in Fiction and Drama*. Ann Arbor: University of Michigan Press, 2005.

Nowatzki, Robert. 2006. "Paddy Jumps Jim Crow: Irish-Americans and Blackface Minstrelsy." *Eire-Ireland* 41(3–4): 162–184.

O'Halloran, Kerry. 2006. *The Politics of Adoption: International Perspectives on Law, Policy and Practice*. Dordrecht: Springer.

Ohanyan-Tri, Emma. 2015. "The Trace of Cultural Ignorance: Russians and Middle Easterners of *24*." *The 2 Shot* March 27. the2shot.wordpress.com.

Orleck, Annelise. 2001. "Soviet Jews: The City's Newest Immigrants Transform New York Jewish Life." In *New Immigrants in New York*. ed. Nancy Foner, 111–114. New York: Columbia University Press.

Palumbo-Liu, David. 2012. "Conclusion." In *The Deliverance of Others: Reading Literature in a Global Age*, 179–196. Durham: Duke University Press.

Park, Madison. 2008. "Prison for Child's Death." *Baltimore Sun* April 18. articles.baltimoresun.com.

Passel, Jeffrey S., and D'Vera Cohn. 2014. "Unauthorized Immigrant Totals Rise in 7 States, Fall in 14." *Pew Hispanic Center* November 18. www.pewhispanic.org.

Passel, Jeffrey S., D'Vera Cohn, and Ana Gonzalez-Barrera. 2012. "Net Migration from Mexico Falls to Zero—and Perhaps Less." *Pew Hispanic Center* April 23.

Patico, Jennifer. 2009. "For Love, Money, or Normalcy: Meanings of Strategy and Sentiment in the Russian-American Matchmaking Industry." *Ethnos* 74(3): 307–330.

Pearce, Matt. 2016. "A Look at the K-1 Visa That Gave San Bernardino Shooter Entry into U.S." *Los Angeles Times* December 17. www.latimes.com.

Penguin Books. n.d. "Reader's Guide: *Petropolis*." Reading Guides. www.penguin.com.

Pew Research Center. 2013. "A Portrait of Jewish Americans." *Pew Research Center* October 1. www.pewforum.org

Phillips, Michael. 2006. *White Metropolis: Race, Ethnicity, and Religion in Dallas, 1841–2001*. Austin: University of Texas Press.

Piketty, Thomas. 2014. *Capital in the Twenty-First Century*. Cambridge: Belknap Press.

Portes, Alejandro, and Ruben G. Rumbaut. 2001. *Legacies: The Story of the Immigrant Second Generation*. Berkeley: University of California Press.

Preston, Julia. 2012. "Record Number of Foreigners Were Deported in 2011, Officials Say." *New York Times* September 12. www.nytimes.com.

Provine, Doris Marie, and Roxanne L. Doty. 2011. "The Criminalization of Immigrants as a Racial Project." *Journal of Contemporary Criminal Justice* 27(3): 261–277.

Quinlan, Margaret M., and Benjamin R. Bates. 2008. "Dances and Discourses of (Dis) ability: Heather Mills's Embodiment of Disability on *Dancing with the Stars*." *Text & Performance Quarterly* 28(1–2): 64–80.

Rands Lyon, Tania. 2007. "Housewife Fantasies, Family Realities in the New Russia." In *Living Gender after Communism*, ed. Janet Elise Johnson and Jean C. Robinson, 25–39. Bloomington: Indiana University Press.

Raphael-Hernandez, Heike, and Shannon Steen, eds. 2006. *AfroAsian Encounters: Culture, History, Politics*. New York: NYU Press.

Reagan, Patricia B., and Randall J. Olsen. 2000. "You Can Go Home Again: Evidence from Longitudinal Data." *Demography* 37(3): 339–350.

Reddy, Sumathi. 2011. "'Russian Dolls' Exposed." *Wall Street Journal* August 5. online. wsj.com.

Reid, Theresa. 2006. *Two Little Girls: A Memoir of Adoption*. New York: Berkley Books.

Reilly, Matthew. 2001. "The Short Life of Viktor Alexander Matthey." *Star-Ledger* October 28. www.nj.com.

Robila, Mihaela. 2010. *Eastern European Immigrant Families*. New York: Routledge.

Roediger, David. 2005. *Working toward Whiteness: How America's Immigrants Became White*. New York: Basic Books.

———. 2008. *How Race Survived US History: From Settlement and Slavery to the Obama Phenomenon*. London: Verso.

Rogin, Michael. 1996. *Blackface, White Noise: Jewish Immigrants in the Hollywood Melting Pot*. Berkeley: University of California Press.

Rosenfeld, Alvin H, ed. 2008. *The Writer Uprooted: Contemporary Jewish Exile Literature*. Bloomington: Indiana University Press.

Rowe, Michael. 2010. "Did U.S. Baptist Cross the Line between 'Good Intentions' and Child Kidnapping in Haiti?" *Huffington Post* February 4. www.huffingtonpost.com.

Royal, Derek Parker. 2012. "Cyrillic Cycles: Uses of Composite Narrative in the Russian Émigré Fiction of Ellen Litman and David Bezmozgis." *Studies in American Jewish Literature* 31(2): 238–255.

Ruby, Walter. 2011. "Too Much Bling in Brighton Beach?" *Jewish Week* August 16. www.thejewishweek.com.

Ryabinska, Natalya. 2011. "Media Ownership in Post-Communist Ukraine: Impact on Media Independence and Pluralism." *Problems of Post-Communism* 58(6): 3–20.

Ryan, Karen. 2011. "Failures of Domesticity in Contemporary Russian-American Literature: Vapnyar, Krasikov, Ulinich, and Reyn." *Transcultural* 1(4): 63–75.

Sadowski-Smith, Claudia. 2008. "Unskilled Labor Migration and the Illegality Spiral: Chinese, European, and Mexican *Indocumentados* in the United States, 1882–2007." *American Quarterly* 60.3 (Fall): 779–804.

Saldívar, Ramón. 2013. "The Second Elevation of the Novel: Race, Form, and the Post-race Aesthetic in Contemporary Narrative." *Narrative* 21(1): 1–18.

Sarna, Jonathan D. 1981. "The Myth of No Return: Jewish Return Migration to Eastern Europe, 1881–1914." *American Jewish History* 71(2): 256–268.

Satzewich, Vic. 2000. "Whiteness Limited: Racialization and the Social Construction of 'Peripheral Europeans.'" *Social History/Histoire Sociale* 33(66): 271–289.

Savodnik, Peter. 2010. "Who Will Write the End to the Story of Russian Orphan Artyom Savelyev?" *AOL News* July 2. www.aolnews.com.

Scherman, Rhoda, and Niki Harré, 2008. "The Ethnic Identification of Same-Race Children in Intercountry Adoption." *Adoption Quarterly* 11(1): 45–65.

Schneider, Dorothee. 2013. *Crossing Borders: Migration and Citizenship in the Twentieth-Century United States*. Cambridge: Harvard University Press.

Schreuder, Yda. 1989. "Labor Segmentation, Ethnic Division of Labor, and Residential Segregation in American Cities in the Early Twentieth Century." *Professional Geographer* 41(2): 131–143.

Schwab, Gabriele. 2009. "Replacement Children: The Transgenerational Transmission of Traumatic Loss." *American Imago* 66(3): 277–310.

Schwartz, Margaret L. 2005. *The Pumpkin Patch: A Single Woman's International Adoption Journey*. Louisville: Chicago Spectrum Press.

Senderovich, Sasha. 2016. "How I Convinced My Russian Jewish Grandmother Not to Vote for Trump," *Forward* November 22. www.forward.com.

Serwer, Adam. 2017. "Jeff Sessions's Unqualified Praise for a 1924 Immigration Law." *Atlantic* 1. www.theatlantic.com.

Shinkle, Peter. 2006. "Wal-Mart's Conspiracy to Break Immigration Law: Details Emerge on Nationwide Scheme to Hire Undocumented Immigrants and Undercut Wages of Janitors." *St. Louis Post-Dispatch* July 16. www.alipac.us.

Shteyngart, Gary. 2002. *The Russian Debutante's Handbook*. New York Riverhead.

———2006. *Absurdistan*. New York: Random House.

———. 2010. *Super Sad True Love Story*. New York: Random House.

Simanski, John F. 2014. "Immigration Enforcement Actions: 2013: Annual Report." Department of Homeland Security. Office of Immigration Statistics, September. www.dhs.gov.

Simons, Lisa Anne. 2001. *Marriage, Migration, and Markets: International Matchmaking and International Feminism*. Ph.D. dissertation, University of Denver.

Skripnikova, Ekaterina. 2011. "The Main Bachelor of the Country Maksim Chmerkovskiy: 'I Don't Know What Love Is.'" [Glavnyi kholostiak strany Maksim Chmerkovskiy: 'Ia ne znaiu, chto takoe liubov']. *Moi Kiev* January 24. www.mycityua.com.

Smith, Sidonie, and Kay Schaffer. 2004. *Human Rights and Narrated Lives: The Ethics of Recognition*. New York: Palgrave Macmillan.

Solari, Cynthia. 2010. "Resource Drain vs. Constitutive Circularity: Comparing the Gendered Effects of Post-Soviet Migration Patterns on Ukraine." *Anthropology of East Europe Review* 28(1): 215–238.

Solomon, Nancy. 2002. "Immigrant Dancers." *NPR* June 27. www.npr.org.

Spagat, Elliot, 2013. "At Arizona's Border Morgue, Bodies Keep Coming." *Fox10Phoenix. com* March 12. www.fox10phoenix.com.

Stasi, Linda. 2012. "'stache of Gold." *New York Post* March 9. www.nypost.com.

Steger, Manfred B., and Ravi K. Roy. 2010. *Neoliberalism: A Very Short Introduction.* Oxford: Oxford University Press.

Stromberg, David. n.d. "Russian as an American Language." *Zeek Net* March 7 www. zeek.net.

Stryker, Rachael. 2010. *The Road to Evergreen: Adoption, Attachment Therapy, and Promise of Family.* Ithaca: Cornell University Press.

Suchland, Jennifer. 2011. "Is Postsocialism Transnational?" *Signs* 36(4): 837–862.

———. 2015. "Introduction/Trafficking as Aberration/The Making of Globalization's Victims." In *Economies of Violence: Transnational Feminism, Postsocialism, and the Politics of Sex Trafficking*, 1–23. Durham: Duke University Press.

Sunnucks, Mike. 2016. "Arizona Getting Third Most Syrian Refugees Coming to the U.S." *Phoenix Business Journal* August 30. www.bizjournals.com.

Thai, Hung Cam. 2008. *For Better or For Worse: Vietnamese International Marriages in the New Global Economy.* New Brunswick: Rutgers University Press.

Thoma, Pamela. 2014. "What Julia Knew: Domestic Labor in the Recession-Era Chick Flick." In *Gendering the Recession: Media and Culture in an Age of Austerity*, ed. Diane Negra and Yvonne Tasker, 107–135. Durham: Duke University Press.

Thompson, Ginger. 2010. "Questions Surface after Haitian Airlift." *New York Times* February 23. www.nytimes.com.

Thorn, Kristian, and Lauritz B. Holm-Nielsen. 2008. "International Mobility of Researchers and Scientists: Policy Options for Turning a Drain into a Gain." In *The International Mobility of Talent: Types, Causes, and Development Impact*, ed. Andrés Solimano, 145–167. Oxford: Oxford University Press.

Tolstokorova, Alissa V. 2010a. "Bitter Berries of Better Life: Socio-Demographic Costs of Labour Migration for the Ukrainian Society." *Enquire* 5: 68–94.

———. 2010b. "Where Have All the Mothers Gone? The Gendered Effect of Labour Migration and Transnationalism on the Institution of Parenthood in Ukraine." *Anthropology of East Europe Review* 28(1):184–214.

Trenka, Jeong Jane. 2003. *The Language of Blood.* St. Paul: Minnesota Historical Society.

Trenka, Jeong Jane, Julia Chinvere Oparah, and Sun Yung Shin, eds. 2006. *Outsiders Within: Writing on Transracial Adoption.* Cambridge: South End Press.

Tricarico, Donald. 2007. "Youth Culture, Ethnic Choice, and the Identity Politics of Guido." *Voices in Italian Americana* 18 (1): 34–86.

"The Tsarnaev Family: A Faded Portrait of an Immigrant's American Dream." 2013. *Washington Post* April 27. www.washingtonpost.com.

Tsuda, Takeyuki. 1998. "Ethnicity and the Anthropologist: Negotiating Identities in the Field." *Anthropological Quarterly* 71(3): 107–124.

Tucker, Jill. 2007. "Irish, Latino Catholics March for Immigrant Rights." *San Francisco Chronicle* June 9. www.sfgate.com.

Tunina, Olga, and Rachael Stryker. 2001. "When Local Myths Meet Global Reality: Preparing Russia's Abandoned Children for International Adoption." *Kroeber Anthropological Society Papers* 86: 143–149.

Turner, Graeme. 1996. "The Mass Production of Celebrity: 'Celetoids,' Reality TV and the 'Demotic Turn.'" *International Journal of Cultural Studies* 9(2): 153–165.

Tyson, Alec, and Shiva Maniam. 2016. "Behind Trump's Victory: Divisions by Race, Gender, Education." *Pew Research Center* November 9. www.pewresearch.org.

Uba, George Russell. 2007. "From Signifying to Performance: International Ballroom Dance and the Choreographies of Transnationalism." *Journal of Asian American Studies* 10(2): 141–167.

Ulinich, Anya. 2007a. "Modern Love: Dreaming of a Life of Privilege, but First . . ." *New York Times* March 11. www.nytimes.com.

———. 2007b. *Petropolis*. New York: Penguin.

———. 2008. "The Nurse and the Novelist." *PEN America* September 8. www.pen.org.

US Department of State. Bureau of Consular Affairs. 2015. "FY 2014 Annual Report on Intercountry Adoption." travel.state.gov.

———. 2016. "FY 2015 Annual Report on Intercountry Adoption." travel.state.gov.

———. n.d. "Statistics." travel.state.gov.

van IJzendoorn, Marinus H., Femmie Juffer, and Caroline W. Klein Poelhuis. 2005. "Adoption and Cognitive Development: A Meta-Analytic Comparison of Adopted and Nonadopted Children's IQ and School Performance." *Psychological Bulletin* 131(2): 301–316.

Vapnyar, Lara. 2003. *There Are Jews in My House*. New York: Pantheon Books.

———. 2006. *Memoirs of a Muse*. New York: Pantheon Books.

———. 2008. *Broccoli and Other Tales of Food and Love*. New York: Anchor Books.

———. 2011a. "The Real Reason I Find 'Russian Dolls' Offensive." *Wall Street Journal* August 25. blogs.wsj.com.

———. 2011b. "What Makes a Russian Jewish American Writer? An Interview with Author Lara Vapnyar." *pjcmedia* December 6. www.pjcmedia.org.

Varzally, Allison. 2009. "Vietnamese Adoptions and the Politics of Atonement." *Adoption & Culture* 2: 159–201.

Wadhwa, Vivek, AnnaLee Saxenian, Richard Freeman, Gary Gereffi, and Alex Slakever. 2009. "America's Loss Is the World's Gain: America's New Immigrant Entrepreneurs, Part IV." UC Berkeley School of Information and Ewing Marion Kauffman Foundation. www.kauffman.org.

Waldinger, Roger. 2012. "Immigration and Transnationalism." In *Encyclopedia of Global Studies*, ed. Helmut K. Anheier and Mark Juergensmeyer, 882–884. Thousand Oaks: Sage.

Walker, Max, and Raquel Cervantes. 2017. "Protests Return for Second Day at Sky Harbor over President Trump's Immigration Executive Order." *ABC 15 Arizona* January 29, www.abc15.com.

Wallace-Wells, Benjamin. 2017. "The Trump Administration's Dark View of Immigrants." *New Yorker* February 2, http://www.newyorker.com.

Wanner, Adrian. 2011. *Out of Russia: Fictions of a New Translingual Diaspora*. Evanston: Northwestern University Press.

———. 2012. "Russian Jews as American Writers: A New Paradigm for Jewish Multiculturalism?" *MELUS: Multi-Ethnic Literature of the US* 37(2): 157–176.

———. Forthcoming. "'There Is No Such City': The Myth of Odessa in Twenty-First Century American Immigrant Writing." Unpublished manuscript.

Waters, Mary C. 1990. *Ethnic Options: Choosing Identities in America*. Berkeley: University of California Press.

Waters, Mary C., Van C. Tran, Philip Kasinitz, and John H. Mollenkopf. 2010. "Segmented Assimilation Revisited: Types of Acculturation and Socioeconomic Mobility in Young Adulthood." *Ethnic and Racial Studies* 33(7): 1168–1193.

Weber, Donald. 2004. "Permutations of New-World Experiences Rejuvenate Jewish-American Literature." *Chronicle of Higher Education* 51(4): B 8–10.

Weir, Fred. 2010. "Russia's Medvedev to Sign International Adoption Accord." *Christian Science Monitor* June 22. www.csmonitor.com.

Whitmire, Lou. 2010. "Ohio Family Knows Tennessee Mom's Plight." *Zanesville Times Recorder* April 19. www.zanesvilletimesrecorder.com.

"Why Russian-American Jews Are Ballroom Dance Leaders." 2015. *NPR* June 18. www.npr.org.

Wilson, Andrew. 1997. *Ukrainian Nationalism in the 1990s: A Minority Faith*. Cambridge: Cambridge University Press.

———. 2002. "Elements of a Theory of Ukrainian Ethno-National Identities." *Nations and Nationalism* 8(1): 31–54.

Wilson, Samantha L. 2003. "Post-Institutionalization: The Effects of Early Deprivation on Development of Romanian Adoptees." *Child and Adolescent Social Work Journal* 20(6): 473–83.

Wingert, Pat. 2007. "When Adoption Goes Wrong." *Newsweek* December 8. www.newsweek.com.

World Bank. 2017. "Ukraine." www.worldbank.org.

Yoon, Dong Pil. 2004. "Intercountry Adoption: The Importance of Ethnic Socialization and Subjective Well-Being for Korean-Born Adopted Children." *Journal of Ethnic and Cultural Diversity in Social Work* 13(2): 71–89.

Zeltzer-Zubida, Aviva, and Kasinitz, Philip. 2005. "The Next Generation: Russian Jewish Young Adults in Contemporary New York." *Contemporary Jewry* 25(1): 193–225.

Zirin, Dave. 2013. "A Fighter by His Trade: Tamerlan Tsarnaev, Sports and the American Dream." *Nation* April 29. www.thenation.com.

Zong, Jie, and Jeanne Batalova. 2014. "Korean Immigrants in the United States." *Migration Information Source*. www.migrationpolicy.org.

INDEX

Adaptation: Asian Americans, 11, 152, 162; enforced, 72–76, 78; immigration studies in, 6, 10, 53–54; in Jewish American literature, 19, 112, 114; Jewish immigrants, 9, 21, 35, 112, 137; marriage migrants, 76, 78, 83; post-Soviet dancers, 6, 17; post-Soviet immigrants, 6, 9, 17, 18, 19, 24, 25, 26, 163; post-Soviet adoptees, 19, 88, 103; in post-Soviet literature, 113, 114, 132; segmentation theory, 54; racialization and, 53–54, 88, 137; transnationalism and, 43; upward mobility and, 6, 17, 21, 24, 53, 137

Adoption. *See* Transnational adoption

Adoption studies, 86; adoption from Asia, 15, 85, 86; adoption from Eastern Europe, 85–86, 87–88; disability and, 85; race and, 85, 88

Adoptive invisibility. *See* Transnational adoption

Akhtiorskaya, Yelena, 183n6; 187

Alba, Richard, 13, 14, 54, 151, 187

Alien Fiancées and Fiancés Act (1946), 72

Alien Registration Act (1940), 143

American Community Survey (ACS), 1, 5–6, 52, 58, 173n1, 173n2

American Dream: upward mobility and, 6, 29, 136, 161, 162–163. *See also* Adaptation

Anticommunism, 88, 90–92, 93, 163

Anti-immigration sentiment, 48, 135, 136, 141, 143, 148, 153, 156, 158, 158. *See also* De-Americanization

Aranda, Elizabeth, 70, 187

Arizona Senate Bill 1070 (2010), 16, 20, 133, 135, 139–147, 167

Assimilation: immigration studies and, 6, 10, 53–54; segmentation theory and, 54. *See also* Adaptation

Atanasoski, Neda, 6, 163, 187

Attachment disorder, 84–85, 107–108; adoptee abuse, 85, 108; adoptee death, 108; attachment therapies, 85, 107–108; Reactive Attachment disorder (RAD), 84–85, 107–108. *See also* Transnational adoption

Bachelor, Ukraine (*Kholostiak*), 45–47. *See also* Chmerkovskiy, Maksim

Ball, Deborah Yarskike, 65, 187

Ballroom dancing, 27–28; post-Soviet immigrants, 28–30, 44; spray tanning, 32–36; USSR, 28; International style, 28; Latin style, 35; US style, 28. *See also* Dance sport

Banerjee, Payal, 10, 63, 64, 118, 187, 188

Barrett, James R., 13, 21, 137, 175n15, 188

Bartholet, Elizabeth, 109, 182n17, 188

Beagley, Kristoff (Daniil Bukharov), 84–85

Bellin, Roger, 148, 188

Bergquist, Kathleen Ja Sook, 90, 188

Bimmel, Nicole, 180n3, 188

Biressi, Anita, and Heather Nunn, 24, 25, 188

Birth culture. *See* Transnational adoption

Birth mother discourse. *See* Transnational adoption

ABOUT THE AUTHOR

Claudia Sadowski-Smith is Associate Professor of English at Arizona State University. She is the author of *Border Fictions: Globalization, Empire, and Writing at the Boundaries of the United States* (2008) and the editor of *Globalization on the Line: Culture, Capital, and Citizenship at U.S. Borders* (2002).